D0761188

Keynes

ROBERT SKIDELSKY

Keynes
The Return of the Master

ALLEN LANE
an imprint of
PENGUIN BOOKS

ALLEN LANE

Published by the Penguin Group
Penguin Books Ltd, 80 Strand, London WC2R ORL, England
Penguin Group (USA) Inc., 375 Hudson Street, New York, New York 10014, USA
Penguin Group (Canada), 90 Eglinton Avenue East, Suite 700, Toronto, Ontario, Canada M4P 2Y3
(a division of Pearson Penguin Canada Inc.)
Penguin Ireland, 25 St Stephen's Green, Dublin 2, Ireland
(a division of Penguin Books Ltd)
Penguin Group (Australia), 250 Camberwell Road, Camberwell, Victoria 3124, Australia
(a division of Pearson Australia Group Pty Ltd)
Penguin Books India Pvt Ltd, 11 Community Centre, Panchsheel Park, New Delhi – 110 017, India
Penguin Group (NZ), 67 Apollo Drive, Rosedale, North Shore 0632, New Zealand
(a division of Pearson New Zealand Ltd)
Penguin Books (South Africa) (Pty) Ltd, 24 Sturdee Avenue, Rosebank, Johannesburg 2196, South Africa

Penguin Books Ltd, Registered Offices: 80 Strand, London WC2R ORL, England

www.penguin.com

First published 2009
2

Set in 10.5/14 pt PostScript Linotype Sabon
Typeset by Rowland Phototypesetting Ltd, Bury St Edmunds, Suffolk
Printed in England by Clays Ltd, St Ives plc

ISBN: 978-1-846-14258-1

www.greenpenguin.co.uk

To Mikhail Gutseriev

Contents

CONTENTS

Preface

The economist John Maynard Keynes is back in fashion. That guardian of free-market orthodoxy the *Wall Street Journal* devoted a full page spread to him on 8 January 2009. The reason is obvious. The global economy is slumping; 'stimulus packages' are all the rage. But Keynes's importance is not just as a progenitor of 'stimulus' policies. Governments have known how to 'stimulate' sickly economies – usually by war – as long as they have known anything. Keynes's importance was to provide a 'general theory' which explains how economies fall into slumps, and to indicate the policies and institutions needed to avoid them. In the current situation no theory is better than bad theory, but good theory is better than no theory. Good theory can help us avoid panic responses, and give us insight into the limitations of both markets and governments. Keynes, in my view, provides the right kind of theory, even though his is clearly not the last word on events happening sixty-three years after his death.

Keynes is relevant for another reason. The crisis has brought to a head wider issues concerning the explanation of human behaviour and the role of moral judgements in economics. These touch on attitudes to economic growth, globalization, justice, the environment and so on. Keynes had important things to say about these matters. To take just one: If growth is a means to an end, what is the end, how much growth is 'enough', and what other valuable human purposes may be pre-empted by a single-minded concentration on economic growth?

The economic hurricane now raging gives us an immense opportunity to reorient economic life towards what is sensible, just and good. Keynes remains an indispensable guide to that future.

My own stimulus for writing this short book was given by my

ix

agent, Michael Sissons, to whom I owe an enormous debt of gratitude over forty years of association and friendship. I have also benefited enormously from the encouragement and advice of my publisher, Stuart Proffitt.

Although the historical Keynes is familiar territory to me, my three researchers at the Centre for Global Studies – Pavel Erochkine, Louis Mosley and Christian Westerlind Wigstrom – have given me invaluable help in transforming him into a figure relevant to the contemporary world. Christian Westerlind Wigstrom has helped clarify numerous points of theory, and is responsible for the statistical analysis in Chapter 5.

I would also like to thank Andrew Cox, Bob Davenport, Paul Davidson, Meghnad Desai, V. R. Joshi, Geoff Miller, Landon Rowland and my sons, Edward and William, for reading the manuscript, in whole or part, and making helpful suggestions. Edward in particular has sharpened my understanding of Keynes as a moralist. The House of Lords Library has been a valuable research resource. Any mistakes of fact or interpretation are my responsibility alone.

An important advantage I would claim for this book is that, although its subject matter is mainly economics, it is written from a vantage point outside that of the economics profession. My first academic study – and love – was history, and though I studied economics later, and was indeed a member of the economics department at the University of Warwick, I am not a professional economist. I would describe myself as an economically literate historian. The advantage I would claim is that of not having been brainwashed to see the world as most economists view it: I have always regarded their assumptions about human behaviour as absurdly narrow. For reasons which will become clearer as the book goes on, I have come to see economics as a fundamentally regressive discipline, its regressive nature disguised by increasingly sophisticated mathematics and statistics.

Not having been trained formally as an economist has an important drawback: I find mathematics and statistics 'challenging', as they say, and it is too late to improve. This has, I believe, saved me from important errors of thinking – like imagining the world to be an urn, or believing in induction as the source of knowledge. On the other hand, it has no doubt led me to underestimate the contribution of mathematics as an aid to rigorous thinking, and statistics as a check on our fancy. History, politics, sociology, psychology and anthropology are suggestive, not conclusive, disciplines: they cannot prove (or more importantly disprove) any hypothesis. They should perhaps be more like economics, and economics should be more like them. That is why I was drawn to Keynes: he was a man of many parts. I have heard economists say he was a brilliant thinker, but a bad theorist. They objected to his '*ad hoc*' theorizing – inventing bits of theory to explain unusual events, rather than building up his theory from secure micro-foundations. His wife called him 'more than an economist'. I am less than an economist, but perhaps this makes me better able to appreciate his greatness.

Keynes, of course, is no one's property; and, while economists may disagree with some of my interpretations, this book will have achieved its purpose if it brings Keynes to life for a world struggling once again with the riddles of economies and the perplexities of moral life in an age of actual and potential abundance.

Once I started writing this book, on 1 January 2009, I stopped reading the newspapers on a daily basis to avoid filling up my mind with 'noise'. Any coherence my argument may have stems from this act of self-denial.

Robert Skidelsky
15 July 2009

Introduction

We have been living through one of the most violent collapses in economic life seen in the last hundred years. Yet economics – the scientific study of economic life – has done an exceptionally poor job in explaining it. For, according to mainstream economic theories, a downturn on this scale should not have happened. And we also have precious little idea about how to stop a succession of such crises bearing down on us in future. To get a handle on both sets of issues we need John Maynard Keynes.

In a way, this is to be expected. For twenty years or so, mainstream economics has taught that markets 'clear' continuously. The big idea was that if wages and prices are completely flexible, resources will be fully employed. Any shock to the system will result in instantaneous adjustment of wages and prices to the new situation.

Admittedly, this system-wide responsiveness depended on economic agents having perfect information about the future. This is manifestly absurd. Nevertheless, most mainstream economists believed that economic actors possess enough information to lend their theorizing a sufficient dose of reality.

This so-called 'efficient market theory' should have been blown sky high by last autumn's financial breakdown. But I doubt that it has been. Seventy years ago, John Maynard Keynes pointed out its fallacy. When shocks to the system occur, agents do not known what will happen next. In the face of this uncertainty, they do not readjust their spending; instead, they refrain from spending until the mists clear, sending the economy into a tailspin.

It is the shock, not the adjustments to it, that spreads throughout the system. The inescapable information deficit obstructs all those smoothly working adjustment mechanisms – i.e. flexible wages and flexible interest rates – posited by mainstream economic theory.

An economy hit by a shock does not maintain its buoyancy; rather, it becomes a leaky balloon. Hence Keynes gave governments two tasks: to pump up the economy when it starts to deflate, and to minimize the chances of serious shocks happening in the first place.

Today, the first lesson appears to have been learned: various bailout and stimulus packages have stimulated depressed economies sufficiently to give us a reasonable expectation that the worst of the slump is over. But, judging from recent proposals in the United States, the United Kingdom and the European Union to reform the financial system, it is far from clear that the second lesson has sunk in. A few cosmetic reforms, it now seems to be agreed, are all that is needed. This is to set the scene for the next crisis. For thirty years or so after the Second World War, Keynesian economics ruled the roost, at least in the sense that Keynesian policy – trying to keep economies fully employed and growing on an even keel – was part of the normal toolkit of governments. Then it was thrown out, as economics reverted to its older doctrine that market economies were internally self-correcting and that it was government intervention which made them behave badly. The free-market era of Reagan and Thatcher dawned.

The story of the decline and fall of the Keynesian revolution, and what has happened to economics generally, is a fascinating intellectual detective story in its own right, which charts the trajectory from President Nixon's 'We are all Keynesians now' in 1971 to Robert Lucas's 2009 remark 'I guess everyone is a Keynesian in the foxhole.'[1]

The decline of Keynesianism is a key theme of this book, because I believe with Keynes that ideas matter profoundly, 'indeed the world is ruled by little else'.[2] I therefore believe that the root cause of the present crisis lies in the intellectual failure of economics. It was the wrong ideas of economists which legitimzed the deregulation of finance, and it was the deregulation of finance which led to the credit explosion which collapsed into the credit crunch. It is hard to convey the harm done by the recently dominant school of New Classical economics. Rarely in history can such powerful minds have devoted themselves to such strange ideas. The maddest of these is the proposition that market participants have correct beliefs on average about what will happen to prices over an infinite future. I am naturally much less critical of the New Keynesian school, which disputes the terrain of macroeconomics with the New Classicals, but I am still quite critical, because I believe that in accepting the theory of rational expectations, which revives in mathematical form the classical theory which Keynes rejected, they have sold the pass to the New Classicals. Having swallowed the elephant of rational expectations, they strained at the gnat of the continuous full employment implied by it, and developed theories of market failure to allow a role for government.

The centrepiece of Keynes's theory is the existence of inescapable uncertainty about the future, and this is the main subject of Chapter 4, with Chapter 3 being an account of the influence in developing it of his experience as an investor during the turbulent period of the Great Depression. Taking uncertainty seriously – which few economists today do – has profound implications not just for how one does economics and how one applies it, but for one's understanding of practically all aspects of human activity. It helps explain the rules and conventions by which people live. I lay particular emphasis on its implications for how the social sciences should use language. Keynes always tried to present his essential thoughts – which he called 'simple and . . . obvious' – in what may loosely be called high-class ordinary language. This was not just to amplify his persuasive appeal, but because he thought that economics should be intuitive, not counter-intuitive: it should present the world in a language which most people understand. This is one reason why he opposed the excessive mathematicization of economics, which separated it from ordinary understanding. He would have been very hostile to the linguistic imperialism of economics, which appropriates important words in the common lexicon, like 'rational', and gives them technical meanings which over time change their ordinary meanings and the understandings which they express. The economists' definition of rational behaviour as behaviour consistent with their own models, with all other behaviour dubbed irrational, amounts to a huge project to reshape humanity into people who believe the things economists believe about them. It was consistent with Keynes's attitude to language to prefer *simple* to *complex* financial systems. He would have been utterly opposed to financial innovation beyond the bounds of ordinary understanding, and therefore control. Complexity for its own sake had no appeal for him.

My hope is that the current slump will cause the New Keynesians and others to take uncertainty seriously. But that probably requires a major institutional change in the way in which economics is taught and transmitted. This book ends with a proposal to reform the teaching of economics to encourage economists to think of it as a moral, not natural, science.

Keynes, of course, did not have the last word to say about the causes of economic malfunctions. His theories have to be adapted to a crisis precipitated by banking, rather than stock-market, failure. But my contention is that he provided the right kind of theory to explain what is now happening; and since, in my view, financial crises which lead to failures in the 'real' economy are a normal part of the operation of unmanaged markets, he can claim to have produced a 'general theory' which directs us to how to make markets safe for the world, as well as making the world safe for markets.

But let's get Keynes – and Keynesianism – right. In the US, more than in Britain, he is considered a kind of socialist. This is wrong. Keynes was not a nationalizer, nor even much of a regulator. He came not exactly to praise capitalism, but certainly not to bury it. He thought that, for all its defects, it was the best economic system on offer, a necessary stage in the passage from scarcity to abundance, from toil to the good life.

Keynes is also considered to be the apostle of permanent budget deficits. 'Deficits don't matter.' This was not Keynes: it was Glen Hubbard, chairman of George W. Bush's Council of Economic Advisers in 2003. It may surprise readers to learn that Keynes thought that government budgets should normally be in surplus. The greatest splurgers in US history have been Republican presidents preaching free-market, anti-Keynesian, doctrines: the one fiscal conservative in the last thirty years has been Democratic president Bill Clinton.

Nor was Keynes a tax-and-spend fanatic. At the end of his life he wondered whether a government take of more than 25% of the national income was a good thing.

Nor did Keynes believe that *all* unemployment was caused by failure of aggregate demand. He was close to Milton Friedman in viewing a lot of it as due to inflexible wages and prices. But he did not believe that that was the problem in the 1930s. And he believed that, except in moments of excitement, there would always be 'demand-deficient' unemployment, which would yield to government policies of demand expansion.

Keynes was not an inflationist. He believed in stable prices, and for much of his career he thought that central governments could achieve price stability by limiting money growth – another link with Friedman. But he thought it was idiotic to worry about inflation when prices and output were in free fall.

It makes some sense to think of Keynes as an economist for depressions – that is, for one kind of situation. He has been criticized for offering not a 'general theory', as he claimed, but a depression theory. I think this is wrong, for two reasons.

First, Keynes believed that deep slumps were always possible in a market system left to itself, and that there was therefore a continuous role for government in ensuring that they did not happen. His demonstration that they were not 'one in a century events', but an ever-present possibility, is at the heart of his economic theory.

Second, Keynes was a moralist. There was always, at the back of his mind, the question: What is economics for? How does economic activity relate to the 'good life'? How much prosperity do we need to live 'wisely, agreeably, and well'? This concern was grounded in the ethics of G. E. Moore, and the shared life of the Bloombsbury Group. Broadly, Keynes saw economic progress as freeing people from physical toil, so they could learn to live like the 'lilies of the field', valuing today over tomorrow, taking pleasure in the fleeting moment. I give an account of his ethical ideas in Chapter 6.

This book shifts the accepted interpretation of what was important in Keynes's theory. The early interpretations of Keynes centred not on his view of why things went wrong, but on why they *stayed* wrong. He established, as economists say, the possibility of 'underemployment equilibrium'. This was the important message for policymakers at the time: it suggested that policy intervention could achieve a superior equilibrium. Today – and understandably at this stage in the economic meltdown – we are more interested in the causes of the instability of the financial system. This was not the main topic of the

General Theory of Employment, Interest and Money (1936), which was written at or near the bottom of the Great Depression. Nevertheless, Keynes did write a crucial chapter – Chapter 12 – which explained why financial markets are unstable, and a year later, in summing up the main ideas of the *General Theory*, he put financial instability at the centre of his theory. In this Keynes it is 'radical uncertainty' which both makes economies unstable and prevents rapid recovery from 'shocks'. The shift in focus from the Keynes of 'underemployment equilibrium' to the Keynes of 'uncertain expectations' allows for a direct confrontation between contemporary theories of risk and risk management and Keynes's theory of uncertainty and uncertainty reduction.

Keynes had a political objective. Unless governments took steps to stabilize market economies at full employment, the undoubted benefit of markets would be lost and political space would be opened up for extremists who would offer to solve the economic problem by abolishing markets, peace and liberty. This in a nutshell was the Keynesian 'political economy'. Keynes offers an immensely fruitful way of making sense of the deep slump now in progress, for suggesting policies to get us out of the slump, for ensuring, as far as is humanly possible, that we don't continue to fall into pits like the present one, and for understanding the human condition. These are the things which make Keynes fresh today. That is why I have written this book.

PART I

The Crisis

I

What Went Wrong?

ANATOMY OF A CRISIS

What Needs to be Explained

All epoch-defining events are the result of conjunctures – the correlation of normally unconnected happenings which jolts humanity
out of its existing rut and sets it on a new course. Such fortuitous
conjunctures create what Nassim Taleb called Black Swans – unexpected events carrying huge impacts. A small number of Black
Swans, Taleb believes, 'explain almost everything in our world'.[1] The
economic crisis today is a Black Swan – a storm out of an almost
cloudless sky, unexpected, unpredicted, falling on a world thinking
and acting on the assumption that such extreme events were things of
the past, and that another Great Depression could not occur.

How and why did it happen? It originated, as we all know, in a
banking crisis, and the first attempts to understand the crisis focused
on the sources of banking failure.

The most popular explanation was the failure of banks to 'manage'
the new 'risks' posed by 'financial innovation'. Alan Greenspan's
statement that the cause of the crisis was 'the underpricing of risk
worldwide' was the most succinct expression of this view.[2] In this
interpretation, the banking crisis – and hence the world slump to
which it has led – was caused by the technical failure of risk-
management models, and especially their inability to manage the risk
of the entire financial system breaking down. Particular attention was
paid to the role of the American sub-prime mortgage market as the
originator of the so-called 'toxic assets' which came to dominate bank

balance sheets. Early remedies for the slump focused on 'bailing out' or refinancing the banks, so they could start lending again. These were followed by 'stimulus' packages – both monetary and financial – to revive the declining real economy.

Now that we are – or may be – over the worst of the crisis, attempts have been made to try to understand its deeper causes. Two theories may be distinguished: 'money glut' and 'saving glut'. Conservative economists blame the crisis on loose fiscal and monetary policy which enabled Americans to live beyond their means. In particular, Alan Greenspan, chairman of the US Federal Reserve in the critical years leading up to 2005, is said to have kept money too cheap for too long, thus allowing an asset bubble to get pumped up till it burst. The Keynesian view sees cheap money in the US as a response to a 'global saving glut' originating in East Asia and the Middle East. It was the rise in US interest rates in 2005, bringing the housing boom to an end, which caused the American economy to collapse. As we shall see, these are a rerun of the debates between conservative and Keynesian economists about the causes of the Great Depression.

The Crisis: A Thumbnail Sketch

Complex in its detailed unfolding, the economic crisis which struck in 2007–8 is easy enough to grasp in outline. A global inverted pyramid of household and bank debt was built on a narrow range of underlying assets – American house prices. When they started to fall, the debt balloon started to deflate, at first slowly, ultimately with devastating speed. Many of the bank loans had been made to 'sub-prime' mortgage borrowers – borrowers with poor prospects of repayment. Securities based on sub-prime debt entered the balance sheets of banks all round the world. When house prices started to fall, the banks suddenly found these securities falling in value; fearing insolvency, with their investments impaired by an unknown amount, they stopped lending to each other and to their customers. This caused a 'credit crunch'.

It all developed with astonishing speed. Commodity prices started to fall from July 2008. Collapsing confidence, precipitated by the bankruptcy of Lehman Brothers in September, caused the stock markets to plunge. Once banks began to fail and stock markets to fall, the economy started to slide. This has brought about generalized conditions of slump throughout the world, which have deepened throughout 2009. Unlike in the Great Depression, governments have introduced reflationary packages, which at least promise that the slump will not spiral all the way down into a deep depression as in the 1930s. But most analysts expect the fall in output to continue through 2009. Here are the main landmarks on the road to ruin.

The Collapse of the Housing Bubble

American house prices rose 124% between 1997 and 2006, while the Standard & Poor's 500 index fell by 8%: half of US growth in 2005 was house-related. In the UK, house prices increased by 97% in the same period, while the FTSE 100 fell by 10%. Between 1994 and 2005, US home ownership rose from 64% to 69%. The average price of an American home, which had long hovered around three times the average wage, was, by 2006, 4.6 times the average wage.

Two forces were behind the housing boom. First, the Clinton administration encouraged government-backed institutions like Fannie Mae – set up in 1938 to make home loans affordable to low-income groups – to expand their lending activities. Second, private mortgage lenders, having exhausted the middle-class demand for mortgages, started vacuuming up 'Ninjas' – borrowers with no income, no job, no assets. Borrowers were enticed by 'teaser' rates: very low, almost zero, introductory interest rates on an adjustable-rate mortgage (ARM), which then went up sharply after a year or two. With defaults at a historic low between 2003 and 2005, there seemed little risk in this extension of mortgage lending, even though a third of the 'sub-prime' loans were for 100% or more of the home value, and six times the annual earnings of the borrower. By 2006, more than a fifth of all new mortgages – some $600 million worth – were sub-prime. The ease of refinancing magnified consumer indebtedness. Mortgage equity withdrawals to buy consumer durables and second homes shot up from $20 billion in the early 1990s, or 1% of personal consumption, to between $600 billion and $700 billion in the mid-2000s, or 8–10% of personal-consumption expenditure. There were similar housing booms in Spain, France and Australia, but the US and the UK stand out by their reliance on debt financing. By the end of 2007, UK household debt had reached 177% of disposable income, mortgage debt 132%. Martin Wolf wrote in the *Financial Times* in September 2008 that the monetary authorities of the United States and Britain had turned their populations into 'highly leveraged speculators in a fixed asset'.[3] Wolf's remark is given point by the fact that the ratio of new builds to house sales fell from almost 50% in 1999–2000 to just over 20% in 2007–8. Most house purchasers, that is, were engaged in swapping titles to existing properties rather than investing in new properties.

In 2005–6 two blows hit the housing market: a rise in the cost of borrowing and a downturn in house prices. Between June 2004 and July 2006 the Federal Reserve, seeking to dampen inflation and return short-term interest rates to a more normal level, raised the federal funds rate from 1% to 5.25%, and it kept it there until August 2007. US house prices declined by 26.6% between 2006 and 2008. By August 2007, 16% of sub-prime mortgages with adjustable rates had defaulted. The sub-prime losses of 2007 were 'a bullet that fatally wounded the banks'.[4] They demolished their risk models. David Viniar, chief financial officer of the smartest investment bank on Wall Street, Goldman Sachs, told the *Financial Times* in August 2007 that his team were 'seeing things that were 25-standard deviation moves, several days in a row',[5] or, in other words, events which, according to their model, could only occur every 10^{140} years. The absurdity of this statement was captured by Jon Danielsson's calculation that Goldman Sachs had therefore suffered a once in-every-fourteen-universes loss on several consecutive days.[6] More prosaically, it would also turn out that Moody's, the US credit-rating agency, had been incorrectly awarding triple-A ratings to billions of dollars' worth of financial instruments because of a coding error in their model.[7]

Financial Innovation

The housing boom was built on securitization, and it was through securitization that sub-prime mortgages entered the world banking system. Securitization is the process of bundling up individual mortgages and then slicing and dicing them into different securities – tailored to the requirements of different investors – which can be sold on by the originating bank. In this way the risks attached to lending money to sub-prime borrowers could be widely spread. Guaranteed by investment-grade credit ratings, and insured by credit-default swaps, these poisoned sausages were snapped up by investors the world over hungry for 'yield lift' to offset historically low interest rates on government bonds. Their marketability hugely increased the possibilities of leverage – or borrowing – by their holders, and thus led directly to the build-up of debt.

The securitization of mortgages was not new; its explosion after 2000 was the result of three deregulating policy decisions: the repeal in 1999 of America's Glass–Steagall Act of 1933, which had forbidden retail banks to engage in investment activities such as underwriting and selling securities; the decision by the Clinton administration not to regulate credit-default swaps; and the 2004 decision by the US Securities and Exchange Commission to allow banks to increase their leverage ratios – the ratio of total liabilities to net worth – from 10:1 to 30:1. The Basel agreements of 1992 and 2004 attempted to control the consequences of financial deregulation by setting a maximum leverage ratio for global banks. However, the definitions of 'capital' and 'assets' were left sufficiently fuzzy for banks to be able to 'game' the regulations by inflating their measures of capital to include mortgage-backed securities. This explains the puzzle why 'banks were caught with huge amounts of mortgage-backed debt when the point of securitization – turning assets into securities – is to be able to sell loans'.[8] Even today it is unclear how many trillions of these toxic assets remain on the balance sheets of financial institutions, or what they are worth.

Never in the history of finance has the market for dreams of instant wealth been so massively accommodated. The dependence of the whole rickety structure on continually rising house prices was rarely made explicit. If the housing market started to fail, these paper securities would become, as Warren Buffett predicted in 2002, 'financial weapons of mass destruction'.[9]

The Banking Crisis and Financial *Dégringolade*

The weakest banks – those that depended most heavily on short-term money-market funding to finance their lending – were the first to be exposed. In August 2007 BNP Paribas, France's biggest bank, was forced to suspend redemptions from three of its investment funds, blaming the 'complete evaporation of liquidity in certain market segments of the US securitization market'. On 13 September 2007 the British bank Northern Rock, which had been offering home loans of up to 125% of the value of the property and 60% of whose total lending was financed by short-term borrowing, applied for emergency support from the Bank of England, prompting the first run on a British bank for over a century. Eventually, on 17 February 2008, Northern Rock was nationalized at a cost of £100 billion, the first British nationalization since the 1970s. The fifth-largest US investment bank, Bear Stearns, which had invested heavily in the sub-prime mortgage market, was sold to JP Morgan Chase on 16 March 2008 for a knockdown price of $1.2 billion, narrowly avoiding bankruptcy. The Federal Reserve provided Bear Stearns with a loan against which the bank pledged as collateral part of its now illiquid mortgage-backed securities, so that it could avoid having to dump them on a failing market. The governments of the world had embarked on the long and arduous process of rescuing their banking systems from collapse, and saving their economies from meltdown.

In September–October 2008 the financial crisis turned into a classic panic. The institutions panicked first and locked up liquidity, followed by individual investors, unnerved by the waterfall of bad news. In the fourth quarter of 2008, all the famous names in American investment banking started toppling. On 7 September the US government took Fannie Mae and fellow mortgage underwriter Freddie Mac into 'conservatorship', or public ownership, after their share prices collapsed, guaranteeing $12,000 billion worth of debt. On 15 September it allowed the private investment bank Lehman Brothers, one of the most famous names in Wall Street, to go bankrupt, owing $600 billion. It was said to be the biggest corporate bankruptcy in American history. Many believed that it was the failure of the US government to bail out Lehman that started the rush for the exit. Merrill Lynch was sold to Bank of America to avoid the same fate. The day after Lehman was allowed to collapse, the US government took a 79.9% stake in AIG, the world's largest issuer of financial insurance, whose share price had collapsed by 95%, in return for a loan facility of $85 billion. On 21 September Goldman Sachs, the world's largest investment bank, and Morgan Stanley converted their legal status from investment banks to holding banks, to allow them to borrow from the Federal Reserve's discount window on more favourable terms in return for greater government supervision. On 25 September came the failure of Washington Mutual, which went into receivership following a bank run when customers withdrew $16.7 billion.

How close was the American banking system to collapse? Paul Kanjorski (Democrat congressman for Pennsylvania, and chairman of the Capital Markets Subcommittee) gave a melodramatic account on TV of the near-meltdown of American banks in the wake of the Lehman bankruptcy. Kanjorski claims to be repeating an account of events given to him by US Treasury Secretary Henry Paulson and Fed Reserve chairman Ben Bernanke:

On Thursday [18 September], at 11 a.m. the Federal Reserve noticed a tremendous draw-down of money-market accounts in the US; [money] to the tune of $550 billion was being drawn out in the matter of an hour or two. The Treasury opened up its window to help and pumped a $105 billion in the system and quickly realized that they could not stem the tide. We were having an electronic run on the banks. They decided to close the operation, close down the money accounts and announce a guarantee of $250,000 per account so there wouldn't be further panic out there.

If they had not done that, their estimation is that by 2 p.m. that after-noon $5.5 trillion would have been drawn out of the money-market system of the US; [this] would have collapsed the entire economy of the US, and within 24 hours the world economy would have collapsed. It would have been the end of our economic system and our political system as we know it.[10]

However exaggerated the details, panic undoubtedly gripped the Treasury and the Fed at the time of Lehman's collapse. Without a comprehensive bailout plan 'we may not have an economy on Monday' Fed chairman Bernanke told Congress on Thursday 18 September.[11] Mervyn King, governor of the Bank of England, declared that 'Not since the beginning of the First World War has our banking system been so close to collapse.'[12] (For the 1914 crisis, see Chapter 3.)

The first nation-wide rescue package came on 25 September, when Treasury Secretary Paulson announced a $700 billion bailout plan, the Troubled Asset Relief Program (TARP), to buy up distressed assets; this was followed by the Fed's promise to make $600 billion available for the same purpose. But the roll-call of failure continued: Wachovia, Pentagon Capital Managment, Peloton Partners, Drake, Andor Capital Managment Sowod, GO Capital, RedKite, RAB Capital PLC.

British investment banking was dealt a near-lethal blow at the same time. On 17 September 2008 Lloyds TSB announced a £12 billion takeover of HBOS (Halifax Bank of Scotland) amid fears that HBOS would collapse. HBOS had taken on a disproportionate share of riskier mortgages, and was only 58% funded by depositors. The price offered by Lloyds was £2.32 a share, for a company which a year before was trading at £10 a share. This was the biggest merger in Britain's banking history, and said to have been brokered in person by Prime Minister Gordon Brown, who brushed aside competition rules. (The merger was granted final legal approval on 12 January 2009.) The newly combined businesses were left with 28% of the UK mortgage market and a third of Britain's current accounts. The tabloids, by now howling for blood, demanded that the Royal Bank of Scotland cancel its celebrity-sponsorship contracts, including one with Scottish tennis star Andy Murray. On 29 September Bradford & Bingley (a demutualized former building society), which had the largest share of the buy-to-let market, was nationalized at a cost of £41.3 billion, with its branch network sold to the Spanish bank Santander.

British and other countermeasures followed the American pattern. On 8 October the British government announced it was putting up

£37 billion to buy 'preference shares' (given priority in receiving dividends, and without voting rights) in distressed banks. It took a 43% stake in the new Lloyds Banking Group and a 58% stake in the Royal Bank of Scotland on top of its 70% stake in Northern Rock. The Icelandic, German and Benelux governments also bailed out parts of their banking systems in September. In October, central banks in the US, the UK, the EU, Sweden, Switzerland and Canada cut interest rates by 0.5%, and in China by 0.27%, in a coordinated attempt to ease credit conditions. IMF loans went to Iceland and Pakistan.

What had been happening in all these cases was a collapse in the asset side of banks' balance sheets. Banks have always borrowed short and lent long. But worldwide banking deregulation – notably the 1999 repeal of the US Glass–Steagall Act – allowed commercial banks to become investment banks as well. In addition to investing their depositors' money, they became highly leveraged speculators in the newly developed securities, with a hubris given by their faith in their 'risk-management' models. Now, as homeowners defaulted on their mortgages, the investments had turned illiquid, and bank borrowings from the wholesale – or inter-bank – money markets were due for repayment or refinancing. Banks were finding it increasingly hard to raise fresh money from other banks. The credit freeze spread from the wholesale to the retail market: from the banks to their customers. The scene was set for a classic downward slide from banking failure to commodity and stock-market failure and to decline in the real economy.

Up to about mid-2008 there was considerable *Schadenfreude* in emerging markets as they saw the giants of the world economy topple. Banks in Russia, China, the Middle East and even Japan were less exposed to toxic securities, and looked forward to a further shift of world economic power in their favour, as their 'sovereign funds' got their opportunity to buy up Western banks at knockdown prices. After mid-2008, this confidence started to fade as failing commodity prices and export markets sucked them into the maelstrom.

Collapse of Commodity Prices

Two forces drove the rise in commodity prices in the decade after the 1997/8 East Asian financial crisis: rising demand, particularly from the booming East Asian economies, and speculation. Chinese oil consumption alone increased by 870,000 barrels per day in 2006–7. But it was speculation that caused the 'spike' of 2008, when crude oil reached $150 a barrel. Most of the volume on commodity markets consists of 'financial operations' – people buying crude oil not to consume it, but to resell it to refineries at a later date (before they have physically to receive it). So expectations of lower global demand in the future were bound to reduce prices now.

The most general IMF commodity-price index (fuel + non-fuel) peaked in July 2008 at 218 (2005 = 100) and dropped to its lowest level in December, when it was down at 98, recovering to 102 in January 2009 and falling again to 100 by March. As in the 1920s and early 1930s, commodity prices had fallen far more than industrial prices, because supply cannot quickly adjust when demand falls in these markets.

Did the commodity-price boom of 2007–8 have a deflationary influence on the non-energy economies in the run-up to the financial meltdown? Experience of the early 1970s, particularly of the OPEC price hikes, suggests that it may have had. Rising energy costs cause people to cut spending on non-energy goods. The combination of rising energy prices and falling demand caused the 'stagflation' of the 1970s. But today the energy and commodities sector is a much lower proportion of Western countries' GDP than it was in the 1970s, and the general price level has remained stable in the last ten years. The downturn in commodity prices in 2008 would have been marginally beneficial to non-commodity producers, but any such effect was totally swamped by the losses of the speculators and the dampening of confidence.

The sequence is clear. Expectations of significantly lower future demand pricked the commodity bubble. Traders and investors sold commodities and converted their positions to cash. This is why commodity prices fell so precipitously around the time of the Lehman Brothers bankruptcy. Interest rates in emerging markets soared, and all currencies fell against the dollar and the yen as speculators sought safe havens for their money. Commodity producers like Russia now felt the full brunt of the storm.

Collapse of Stock Markets

The collapse of bank shares and commodity prices dragged down the stock market. From the autumn of 2008, stock markets the world over went into steep decline. The Dow Jones fell by a third over the year (from 12,000 to 8,000); London's FTSE 100 by 31.3%; Franfurt's DAX by 40.4%; Paris's CAC by 42.7%; Japan's Nikkei by 42%. The Russian RTS index fell by 80%, largely because of falling oil prices. Most of these losses came in the fourth quarter. Large frauds were exposed, as they always are in bear markets, most notably that of Bernie Madoff, the former chairman of the NASDAQ exchange, who pleaded guilty to running a pyramid or Ponzi scheme of epic proportions, which caused investors losses of tens of billions of dollars. The fall in the stock market continued into 2009 and reached a low in March, when all major stock indices had fallen by another 25% since New Year. At the time of writing (beginning of May) a rapid recovery is in progress. The Dow Jones has increased by 28%, the FTSE 1000 by 23%, the DAX by 32% and the Nikkei by 26%. It is hard to see how this rally can be sustained as long as the real economy continues to slide.

Collapse of the Real Economy

Writing in the *Financial Times* in November 2007, Martin Wolf thought that a 'plausible view of the future . . . is that the US will experience a lengthy period of sluggish growth over the next two years'.[13] This was reasonable at the time. In its quarterly report of December 2007, the OECD expected economic growth in its member countries in 2008 to be 2.3% – just slightly below the 1995–2004 average of 2.7%. This was gradually revised downward as the year wore on, and by December 2008 the OECD was forecasting negative growth in both 2009 and 2010. These quarterly forecasts are well-known 'lagging indicators', since they fail to capture worsening, or for that matter improving, trends. In December 2007 the OECD expected unemployment to remain below 6% (1995–2004 average 6.6%) in 2008. The 2008 outcome was close to 7%, with the US unemployment rate up to 7.2%.

Before the slump hit, consumption had been maintained by an increase in paper wealth through the rise in house and stock-market prices. The reversal of this process led to a decline in consumer spending and therefore a decline in firms' profit expectations. Faced with weakening final demand, firms found themselves with excess inventories, and unable to finance them. To preserve cash, they cut dividends, employment, capital spending and output. They dumped stock and discounted prices in the fourth quarter of 2008. The normally self-congratulatory 'World Economic Forum' at Davos in late January 2009 resembled nothing so much as a wake of punch-drunk boxers, barely able to mumble their platitudes as the blows from a collapsing economy rained down on them.

Differences in output forecasts reflect differences in vulnerabilities. The outsize role of finance in the British economy – generating 30% of GDP, as compared to 8% in the US – puts the UK at special risk. Britain's global banks carry liabilities that dwarf the nation's output. The manufacture and selling of debt by the City of London has been the major British growth industry of the last ten years, far outstripping the growth of all real assets except housing and all services except hairdressing. With the financial sector in free fall, Britain has little enough left to sell, though the depreciation of the pound will bring some relief. Commodity-based economies like Russia and Venezuela are clearly at risk from falling commodity prices. Australia, one of few developed economies without a banking failure, is also hit by collapsing food and commodity prices. The major export economies are vulnerable to the collapse of export demand. The Japanese economy has been hugely hit by the decline in exports, with GDP falling at an annualized rate of 12.7% – much more than in the US or the Eurozone. 'There is no doubt that this is the worst economic crisis of the postwar era,' said economic and fiscal minister Kaoru Yosano.[14] Chinese exports registered their biggest decline for a decade, with rioting breaking out among internal migrants sucked into the towns from the countryside by double-digit export-led growth. Growth in

African countries will fall as a result of the steep fall in prices for commodities such as oil, copper and coffee, but also because of the dwindling Western market for African manufactures. In Latin America, real GDP growth is expected to be less than half of what it was in 2008, largely as a result of falling commodity prices, but also because of stock-market collapses.

How Long Will It Last?

How long will the slump last? This is the worst global turndown since the Great Depression. But it is highly unlikely to be as bad. The years 1929–32 saw twelve successive quarters of economic contraction. If repeated, this would mean the economic slide will continue till mid-2011. But the present contraction will be neither as deep nor as long, and this for two reasons. First, the will to international cooperation is stronger. Second, we do have Keynes. To be a Keynesian 'in the foxhole' is not enough. But it is better than to be a classical economist in the foxhole, which was the only intellectual support that perplexed policymakers had available during the Great Depression. Governments at that time made heroic efforts to balance their budgets; they allowed banks to fail and households to default on their mortgages; they stuck to the gold standard, which kept interest rates high for the first two years of the slump. Today the intellectual climate is different. The 'stimuli' which have been put in place will stop the slide into another Great Depression. The financial system will be cleaned up, and money will become very cheap, but the collapse of confidence will continue to depress new investment for years ahead.

The latest projections are worth noting, if only for the record. The April 2009 IMF projection is for a world output decline of 1.3% in 2009, with output expected to recover, by 1.9%, in 2010. The output projection for the advanced economies is the worst: 3.8% decline in 2009, and zero growth in 2010. Notable outliers are Russia, with minus 6.0% in 2009 and plus 0.5% in 2010, and the UK, with minus 4.1% in 2009 and minus 0.4% in 2010, as against UK Chancellor Alistair Darling's projections in his 22 April budget of minus 3.5% in 2009 and plus 1.25% in 2010.

Advanced economies suffered a 7.5% decline in real GDP in the last quarter of 2008, emerging economies 4%. Overall, global GDP contracted 6.25% (annualized) in the same period (a swing from 4% growth one year earlier), and has fallen almost as fast in the first quarter of 2009.

The twelve-month headline global inflation rate fell below 1% in February. Total global write-downs are estimated to reach $4.1 trillion – two-thirds in banks, the rest in insurance companies, pension funds and hedge funds etc. The world fiscal deficit will jump to 10.5% of GDP in 2009, from less than 2% in 2007, with half of the deterioration reflecting the impact of fiscal stimulus and financial support.

These projections are sure to be revised by the time this book appears, but whether for the better or the worse it is impossible to say. 'Policy responses', noted the IMF, 'have been rapid, wide-ranging, and frequently unorthodox, but were too often piecemeal and have failed to arrest the downward spiral.'[15]

RESCUE OPERATIONS

Rescuing the Banking System

The earliest aim of the rescue operations was to get banks to restart lending. Following the lead of British prime minister Gordon Brown, governments in the US and the EU committed themselves, in October 2008, to coordinated 'recapitalization' of their banking industries – that is, to buy shares in distressed banks. This was run in parallel with commitments to guarantee, insure or buy up toxic assets on the banks' balance sheets, the global cost of which was estimated at $5 trillion. It was hoped that recapitalization plus contingent guarantees would give banks the equity cushion to start lending. But the banks took the money and just sat on it. Early this year, with no sign of significant easing of credit conditions, signs that the trouble in the banks had not been cured – Bank of America and Citigroup in the US and the Royal Bank of Scotland and Lloyds Banking Group in the UK reported huge 2008 losses – and the real economy still sliding, a further round of bank rescue operations was launched. At the end of February the

British government promised to insure £550 billion worth of the loan portfolios of Royal Bank of Scotland and Lloyds Banking Group. Frank Partnoy noted in the *Financial Times* on 19 January that 'given declining assets and increasing liabilities many – perhaps most – big banks [in the US] are essentially insolvent and have been for a long time.'[16]

What started as a liquidity crisis – an inability of banks to borrow in the wholesale market to meet their current liabilities – rapidly turned into a solvency crisis – an insufficiency of bank capital to cover liabilities. Governments have tackled both solvency and liquidity issues in tandem: they bought bank shares and, by simultaneously buying or guaranteeing or insuring banks' 'toxic' assets, they hoped to unfreeze the wholesale market.

However, there was a major problem with the bailout projects. With growing unemployment, home repossessions and loan defaults, the value of the banks' securities continued to fall. Government recapitalization and insurance schemes were continually having to catch up with bad news.

There seemed to be two possible ways out of this bind. The first was to create a 'bad bank'. The state would buy up toxic securities from a range of banks at an agreed or imposed price and hold them. This would force banks to declare large losses, but by removing these illiquid assets from their balance sheets it would give them the confidence to start lending again. On 23 March, Timothy Geithner, Barack Obama's Treasury Secretary and former chairman of the New York Fed, unveiled a more sophisticated version of Paulson's original TARP scheme. Instead of buying the troubled assets directly, Geithner proposed to lend private investors the money to do so. But he faced the same problem: if the assets turned out to be worthless, the taxpayer would end up bearing the cost. The latest phase in US policy has been to subject the nineteen leading American banks to 'stress tests' to establish the extent of the losses they face, and to force the recapitalization needed to absorb them.

Bank nationalization was offered as one way to avoid the need to agree a price with the banks for toxic securities on their balance sheets. Surprisingly, this solution was supported by Alan Greenspan himself, as something one might have to do 'once in a hundred years'.[17] The

Swedish precedent of 1992 was cited, in which the Swedish government took huge stakes in the country's banks, which it was then able to sell successfully. But the Swedish banks had at least backed tangible assets, whereas the 'value of our financial garbage – sub-prime mortgages, CDOs [collateralized debt obligations] and derivatives – may eventually prove ethereal'.[18]

The rescue operations raised serious ethical issues. Henry Paulson went straight from being chairman and CEO of Goldman Sachs in 2006 to being Secretary of the US Treasury. His bailout of AIG put $12.9 billion of taxpayers' money into Goldman Sachs's pockets. A system in which owners are allowed to profit from good bets, while being insured by the taxpayer against bad ones, rightly brings capitalism into disrepute.

Stimulus Packages

Cutting interest rates is the classic response to an economic downturn. However, it has its limitations. First, banks do not lend to customers at the rate set by central banks. As the value of bank investments fell, banks allowed the interest-rate spread between the wholesale and retail cost of borrowing to go up substantially, to compensate for their losses. Twelve months before the crisis, the spread between the three-month dollar LIBOR (or inter-bank lending) rate and the three-year mortgage-rate average was 0.97 percentage points; in February 2009 it was 3.87 percentage points. Second, if prices start falling, there is no way of stopping the real (or inflation-adjusted) interest rate from rising, as the nominal rate cannot go below zero. Japan discovered this in the late 1990s. Finally, investment is governed not just by the cost of borrowing, but by the expectation of profit. If the expectation of profit falls below the cost of borrowing, no money will be borrowed.

It only slowly became clear that the crisis had turned from a *lending* into a *spending* crisis: even though money was becoming cheaper, people weren't borrowing. Keynes put this in a nutshell near the bottom of the Great Depression:

Cheap money means that the riskless, or supposedly riskless, rate of interest will be low. But actual enterprise always involves some degree of risk. It may still be the case that the lender, with his confidence shattered by his experience, will continue to ask for new enterprise rates of interest which the borrower cannot expect to earn ... If this proves to be so, there will be no means of escape from prolonged and perhaps interminable depression except by state intervention to promote and subsidize new investment.[19]

So the scene was set for a more direct 'stimulus'.*

The theory behind the stimulus is one of the bequests of the Keynesian revolution. The authorities forecast the 'output gap' over, say, the next twelve months – the amount by which, because of the decline in total spending, actual output in the economy is expected to fall short of potential output. This gives a number for the extra spending which is required to fill the gap. Very crudely, if, starting at full employment, GDP is expected to fall by 5%, the government should inject 5% of extra spending into the economy.

On 17 February 2009 President Obama signed into law a $787 billion fiscal stimulus, calling it 'the most sweeping recovery package in our history'. Amounting to just over 5% of US GDP, over two to three years, it provided a mixture of tax cuts, infrastructure spending, energy investments and basic research, as well as emergency spending for unemployment benefits, health care and food aid. A few months earlier, in November 2008, China had promised to spend $586 billion on infrastructure and social projects – a much higher proportion of its national income than the US stimulus. The same month, the British government announced a £20 billion package of tax breaks and lending to businesses and homeowners. In December, France unveiled a €26 billion package, and Japan announced an extra ¥12 trillion of spending. By January, even Germany, whose chancellor, Angela Merkel, had derided the autumn round of fiscal stimuli as 'a senseless race to spend billions', had unveiled a package worth €50 billion. Stimulus packages round the world have included subsidies to motor-car manufacturers, cash payments to households, and public

---

*Stimulus' entered the lexicon when, in the aftermath of the 11 September 2001 attacks, President Bush announced a fiscal 'stimulus package' amounting to $190 billion, or nearly 2% of US GDP over twelve months. This was hailed as the biggest stimulus in a single year since 1975. 'Crude Keynesianism has risen from the dead,' complained Milton Friedman.

investment in schools, housing, road and railways. These discretionary increases in government spending are in addition to the 'automatic stabilizers' which send the budget into deficit whenever unemployment rises. One may expect a further succession of stimulus packages over the course of 2009.

So far these stimuli have been financed mainly by borrowing from the public – that is, by selling them long-dated bonds. Up to now this has been cheap enough. The reason is that normally government debt is the most secure investment. However, as government deficits grow, governments may have to offer higher interest rates to induce people to hold ever larger stocks of such debt; the higher interest payments will in turn increase the size of the deficit, requiring more borrowing, and so on.

Financing rescue operations through bond issues is complicated by the fact that, unlike in 1929, most Western governments started this downturn with already sizeable deficits. This means that the recession is forcing governments to run record deficits as percentages of peacetime GDP. The UK has one of the weakest fiscal positions in the world. The Chancellor, Alistair Darling, has predicted that, on the basis of existing commitments, public-sector net borrowing will rise to 12.4% of UK GDP in 2009 and 9.1% in 2010, exceeding the post-war high of 7.8% in 1993 and far above the 6.9% reached in 1976, when Britain had to call in the IMF. Similarly, 'the US government faces huge and potentially debilitating structural deficits as far as the eye can see.'[20] In March 2009, following the failure of a government bond issue, Mervyn King questioned whether Britain could afford any further fiscal stimulus,[21] which seemed to knock out Brown's intention to go for a further big stimulus agreement at the G20 meeting on 2 April. Technically, a government can become insolvent when people no longer wish to hold its long-dated paper. (Nowadays few governments are willing to pledge their population as collateral.) Government defaults are rare, but not unknown: the Russian government defaulted on its dollar and euro-denominated bonds in 1998. But, even before that point is reached, the creditworthiness of the government may become so impaired that it can borrow only at prohibitive interest rates.

There are still many economists – though fewer than during the

Great Depression – who oppose the orthodox form of stimulus by bond issues on theoretical grounds. We will meet up with them in Chapter 2. If the government finances its deficit by borrowing from the public, they say, it will simply divert spending from the private to the public sector. This proposition would be true only at full employment. If resources are idle it is false. A more subtle argument is that of 'psychological crowding out'. If confidence in government policy is impaired, the government may have to pay an increasing price for its debt. This will force up the cost of borrowing for the private sector as well.

At this point, 'quantitative easing' comes into the picture. There are two main forms of it. The government can sell securities to the central bank in exchange for cash, which it then uses to meet its excess of its spending over revenue. This is 'printing money' proper. Or the central bank can inject cash into the economy by buying government bonds. The idea is that banks swap their securities for cash and then expand their lending against their higher cash reserves. Central banks have been doing the latter. In mid-March 2009 the Fed announced that it would buy $300 billion of long-term Treasury bonds on the open market. Fed chairman Bernanke, who has closely studied the policy failures of the Fed in 1930–31, said these measures were 'justified by the extraordinary circumstances'.[22] On 4 March Mervyn King announced that the Bank of England would inject £75 billion over three months into bank and company balance sheets by buying government bonds and corporate securities; it followed up with another £55 billion. The European Central Bank announced a policy of quantitative easing in May 2009.

For monetarists, the aim of quantitative easing is simply to increase the money supply in the economy, restoring the rate of money growth which had fallen during the downturn. Enlarging banks' cash reserves would, other things being equal, increase bank lending, and thus increase the money supply by a multiple of the cash injection.[23] But other things are rarely equal. As Keynes pointed out, 'If money is the drink which stimulates the system to activity . . . there may be several slips between the cup and the lip.'[24] If the banks' desired ratio of cash reserves to total deposits is increasing, as may well be the case if they hold a lot of toxic assets, they will not lower the interest rates which they charge on loans; lowering the rate of interest will not increase the rate of borrowing if profit expectations are falling more quickly than the rate of interest; and, even if some people are stimulated to invest more, economic activity may not rise if other people are simultaneously increasing their saving to pay off debt. In technical terms, the money multiplier – the change in the total money stock for any change in the quantity of injected cash – may be quite small, or even negative. For Keynesians it is the spending of money, not its creation, which provides the 'stimulus'. The virtue of quantitative easing is that it may lower the cost at which a government has to borrow money from the public to finance its own spending. But this effect depends on the expectations the public holds about government policy. If the public expects the government to inflate away its debt, the rate of interest they will demand for lending the government money will rise in line with the anticipated rate of inflation. This may be starting to happen in the US and UK, with the markets pushing up yields on long-dated Treasury bonds, even as base rates fall towards zero.

Thus the stimulating effects of either fiscal or monetary expansion may be disappointingly small. The truth is that there is no easy way of digging yourself out of a hole. It is far more important is to take precautions against falling into one.

BLAME GAMES

Whenever anything goes badly wrong, our first instinct is to blame those in charge – in this case, bankers, credit agencies, regulators, central bankers and governments. We turn to blame the ideas only when it becomes obvious that those in charge were not exceptionally venal, greedy or incompetent, but were acting on what they believed to be sound principles: bankers in relying on risk-management systems they believed to be robust, governments in relying on markets they believed to be stable, investors in believing what the experts told them. In other words, our first reaction to crisis is scapegoating; it is only by delving deeper into the sources of the mistakes that the finger can be pointed to the system of ideas which gave rise to them.

Blaming the Bankers

Bankers have been the easiest targets, and understandably. They controlled trillions of dollars of wealth. They ruined their shareholders, their customers, their employees and the economy, while continuing to collect large bonuses. They had ridden a boom in which nearly all profits went into private hands, followed by a gigantic bust in which taxpayers became liable for their losses. Spectacular payments for success may be acceptable; spectacular rewards for failure – especially if unaccompanied by contrition – are obscene. 'Bring back the guillotine ... for bankers,' cried Britain's Liberal Democrat Treasury spokesman Vince Cable in the *Daily Mail* on Monday 9 February 2009. 'The bonus-hunting bankers ... stand charged with destroying wealth on an epic scale. Foolish, greedy, irresponsible behaviour and excessive risk-taking led to massive losses ... which [are] now costing millions their jobs and many their homes.'[25] 'Betting our cash for personal gain' should be outlawed thundered Will Hutton in *The Observer* on 25 January 2009.[26]

Others stressed perverse incentives: short-term bonuses encouraged reckless and excessive lending. Securitization meant that loan originators had no stake in a borrower's continued solvency. Others put failures of corporate governance at the root of the crisis, especially the lack of proper accountability of senior management to shareholders and boards of directors, the inability of senior management to control traders, and so on.

The general approval of downsizing executive salaries and bonuses in bailed-out or state-assisted banks overwhelmed the bankers' defence that they needed to pay the 'going rate' for talent. Sir Fred 'The Shred' Goodwin of the Royal Bank of Scotland, who accumulated millions while he led his institution to insolvency, and collected a huge pension on his forced retirement, has had his Edinburgh house stoned.

Those who recalled banks' predatory selling of mortgage loans to the impecunious asked, Why are they now charging extortionate rates for the money governments are pumping into them? The bankers' defence that if they started lending again too quickly they would be in even worse shape cut little ice even with the financial press. 'Banks have gathered the capital furnished by government into one lovely pile on which they now gloatingly writhe, like Smaug, the dragon in *The Hobbit*,' wrote Johnathan Guthrie in the *Financial Times* of 12 February 2009. 'This is technically referred to as "rebuilding the balance sheet".'[27]

Bankers naturally disagreed. Thus Lloyd Blankfein, CEO of Goldman Sachs:

If we abandon, as opposed to regulate, market mechanisms created decades ago, such as securitization and derivatives, we may end up constraining access to capital and the efficient hedging and distribution of risk. Most of the past century was defined by markets and instruments that fund innovation, reward entrepreneurial risk-taking and act as an important catalyst for economic growth. History has shown that a vibrant, dynamic financial system is at the heart of a vibrant, dynamic economy.[28]

In fact 'history shows' that the superior global economic performance of the golden age from 1951 to 1973 was achieved without most of the paraphernalia of financial engineering of the following years.

Nevertheless, there is something disagreeable about the mass hysteria directed against the bankers, reminiscent of ancient witch-hunts, pogroms and human sacrifices at times of poor harvests. It is also counterproductive. Unless one is prepared to take over the banking system oneself, one cannot attack bankers for reckless lending and then expect them to lend, any more than one can condemn excessive profits and expect businessmen to invest. Also, the polemics missed something. What does it mean to say bankers were 'greedy'? The concept of greed is incomplete unless one has a notion of what is 'enough', which we lack. The more thoughtful realized that bankers' failures were part of a wider intellectual and regulatory failure, as well as a moral climate which celebrated moneymaking above all other activities. Bankers were scapegoats for the whole Reagan–Thatcher era, which exalted finance and humbled industry, and which had allowed the fruits of progress to accrue disproportionately to the rich and super-rich. (The new class struggle, the quip had it, was between the haves and the have-yachts.)

Moreover, in following 'risk-management' models which they barely understood, bankers acted, in their own lights, correctly.

Indeed, had they acted otherwise, they might have been held culpable for failing to 'maximize shareholder value'. Their behaviour, while selfish and self-satisfied, was in the highest degree *conventional*. They swallowed the whole securitization philosophy without understanding its ramifications. Many of them no doubt felt they were conferring a public benefit by enabling poor people to acquire homes and other desirable goods. Keynes hit the nail on the head when he wrote, 'The "sound" banker, alas! is not one who sees danger and avoids it, but one who, when he is ruined, is ruined in a conventional and orthodox way along with his fellows so that no one can really blame him.'[29]

Blaming the Credit-Rating Agencies

High on the list of villains are the credit-rating agencies: Fitch Ratings, Moody's Investor Services and Standard & Poor's. 'They were a significant cause of the crisis. They helped fire the fatal bullet by giving unreasonably high credit ratings to "super senior" tranches of sub-prime mortgage-backed collateralized debt obligations.'[30] The problem came to light when it turned out that securities with high amounts of sub-prime debt in them had been given triple-A ratings.

Again, the more thoughtful refrained from merely pillorying the credit-rating agencies. They pointed out one obvious problem: that the raters are paid by the issuers of the debt, and therefore had a strong incentive to underprice the risk to the buyer. In the downswing, the incentive is exactly the reverse – to overprice risk in order to retain a battered reputation for integrity. A downgrade means that a company automatically has to pay more for financing its debt or taking on fresh borrowing (its risk of default is expected to be higher). Downgrading thus raises the cost of capital just when economic conditions require lowering it.

But again the problem lies deeper. It was securitization which exalted the credit-rating agencies, by cutting the close link between sellers and buyers of mortgages. If banks held the mortgages they issued, there would be less need for credit-rating agencies.

Blaming Hedge Funds

Hedge funds are rather mysterious to the ordinary investor, even more so to the general public, and hit the headlines only when a famous hedge-fund manager like George Soros of Quantum Fund makes a fortune betting against a currency (as he did against the pound in 1992). Hedge funds are supposed to stabilize financial markets by 'shorting' – taking bets that a security will fall in value. This is supposed to moderate gains on the upside, but protect against loss. By 2008 the 10,000 largest hedge funds controlled an estimated $2 trillion of the world's capital. The problem was that they were so overleveraged – that is, overborrowed – that, when the prices of their investments fell, they were faced with margin calls which they could not meet. Their inability to refinance their positions left the prime brokers holding a whole lot of unsellable assets.[31] Thus, far from making the market more liquid, hedge funds added to its illiquidity by helping to bankrupt the lending institutions. But hedge funds did not cause the crisis; what made it so disastrous was 'the behaviour of large, regulated banks, which have spent the last decade operating with ridiculously high levels of leverage, and purchasing vast quantities of toxic assets'.[32] The European obsession with closing the offshore jurisdictions and tax havens from which hedge-funds operate is part of the scapegoating mania.

Blaming Central Bankers

Alan Greenspan was once called 'master of the financial universe', but his reputation has fallen as far and as fast as the prices of the derivatives whose virtues he for so long extolled. The charge against him is that as chairman of the Federal Reserve Board from 1987 to 2005, he failed to withdraw the punchbowl before the party got out of hand. The cause of the slump, writes Andrew Smithers, was 'quite simply, the incompetence of the central banks, whose excessively easy monetary policies fuelled the asset bubbles, in shares, houses, and financial assets. The Federal Reserve was particularly to blame'.[33] A more serious charge is that the inflation-targeting regime of most central banks, directed at controlling the general price level, ignored the danger of asset-price inflation. But this was an intellectual failure, based on the belief that financial markets were 'efficient'. However, there is a serious defence of Greenspan. This is that, given the world saving glut, keeping money cheap in the USA was the only way to hold a global recession at bay. We shall return to this issue in Chapter 8.

Blaming the Regulators

The most frequently voiced charge against the regulators is that they were captured by vested interests. 'Created to protect investors from financial predators, the [US Securities and Exchange Commission, or SEC] has somehow evolved into a mechanism for protecting financial predators with political clout from investors',[34] runs one comment. Another charge is that globalization has created a regulatory 'race to the bottom', since, with capital internationally mobile, money will flee a heavily regulated jurisdiction for a more lightly regulated one. But again intellectual failure seems more important than venality or incompetence. The 'light-touch regulation' philosophy of the Reagan–Thatcher years stemmed from the notion that markets could regulate themselves, and that heavy-handed regulation was bound to be a check to enterprise.

Blaming Governments

Fatuous pre-crisis optimism – for example, Gordon Brown's fanciful notion that 'the era of boom and bust is over' – has come to haunt politicians. Governments, writes historian Paul Kennedy 'let down their guard'.[35] A better criticism is that they 'bought' the hype about marketization, securitization and globalization. Like the bankers with their micro-forecasting models, they embraced theories which they barely understood, but which they accepted on trust. Maurice Cowling's remark is apposite: 'Politicians only know what they need to know; this need not be much.' What they need to know is enough to gain or retain power. The ideas by which they govern are always supplied from outside politics.

THE REAL FAILURE

To understand the crisis we need to get beyond the blame game. For at the root of the crisis was not failures of character or competence, but a failure of ideas. As Keynes famously remarked, 'The ideas of economists and political philosophers, both when they are right and when they are wrong, are more powerful than is commonly supposed. Indeed the world is ruled by little else.'[36] The practices of bankers, regulators and governments, however egregious, can be traced back to the ideas of economists and philosophers. It is to the ideas of the economists that we now turn, starting with those most recently in fashion. For the present crisis is, to a large extent, the fruit of the intellectual failure of the economics profession.

2

The Present State of Economics

Economics has received a bad press in the present crisis, even from economists. Willem Buiter, a highly respected former member of the Bank of England's Monetary Policy Committee, has written of 'the unfortunate uselessness of most "state of the art" academic monetary economics'.[1] Macroeconomics is divided into two major schools: New Classicals and New Keynesians. The New Keynesians accuse the New Classicals of living in the Dark Ages. The New Classicals accuse the New Keynesians of being pre-Copernican. The two schools are sharply divided over the merits of the 'stimulus'.

In the social sciences, unlike in the natural sciences, there is a variety of opinion, so that it is somewhat misleading to talk of dominant paradigms. In economics, there are many reputable economists who would not accept what I describe below as the central beliefs of the profession. Mostly, though, they are isolated figures in their departments, usually of an older age group. So when I talk of two dominant schools of macroeconomists, the New Classical economists and the New Keynesians, I am referring to the two centres of gravity in macroeconomics today. Moreover, the two schools share much of the same underlying theory, differing mainly in how applicable they think it is to the real world.

FRESHWATERS AND SALTWATERS: A THUMBNAIL SKETCH

Robert Waldmann, professor of economics at Rome University, has given an entertaining summary of the two main American professional positions, which he dubs 'freshwater' and 'saltwater' to distinguish, respectively, Chicago economists from east- and west-coast ones. Since most of the world's top economists have been trained in the United States, these two positions are reasonably representative of the global state of macroeconomic theory:

Roughly freshwater economists [those who teach or were trained at Chicago] consider general equilibrium models with complete markets and symmetric information to be decent approximations to reality. Unless they are specifically studying bounded rationality [a situation in which practical limitations such as computational abilities constrain perfectly rational behaviour] they assume rational expectations, that everyone knows and has always known every conceivable conditional probability. I've only met one economist who claims to believe that people actually do have rational expectations (and I suspect he was joking). However, the freshwater view is that it usually must be assumed that people have rational expectations.

Over near the Great Lakes there is considerable investigation of models in which the market outcome is Pareto efficient [a situation where no one can get better off without someone else getting worse off], that is, it is asserted that recessions are optimal and that, if they could be prevented, it would be a mistake to prevent them.

Saltwater macroeconomics is basically everything else with huge differences between people who attempt to conduct useful empirical research without using formal economic theory and people who note the fundamental theoretical importance of incomplete markets and of asymmetric information and of imperfect competition . . . Market outcomes are generically constrained Pareto inefficient which means that everyone can be made better off by regulations . . .

In the US there is a strong correlation between Fresh and Salt and Right and Left. The correlation is not perfect.

Waldmann makes a point about the training of economists which explains how they come to be hard-wired to think in a certain way:

I have a view of how people can devote so much effort to working out the implications of assumptions which almost no ordinary people would find other than nonsensical if they understood them. Freshwater economics uses difficult mathematical tools. Students in freshwater graduate programs have to learn a huge amount of math very fast. It is not possible to do so if one doesn't set aside all doubts as to the validity of the approach. Once the huge investment has been made it is psychologically difficult to decide that it was wasted. Hence the school gets new disciples by forcing students to follow extremely difficult courses . . . If my information is not out of date, innocents from abroad are the new blood of freshwater economics.[2]

One could add that saltwater programmes impose the same mathematical rigour on their students.

Because New Keynesians are much more interested in policy than New Classicals, they have a bias for developing models which allow some scope for policy intervention. This policy interest dilutes the purity of their acceptance of New Classical theory. For policy must have a window of opportunity to be effective, which, as we shall see, the freshwater school deny. Thus the New Keynesians tend to make use of an escape clause as old as economics itself – the distinction between the long run and the short run. This enables them to inhabit the same theoretical house as the New Classical economists, differing from them only in their view that it takes *longer* for economies to adjust to 'shocks'. In that interval of time lies the chance for the intrusion of common sense.

THE UNDERLYING PREMISES

Although the two schools differ considerably on policy, they share the same underlying theoretical premises. Their quarrels seem to be in the nature of family disputes. Family quarrels can be very bad-tempered.

Buiter has pointed out that the most influential New Classical and New Keynesian theorists work equally in a 'complete markets paradigm': roughly, they assume that markets exist for every possible contingency. In this situation, 'default, bankruptcy and insolvency are impossible.'[3] It is not surprising that Buiter thinks that these theorists are ill-equipped to explain what is happening. Much more seriously, by their influence on the way policymakers think about the world, they have helped create a system which is inefficient, unjust and prone to frequent collapses.

The three interrelated premises of the New Classical macroeconomics are the rational expectations hypothesis (REH), real business cycle theory (RBC) and the efficient financial market theory (EFMT). Together they lie at the heart of contemporary economics. Their inventors have won Nobel Prizes. To the non-economist they will seem mad; but they are the only way most economists today know how to do economics.

RATIONAL EXPECTATIONS

The New Classical economists developed the rational expectations hypothesis to demonstrate the uselessness and even harm of government interference with market processes. The old classical economists believed that, *if* wages and prices were completely flexible, there could be no persistent unemployment. Nevertheless, they accepted that widespread ignorance about future events could make people slow to adjust to change, and that therefore unemployment could persist for some time, justifying government intervention to provide employment. Now see what happens if you abolish the ignorance assumption. Assume that everyone has perfect information about future events. Now the sluggishness disappears. Wages and prices will adjust instantaneously to new conditions, because these conditions will have been anticipated and will already be incorporated in the prices which people charge and expect to pay for their services. No departure from real long-term values is possible even in the short run. Greenspan's 'underpricing of risk worldwide' is impossible. Moreover, because people are always at their preferred position, government efforts to improve their position will be ineffective. The bogey of involuntary or unwanted unemployment is banished. Such unemployment as is observed is a voluntary choice for leisure. Government should get out of the business of second-guessing private preferences. This is the meaning of the rational expectations revolution.

A favourite example of RE thinking is the answer that rational expectations theorists give to the question: What happens when the minister of finance increases the money supply by 10% in order to reduce unemployment? His hope is that this will bring down interest rates. However, the lender – having studied the quantity theory of money – will anticipate that prices will rise by 10%. So, if he wants to maintain, say, a 5% real return on his capital, he will now charge a nominal interest rate of 15% for lending out money. The borrower, also anticipating an inflation rate of 10%, will be willing to pay 15%, since he is only looking for a real return of 5%. So, when the minister of finance increases the money supply by 10%, the only thing that he has achieved is a 10% increase in the price level. Real interest rates, unemployment, output are all unchanged. The government cannot improve on the outcome established by market forces.[4]

On the basis of such homely, but historically important, illustrations from real life, economists built a sophisticated intellectual structure, whose starting point is the existence of extensive and precise knowledge of future events. This is derived from all the information available about both past and present circumstances. The extensive-knowledge assumption implies that economic actors will not make systematic mistakes in predicting the future. This rules out the possibility of large crises except as a result of surprises – things which haven't happened before and which therefore cannot be part of anyone's information. But these are increasingly unlikely as our information, and ability to process it, expands.

Two formal propositions underlie REH. The first is that the expected value of a variable (like the price of a security or a house) is equal to the value predicted by the forecasting model, plus a random error term representing the role of vestigial ignorance or incompetence. The main idea here is that, in forming their expectations, rational individuals make efficient use of all the information available to them. This is generally taken to mean that they behave in ways consistent with the models which generate the forecasts. The random error term means that their forecasts will be consistent with the model only on average. People will go on making mistakes, but, provided these are independent of the information set available to all, and are serially uncorrelated – independent of each other – there is no reason to suppose that they will be biased in one way or the other. The only possible source of bias lies in the model itself. This leads to the second assumption: that the model of the economy used by individuals in making their forecasts is the correct one – that is, that the economy behaves in the way predicted by the model. This in turn assumes that the universe exhibits stability over time: that the future can be inferred from the past and the present. Without some such assumption, the possibility of making correct forecasts is severely restricted. How do people know that they have the right model? The answer is that the world of economic theories or models is subject to a Darwinian learning process, in which inferior models – those which make forecasts disproved by events – are weeded out, just as they are in the natural sciences. Not surprisingly, the correct models turn out to be those favoured by the Chicago school of economists. Rational behaviour boils down to having expectations of future events identical with the predictions of Chicago economists.

The two assumptions concerning efficient use of information and stability of the universe give the required amount of information and predictability to make expectations correct on average. Since the information set on which expectations are based is always up to the minute, at no time is there any ground for changing expectations. If you think that you will change your expectations, you have already changed them, and therefore will not change them in the future. Today's share price depends on today's expectation of what the price will be till the end of time.*

REH was not intended by its adherents to be a literal description of how people actually behave. One of its leaders, Robert Lucas, has always emphasized the fictional character of his models. The predictive performance of REH models is notoriously bad. REH was advanced as a solution to an abstract problem: What conditions of knowledge

---

*The best guess that an agent can make at time t about the value of a variable at time $t+i+j$ is equal to the best guess that he can make about his expectation for the same variable at intermediate time $t+i$. That is, there is no basis for determining any changes in expectation over time.

would be required for markets to be perfectly efficient? Efficiency has always been the normative goal of economics. If the conditions required for market efficiency could be specified, and, over time, realized, then poverty would be eradicated, and the role of government in the economy suitably diminished. Economists therefore set out to build a Platonic world of perfect efficiency, which was nevertheless supposed to have sufficient warrant in terms of human computing abilities and the nature of the universe to make it an acceptable basis for economic theorizing. Unfortunately most policymakers – and even economists – failed to distinguish statements of logical possibility from descriptions of the real world, an ambiguity which REH is happy to accommodate.

Although all mainstream economists adhere to REH, they do so with varying degrees of conviction. In the world of 'strong' rational expectations, all resources are always fully employed. There is no such thing as involuntary unemployment, only voluntary choices for work or leisure. The hugely important policy implication of this belief, as we shall see, is not just that 'stimulus' policies will fail to stimulate, but that they will lead to inferior outcomes. The New Keynesians accept REH, but also admit the existence of 'frictions' which impede almost instantaneous adjustment to new conditions. This allows them to advocate government interventions to improve outcomes.

In the history of thought, REH represents a fusion of the rational-scientific aspirations of the Enlightenment with that belief in the 'wisdom of the crowd' characteristic of American democracy. REH had been germinating in the womb of economics ever since the start of 'scientific' economics in the eighteenth century, requiring only mathematical magic to bring it to full life. But the history of rational expectations is also connected with the democratic character of the American dream. Markets, representing the verdict of millions of individuals pursuing their self-interest, know more and better than governments. The American consumer is queen. Adherents of REH love to stress the democratic character of the rationality claim. It is based on the law of large numbers, which tells us that the larger the group, the more likely is the average choice to be optimal. There is no way in which governments can improve on the crowd's wisdom.

However, although REH economists were concerned to make the

case for unfettered markets, REH is also the answer to the central planner's dream. Just think of those giant linear-programming exercises designed by Soviet mathematicians in the 1960s in the attempt to make central planning rational. The crucial assumption of REH is not perfect competition, but perfect information. Had the Soviet state been able to concentrate the information and computing power now said to be dispersed around free markets, there would have been no technical reason why its choices should not have been perfectly rational in the way postulated by REH. A single Platonic guardian would make no mistakes.

REAL BUSINESS CYCLE THEORY

RBC theorists accept the strong version of the REH: that markets always clear – that is, that demand always equals supply. But if markets always clear, why do we have business cycles? The older generation of theorists had explained such cycles by slowness of wages and prices to adjust to 'shocks'. A change in spending drives the economy away from equilibrium, but 'sticky' wages and/or prices prevent rapid adjustment to a new equilibrium. As wages and prices do not adjust, output does. But REH claimed almost instantaneous adjustment. It seemed to follow, RBC theorists argued, that cycles are due not to temporary deviations from an optimal level of output, but to fluctuations in the level of potential output itself. Business-cycle fluctuations are explained by sequences of real shocks to productivity which reverberate through the economic system. Recessions and periods of high economic growth are the efficient response to changes in the real economic environment – that is what makes the theory a 'real' theory. The changes might involve oil prices, regulations, weather conditions, and so on.

Suppose, for example, that the rate of technological change slows down. As a result, people's marginal productivity will drop, and, as it does so, the real wage will drop. People will react to that change in a rational manner by choosing to work for a lower wage, in the same or an alternative job, or will spend more time with their families. Hence real shocks provoke cycles through efficient reactions by economic agents to their changing economic circumstances. This pattern holds over longer periods. When there is a cluster of new inventions which raise real wages, people will work more, causing output to surge. Where there is a technological slowdown which lowers the real wage, people will work less, causing output to fall. This pattern is what we observe as booms and recessions. Like REH, RBC assumes that markets are efficient in the absence of regulations. The implication is, obviously, that markets should be left as little regulated as possible. In recent years great efforts have been invested in developing the so-called dynamic stochastic general equilibrium (DSGE) RBC models, whose main feature has been the attempt to model decisions over time by using increasingly complicated mathematics.

What RBC theorists have in mind as examples of 'efficient' adaptation to 'real' shocks is brought out by the following snatch of conversation between Robert Lucas, high priest of RBC theory, and Arjo Klamer in the early 1980s. Unemployment in the US was then 9.4%:

KLAMER: My taxi driver here is driving a taxi, even though he is an accountant, because he can't find a job. He is obviously frustrated. It seems a lot of people are running around in that position.

LUCAS: I would describe him as a taxi driver (laughing), if what he is doing is driving a taxi.

KLAMER: But a frustrated taxi driver.

LUCAS: Well, we draw these things out of urns, and sometimes we get good draws, and sometimes bad draws.

Lucas went on to explain that situations of heavy unemployment are best modelled as information problems:

'If you look back at the 1929 to 1933 episode, there were a lot of decisions made that, after the fact, people wished they had not made; there were a lot of jobs people quit that they wished they had hung on to; there are job offers that people turned down because they thought the wage offer was crappy, then three months later they wished they had grabbed. Accountants who lost their accounting jobs passed over a cab driver's job, and now they're sitting on the street while their pal's driving a cab. So they wish they'd taken the cab driver's job. People are making this kind of mistake all the time.

Nevertheless, Lucas did find it hard to understand why these 'mistakes' didn't cancel each other out.[5]

THE EFFICIENT FINANCIAL
MARKET THEORY

It is not easy to see why a world in which the future is perfectly known requires financial markets at all, since such a world is risk-free. All transactions take place at the risk-free rate of interest. Efficient financial market theory recognizes this problem by modifying the knowledge requirement. What is known is not what will happen for certain, but the risk of it happening, which is measurable. EFMT says that the prices of financial instruments – stocks, shares, debts – represent the best possible estimates of the risks attached to ownership of this type of asset, taking into account available information, both public and private. This implies that different financial instruments could give different rates of return depending on their riskiness. EMFT has been the biggest casualty of the current financial meltdown.

Britain's Financial Services Authority has described, with commendable honesty, the 'intellectual assumptions' on which it based its recent regulatory philosophy:

(i) Market prices are good indicators of rationally evaluated economic value.

(ii) The development of securitized credit, since based on the creation of new and more liquid markets, has improved both allocative efficiency and financial stability.

(iii) The risk characteristics of financial markets can be inferred from mathematical analysis, delivering robust quantitative measures of trading risk.

(iv) Market discipline can be used as an effective tool in constraining harmful risk taking.

(v) Financial innovation can be assumed to be beneficial since market competition would winnow out any innovations which did not deliver value added.[6]

From which it followed that:

(i) Markets are in general self-correcting, with market discipline a more effective tool than regulation or supervisory oversight . . .

(ii) The main responsibility for managing risks lies with senior management and boards of . . . individual firms . . .

(iii) Customer protection is best ensured not by product regulation or direct intervention in markets, but by ensuring that wholesale markets are as unfettered and transparent as possible . . .[7]

All bank risk-management models are based on the efficient financial market theory. What they do is establish a range of probabilities within which future events will occur. Technically speaking, the spread of past returns give us a range of uncertainty about future returns. The spread, or the uncertainty of outcomes, is measured by the standard deviation or the variance.

The main assumption underlying these models is that the distribution of risk is captured by a Gaussian bell curve, named after its inventor, Carl Friedrich Gauss (1777–1855). The colloquial name 'the *normal* distribution' indicates the standard view. It is a distribution where the average value is also the most common value. Data points are clustered in the middle. 'Normal distribution' can be represented graphically as a bell curve (see p. 40) with 'thin tails'.*

It is an article of faith in such models that diversification reduces risk: when we hold many assets, the risks which are unique to each one tend to cancel each other out, as they are largely unconnected.

---

*An explanation for most of us. The area underneath the curve sums the full set of probabilities and is therefore equal to 1. The area under the curve between any two points represents the probability that an event occurs between those points. The x-axis is divided into standard deviations, or sigmas, around the mean (average); a standard deviation corresponds to a measure of the average distance of events from the overall average. What the normal distribution is saying is that the probability of an event happening within one standard deviation up or down from the mean is equal to 68%. The probability of an event happening within two standard deviations is 95%, and so on. In other words, the vast majority of events, it is assumed, occur very close to the average. Knowing that all probabilities add up to 1 (the total area underneath the curve) and combining that with the high concentration of probabilities around the mean implies that the area in the tails of the distribution is very small. 'Thin tails' are the statisticians' way of saying that extreme events are very unlikely.

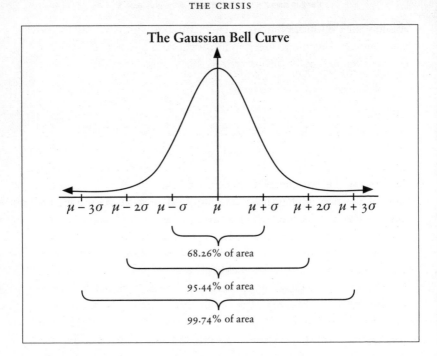

The Gaussian Bell Curve

$\mu - 3\sigma$ $\mu - 2\sigma$ $\mu - \sigma$ μ $\mu + \sigma$ $\mu + 2\sigma$ $\mu + 3\sigma$

68.26% of area

95.44% of area

99.74% of area

The risk-management models ignored the possibility of a correlation or momentum in the movement of risks, typical of a boom or a bust. What happened over the course of 2008 was that suddenly 10% risks became 90% risks or higher, and all at the same time.

A reason often given for why the risk-management models failed is that they relied on data drawn from the very recent past. In Alan Greenspan's words, 'Probability distributions estimated largely, or exclusively over cycles that do not include periods of panic will underestimate the likelihood of extreme price movements . . . Furthermore, joint distributions estimated over periods that do not include panics will underestimate correlations between asset returns during panics.'[8] The only mistake Greenspan acknowledges is that he assumed that senior management would be able to manage risk in a way which would not endanger their firms.

But Greenspan's explanation for failure of the models does not go far enough. The failure is not only a matter of limited data: ultimately, it is a matter of limited applicability. One cannot apply insurance models to non-insurable products. Although both actuarial and micro-forecasting models rely on historical data, the analogy between actuarial models of life, property and casualty insurance and insurance of complex derivatives is false. Although there have been failures in insurance markets (the failure of Lloyds in the late 1980s is a major example), insurers in general haven't suffered the same losses as the investment banks, because the risks they take on are generally measurable. Life-assurance companies can correctly price the premiums they need to cover their payments, because they have reliable, up-to-date, statistics of life expectancy. For them, the future is a statistical reflection of the past. But insurers, relying on a false analogy with life expectancy, have been spreading into a world beyond actuarial risk. They started offering insurance on every type of risk – credit risk, liquidity risk, market risk, legal risk, catastrophic risk, regulatory risk, political risk, compliance risk, reputational risk – all of which they claimed were actuarially calculable in exactly the same way as life assurance. And the big banks and pension funds piled in, because they bought the story. We talk of 'political risk' when we should talk about political uncertainty. We simply do not know what the probability is of the future direction of Russia's economic or political policy. The use of the word 'risk' to cover uninsurable contingencies conveys a spurious precision, which comforts the markets but has no basis in science.

Few of the bank executives and boards who were supposed to manage risk understood the mathematics of risk-management models. This did not prevent them selling them to the public – or themselves. One of the most widely used option-pricing models, the Black–Scholes formula, is based on a 'normal distribution', and ignores the possibility of extreme events. Now, as a result of Black Swans, those executives and boards find their stock options in black holes.

It is ironic that the 2009 FSA review cited above (p. 38) says it is vital to achieve 'external challenge to conventional wisdom assumptions' from academics, when it was academic and business economists who were the main sources of the conventional-wisdom assumptions which brought the financial system crashing down. The review quotes from the IMF Global Financial Stability Report (GFSR) of April 2006:

There is growing recognition that the dispersion of credit risk by banks to a broader and more diverse group of investors, rather than warehousing such risk on their balance sheets, has helped make the banking and overall financial system more resilient.

The improved resilience may be seen in fewer bank failures and more consistent credit provision. Consequently the commercial banks may be less vulnerable today to credit or economic shocks.[9]

This is the equivalent of Professor Irving Fisher's belief in October 1929 that stock prices on Wall Street had reached a 'a permanently high plateau', followed, after its collapse, by his prediction in November that the 'end of the decline of the Stock Market will probably not be long, only a few days more at most'.[10] He was the efficient market philosopher of his day, his optimism perhaps fortified by his huge exposure. He was wiped out.

Critiques of Bell-Curve Economics

Within the academic community, the 'post-Keynesian' school of economists has remained closest to the spirit of Keynes's *General Theory*. Their best-known member,[11] Paul Davidson, has persistently maintained that old classical, New Classical and New Keynesian economists alike have betrayed Keynes's legacy by accepting the 'ergodic' axiom – an axiom which holds that the outcome at any future date is a statistical shadow of past and present market prices. The late Hyman Minsky also followed Keynes's footsteps by depicting a financial system which transforms investment into speculation followed by collapse. Whether the present crisis represents a 'Minsky moment' has been a topic much discussed by financial journalists. Minsky was completely ignored by mainstream economists.

Following the French mathematician Benoît Mandelbrot's argument that forecasting models based on the bell curve ignore dramatic discontinuities in nature, Nassim Taleb highlights the pivotal role of Black Swans. Unlike much of physical science, economics, Taleb argues, is dominated by such rare and extreme events. 'The bell curve ignores large deviations, cannot handle them, yet makes us confident that we have tamed uncertainty.'[12] Thus risk managers supply measures of uncertainty that exclude Black Swans. At times when markets are faced with the most significant changes, economic models cease to work, since they are based on the continuity of previously observed patterns. Typically, these are times when herd behaviour is most obvious. As paraphrased in an interview in the *Wall Street Journal*, Taleb delivered himself of the thought that 'the lesson, evidently, is that it's better to be wrong than alone.'[13] All these attitudes echo Keynes on the snares of statistics.

However, Taleb's Black Swans are not Keynesian. They are highly improbable events, but one can still attach a probability to them – albeit a low one. For Keynes, uncertainty attached to a future event to which no probability can be assigned at all.

George Soros is another critic of the bell-curve view of the world. In his book *The Alchemy of Finance* (1987) he developed the idea of 'reflexivity'. Mistaken opinions about markets reinforce each other. Positive feedback loops lead to cumulative movements up or down. 'Thus, prices typically run up *too high or stay too low* for far too long, because people become fixed in their partial convictions.'[14] Because of reflexivity, momentum carries markets far from equilibrium territory. Nevertheless, equilibrium exists, and the longer the rise, the more savage the fall. Soros provides an excellent theory of herd behaviour, and of why economics is not a natural science. But it is not, as we shall see, Keynes's theory. It is a theory of long deviations from an equilibrium given by objective facts. There is no irreducible uncertainty in his system – the future is still ergodic in the sense that it can be reduced to statistical probabilities based on the past.

To the non-economist, these debates may seem to have little or nothing to do with the crisis and how to get out of it. This is to ignore their influence on policy. The policy regime which followed the Reagan–Thatcher revolution reflected to a large extent the ideas of the New Classical economists. Consumer price stability became the main, and often the only, goal of macroeconomic policy, and monetary policy was considered sufficient by itself to ensure macroeconomic stability. Concern with credit, banking, asset prices, and financial stability was downgraded. Credibility of policy was supposed to be built by responding to events in a systematic way – no surprises. Budgets should be balanced and debt-to-GDP ratios stabilized, since rising debt threatened the solvency of governments, and all deficits did was to raise interest rates and thus 'crowd out' more efficient private activity. To apply these policies one needed independent central banks with mechanical rules – like the so-called Taylor rule, devised in 1993 by the economist John Taylor for relating interest-rate changes to projections of inflation. Efficient financial market theory also lay behind the extensive deregulation of the last twenty years: the repeal of the Glass–Steagall Act, the acceptance of bank self-assessment of risk, the failure to regulate the market for derivatives.

FAILURES TO EXPLAIN THE CRISIS

It was to be expected that, holding the theories they do, the New Classical economists have been embarrassed to admit the crisis. If markets are efficient they cannot fail. Therefore the crisis must be the result of policy mistakes. As we have seen, the favourite mistake for conservative economists is excessive money creation by the monetary authority, leading to bubble and burst. But this admission is damaging to them theoretically, because it destroys the policy ineffectiveness proposition. It assumes that people are fooled by 'money illusion'. But if they had rational expectations, they should not have been.

But New Keynesians also flounder when they try to explain the crisis. The New Keynesians, as we have seen, accept rational expectations, but are nevertheless able to conclude that markets can fail. They achieve this height of common sense by 'relaxing the assumption' of perfect information. Here is New Keynesian Joe Stiglitz: 'Failures in financial markets . . . have highlighted the importance of information imperfection . . . The results were clear: the financial system failed to perform the functions which it is supposed to perform, allocating capital efficiently and managing risk.'[15]

The main source of market failure investigated by the New Keynesians is 'asymmetric information': insiders have an informational advantage over outsiders. The credit customer knows more about his risk of default than the bank does; the insurance buyer knows more about his health than the insurance company does.

Achieving efficient exchange under these conditions is difficult. Suspecting that the insider will use his superior information to cheat, the outsider will pay only a low price, and therefore the insider will want to sell only bad goods. Whether the participants want it or not, only low-quality goods and services get traded.

In the eyes of the New Keynesians, market failure is extensive, ramifying into all markets – labour markets, product markets, financial markets.

The New Keynesians' models seem to fit some current facts rather well, such as banks giving out loans to borrowers who could never pay them back. The flaw of these models is that they assume that someone – the credit customer, the insurance buyer – possesses *perfect* information. However, the present crisis shows that we are in a world of uncertainty, with the blind leading the blind. It is a crisis of symmetric ignorance, not asymmetric information.* As Taleb points out, the bankers were not only greedy, but 'phenomenally skilled at self-deception'.[16] Robert Merton and Myron Scholes, who in 1997 received a Nobel Prize for their work on derivative pricing methods, believed in the models which led to the collapse in 1998 of their hedge fund Long Term Capital Management. They were 'using phoney, bell-curve mathematics while managing to convince themselves that it was a great science and thus turning the entire financial establishment into suckers'.[17] Every general crisis involves self-deception as well as the deception of others. In Donald Rumsfeld's immortal phrase, it is the 'unknown unknowns' which trip us up. If only one person were perfectly informed there could never be a general crisis. But the only perfectly informed person is God, and he does not play the stock market.

The reason why economics has given such a poor account of the origins of the crisis is that there is something essentially incompatible between the economist's view of individual rationality and systemic collapse. Without adding qualifications which strain their logic,

---

*Traders need to be distinguished from bankers. No traders I have talked to believe in anything as silly as efficient markets. What they live on is commissions. They are not interested in holding correctly priced risks, only in selling them on as quickly and frequently as possible. The thing to avoid is to be left holding these securities when the music stops.

economists cannot readily get from their picture of the the individual maximizing his utilities to booms and slumps and the persistence of depressions. The New Keynesian solution is to say that people are rational but have information problems. Another is simply to say that human behaviour is irrational, and therefore efficient markets don't exist. This is the thrust of behavioural economics. But the epistemological source of such irrationality is unexplored. The adoption of 'irrationality' as a general explanation for all 'abnormal distributions' smacks of theoretical panic.[18] Another line of retreat is to say, with Alan Greenspan, that disasters such as the present are (unexplained) once-in-a-century events, and that most of the time markets behave in a perfectly rational way. None of these explanations gets to the heart of the matter, because they all leave out the influence of irreduceable uncertainty on behaviour.

DEBATE OVER THE STIMULUS

The influence of ideas on policy is also clearly shown by the debate over how to escape from the slump. The New Classical economists believe in continuous market clearing. The New Keynesians believe that markets fail due to imperfect information and other frictions: whether they believe that markets *must* fail is less obvious. Normally these schools pursue their separate ways, but on the subject of the stimulus they argue the toss like bad-natured siblings. Broadly speaking, the New Classical economists believe that any stimulating should be done by means of the central bank printing money. New Keynesians believe it should be done by the government running a budget deficit financed by bond issues and itself directly spending the money raised on infrastructure projects.

The case for a monetary stimulus follows the conservative explanation for the slump. Echoing Milton Friedman, Robert Lucas believes that the Great Depression was caused by the Federal Reserve Board not offsetting the collapse in the money supply by open-market operations. Hence he approves of the Fed's injection of an extra $600 billion into the economy. Monetary policy as Bernanke implements it has been the most helpful counter-recession action taken to date, in my opinion, and it will continue to have many advantages in future months. It is fast and flexible. There is no other way that so much cash could have been put into the system as fast as this $600 billion was, and if necessary it can be taken out just as quickly. The cash comes in the form of loans. It entails no new government enterprises, no government equity positions in private enterprises, no price fixing or other controls on the operation of individual businesses, and no government role in the allocation of capital across different activities. These seem to me important virtues.[19]

This concession to reality involves Lucas in theoretical breakdown. For, according to New Classical theory, market economies don't need stimulating. They always respond efficiently to shocks. There is no positive demand for money, and, with agents correctly anticipating inflation, the monetary injection can have no stimulatory effect.

Paul Krugman, on the other hand, has consistently argued for a fiscal stimulus based on government spending. He echoes Keynes on the uncertainty of monetary policy. Rather, 'increased government spending is just what the doctor ordered, and concerns about the budget deficit should be put on hold.' The federal government should 'provide extended benefits for the unemployed . . . provide emergency aid to state and local governments . . . buy up mortgages . . . and restructure the terms to help families stay in their homes. And this is also a good time to engage in some serious infrastructure spending which the country badly needs in any case.'[20]

The New Deal had only 'limited short-run success', Krugman believes, because President Roosevelt's 'economic policies were too cautious.' Obama's people should 'figure out how much help they think the economy needs, then add 50 percent'.[21] Depression economics is back, and 'the usual rules of economic policy no longer apply: virtue becomes vice, caution is risky and prudence is folly . . . To pull us out of this downward spiral, the federal government will have to provide an economic stimulus plan in the form of higher spending.'[22] 'Under current conditions there's no trade-off between what's good in the short run and what's good for the long run.'[23] The bank recapitalization scheme will not be enough: what's needed is closer to 'a full nationalization of a significant part of the financial system'. Krugman echoes most New Keynesians in arguing that the stimulus should take the form of spending, not tax rebates (except to the very poor), since part of the rebates will be saved, not spent.[24]

By contrast, the freshwater economists have been almost unanimously against fiscal stimulus. Typical is the University of Chicago's Gary Becker – also a Nobel laureate – who warned that 'the true value of these government programs may be limited because they will be put together hastily, and are likely to contain a lot of political pork and other inefficiencies.' Becker says that, in that case, spending could do more harm than good. An analysis by a taxpayer group, Americans for Limited Government, shows that Obama's $800 billion stimulus includes $200 million for beautification of the National Mall and millions for new cars for federal bureaucrats.[25] There was also a flap over contraceptive-related spending. If cars and condoms qualify as emergency 'stimulus' spending, what doesn't? These criticisms echo conservative attacks on the New Deal's 'boondoggles'. In fact conservative economic historians argue that the New Deal hindered what would have been a natural recovery from the Depression. John Cochrane, the Myron Scholes professor of finance at the University of Chicago's business school, has argued for lower taxes rather than higher spending, as being good for incentives.[26]

However, beyond the conservative argument that public spending always involves corruption and mis-spending, there is the argument that it will simply divert resources from more efficient private spending, so that its multiplying effect will be zero, or even less than zero. Thus Eugene Fama of the University of Chicago, inventor of the efficient financial market theory:

The problem is simple: bailouts and stimulus plans are funded by issuing more government debt. (The money must come from somewhere!) The added debt absorbs savings that would otherwise go to private investment. In the end, despite the existence of idle resources, bailout and stimulus plans do not add to current resources in use. They just move resources from one use to another.[27]

And John Cochrane:

First, if money is not going to be printed, it has to come from somewhere. If the government borrows a dollar from you, that is a dollar that you do not spend, or that you do not lend to a company to spend on new investment. Every dollar of increased government spending must correspond to one less dollar of private spending. Jobs created by stimulus spending are offset by jobs lost from the decline of private spending. We can build roads instead of factories, but fiscal stimulus can't help us to build more of both.[28]

Robert Barro calls the claims for the stimulatory effects of extra spending 'a voodoo multiplier'. His own empirical work suggests 'a multiplier of zero' (zero stimulating effect) for non-defence outlays. In the medium term, though, the multiplier is likely to be negative, reflecting the adverse effects of larger government on economic growth. He points out that 'although World War II raised US real GDP a lot, this response is not typical for the OECD. In fact, WWII is the biggest economic disaster of the 20th century, out-stripping the Great Depression. This is, of course, because many countries suffered from physical destruction and loss of life.'[29]

Paul Krugman was enraged, pointing out that the conservative argument was a rerun of the 'Treasury View' of the 1920s:

If there was one essential element in the work of John Maynard Keynes, it was the demolition of Say's Law – the assertion that supply necessarily creates demand. Keynes showed that the fact that spending equals income, or equivalently that saving equals investment, does *not* imply that there's always enough spending to fully employ the economy's resources, that there's always enough investment to make use of the saving the economy would have had if it were at full employment.

Getting to that realization was an awesome intellectual achievement. That's why it's deeply depressing to find, not that people like Eugene Fama disagree with Keynes's conclusions . . . but that they're obviously completely unaware of the whole argument.[30]

Krugman added that it was as if some eminent biologists have never heard of the theory of evolution and the concept of natural selection. He claimed that economics had entered a new Dark Age, similar to the early Middle Ages when knowledge known to the Greeks and Romans had been forgotten by the barbarian kingdoms. Freshwaters, on the other hand, believe that saltwater economics is as discredited as the Ptolemaic model or the phlogiston hypothesis.

In a more thoughtful essay, Krugman has tried to give a 'history-of-ideas' explanation for the new Dark Ages.[31] He says that, at the end of the 1960s, saltwater economists began the search for more secure micro-foundations than unexplained wage rigidity to explain why shocks to money seemed to have real effects rather than affecting only the price level. Imperfect information was their answer. But business cycles last too long to rely on imperfect information. So then the profession divided. One group went down the New Keynesian route, arguing that something such as 'menu costs' – the cost of changing the prices on menus, and all price lists, each time the inflation rate changes – must explain the stickiness we actually seem to see. 'This group isn't averse to putting a lot of rationality into its models, but it's willing to accept aspects of the world that seem clear in the data, even if [they] can't . . . be fully explained in terms of deep foundations.'

On the other hand, the freshwaters decided that, since they couldn't come up with a rigorous micro-foundation for price inflexibility, there must not be any price stickiness: recessions are the result of adverse technological shocks, not demand shocks. This group was so convinced of the logical correctness of its position that the schools dominated by it stopped teaching macroeconomics. Students wondered who Keynes was, because he was never mentioned in their courses.

In short, as I said earlier, the New Keynesians put common sense ahead of their logic, while the freshwaters put their logic ahead of common sense. Policymakers are left with an unenviable choice.

CONCLUSION

The case for Keynes is quite simple. He might not have predicted that the financial collapse would occur when it did – indeed, he would have rejected the idea that economic life consists of predictable events – but he would certainly have thought a financial collapse possible, and even likely, given the extent to which governments had abandoned any serious attempt to avert such a thing. An economics infused with his spirit would have set up a system which took precautions against blizzards like this happening. The dominant economics of the last thirty years encouraged and promoted a system in which financial blizzards like this could occur, and more often than once in a hundred years. It did so from a mistaken belief that all risk can be correctly priced and that therefore financial markets are optimally self-regulating. The New Keynesians who challenged the policies of the market fundamentalists were defeated because they accepted their basic premises: and in economics logic is everything. But what kind of logic? It is time to introduce the Master.

PART II

The Rise and Fall of Keynesian Economics

3

The Lives of Keynes

A MANY-SIDED GENIUS

Born in 1883 into an academic family, John Maynard Keynes was a product of Cambridge civilization at its most fertile. His circle included not just the most famous philosophers of the day – G. E. Moore, Bertrand Russell and Ludwig Wittgenstein – but also that exotic offshoot of Cambridge the Bloomsbury Group, a commune of writers and painters, with whom he formed his closest friendships. He was caught up in the intellectual ferment and sexual awakening which marked the passage from Victorian to Edwardian England. At the same time, he had a highly practical bent.

After the First World War, Keynes set out to save a capitalist system he did not particularly admire. He did so because he thought it was the best guarantee of the possibility of civilization. But he was always quite clear that the pursuit of wealth was a means, not an end – the end being to live 'wisely, agreeably, and well'. He did not much admire economics, either, hoping that some day economists would become as useful as dentists.[1] All this made him, as his wife, the ballerina Lydia Lopokova, put it, 'more than an economist'. He himself felt that 'all his worlds' fertilized his economics, giving him a richer, more complex, understanding of human nature than that of the economist's 'economic man'. In fact, given his other interests, he might be seen as the most brilliant non-economist who ever applied himself to the study of economics. In this lay both his greatness and his vulnerability. He imposed himself on his profession by a series of profound insights into human behaviour which fitted the turbulence of his times. But these were never – could never be – properly integrated into the core of his discipline, which expelled them as soon as it conveniently could. In the 1930s Keynes's lifestyle became more conventional as his work became more creative. He died of heart failure in 1946, having worked himself to death in service of his country.

His ideas about how markets worked reflected his personal experiences, particularly as a speculator and investor: in this respect he was like George Soros and Warren Buffett. Of course, these ideas were not straightforward reflections. Keynes was superbly able to use the 'data of experience', his own and others', to develop theoretical insights into how the market system actually worked – in contrast to the pure theorist who averts his eyes from the messiness of reality in contemplation of the beauty of his model. As an economist, Keynes firmly believed in making his assumptions as realistic as possible, in contrast to many theorists at all times for whom *unrealism* of assumptions has been their models' chief merit. Keynes was also extremely practical. He had a lot of the civil servant in his make-up, and spent several years of his life working in government departments, both the India Office and the Treasury. A leading feature of his Civil Service performance was his facility in applying theory to practice. A lot of the theory was made up 'on the hoof', to fit the practical requirements of the moment. His theoretical speculations issued into compact plans of action, which could be slotted into the existing institutions of government, and which could therefore be made to happen without huge convulsions in established practice – or, indeed, the social order. He was an evolutionist, not a revolutionist. Few have paid much attention to Keynes as a philosopher, but his economic work was philosophically inspired, and what he thought about economic life, its purpose and meaning, was controlled by ethics. Like other economists, he had the double character of the scientist and the preacher. So Keynes brought a glittering array of talents to his diagnosis of, and prescriptions for, the diseases of contemporary economies.

What sort of economist was he? In his obituary essay on his teacher Alfred Marshall, Keynes wrote:

The master-economist must possess a rare *combination* of gifts . . . He must be mathematician, historian, stateman, philosopher – in some degree. He must understand symbols and speak in words. He must contemplate the particular, in terms of the general, and touch abstract and concrete in the same flight of thought. He must study the present in the light of the past for the purposes of the future. No part of man's nature or his institutions must be entirely outside his regard. He must be purposeful and disinterested in a simultaneous mood, as aloof and incorruptible as an artist, yet sometimes as near to earth as a politician.[2]

This bore little resemblance to Marshall, but a striking resemblance to one John Maynard Keynes.

He had a universal curiosity, and could not touch any topic without weaving a theory about it, however fanciful. He called the seventeenth-century scientist Isaac Newton 'the last of the magicians',[3] and not the first of the rationalists. In late middle age he used to complain that young economists were not 'properly educated', by which he meant they were not able to draw on a wide culture to interpret economic facts.

He was formidably intelligent. Bertrand Russell, one of the cleverest men of his day, wrote that 'Keynes's intellect was the sharpest and clearest that I have ever known. When I argued with him, I felt that I took my life in my hands, and I seldom emerged without feeling something of a fool.' Others, like the art historian Kenneth Clark, felt he used his brilliance too unsparingly: 'he never dimmed his headlights.'

His mind was mercurial, which meant that he quickly changed his opinion. He liked to play with ideas in a reckless way, but in this manner, as his friend Oswald Falk remarked, 'in spite of false scents, he caught up with the march of events more rapidly than did others.'

Keynes was the most intuitive of economists, with an extraordinary insight into the gestalt of particular situations. He possessed in marked degree the scientific imagination he ascribed to Freud, 'which can body forth an abundance of innovating ideas, shattering possibilities, working hypotheses, which have sufficient foundation in intuition and common experience', though unprovable. He claimed for the economist Thomas Malthus 'a profound economic intuition', and quoted De Morgan's verdict on Newton, 'so happy in his conjectures as to seem to know more than he could possibly have any means of proving'. Keynes also felt sure of his unprovable conjectures.[4]

Keynes ascribed to Malthus 'an unusual combination of keeping an open mind to the shifting picture of experience and of constantly applying to its interpretation the principles of formal thought'. This expressed his own economic philosophy in a nutshell. Economics, he told Roy Harrod in 1938, is a 'science of thinking in terms of models joined to the art of choosing models that are relevant to the contemporary world . . . Good economists are scarce because the gift of using "vigilant observation" to choose good models . . . appears to be a very rare one.'[5] Keynes paid close attention to economic facts, usually in statistical form. He used to say that his best ideas came to him from 'messing about with figures and seeing what they must mean'. He could be as excited as any economist at discovering correlations in the data. Yet he was famously sceptical about econometrics – the use of statistical methods for forecasting the future. He championed the cause of better statistics not to provide material for the regression coefficient, but for the intuition of the economist to play on. He believed that statistical information in the hands of the philosophically untrained was a dangerous and misleading toy.

Keynes was the greatest *persuader* in twentieth-century economics. (Some would allow Milton Friedman to share pride of place with him.) Of today's leading economists, only Paul Krugman and Joe Stiglitz seriously aim to persuade the public. His success as an economist is inseparable from his style, just as the failure (as I would call it) of mainstream economics today is inseparable from *its* style. What was his secret? He lived much of his life in a commune of writers, whose books he read – Virginia Woolf, Lytton Strachey, E. M. Forster – and Lytton Strachey's irony certainly rubbed off on him. He read widely in philosophy. Much of his imagery came from a religious background. But clarity, succinctness, an unerring sense of the fitness of words, and an uncanny ability to use simple language to convey profound thoughts were innate emanations of the quality of his mind. He was a wonderful user of the English language, but even more important was his passionate commitment to communicating his ideas in language which his readers could understand, in words which they might use themselves, and which reflected their experience of what was going on. In the history of public language, this comes closest to the Aristotelian notion of the *enthymeme* – a 'rhetorical logic', appropriate to reasoning about 'things which are variable', and taking its premises from the audience's stock of social knowledge.

Keynes's generalizing passion was often at odds with his uncanny sense of the significant particular. It was his very ability to 'touch the abstract and concrete in the same flight of thought' which is such a dazzling, but also bewildering, feature of his economics. To one contemporary, Kurt Singer, he evoked 'by gesture, eye and word . . . the figure of a bird, of incredible swiftness, drawing circles in high altitudes, but of deadly precision when suddenly sweeping down on some particular fact or thought'. Fellow economists often accused him of mixing up the abstract and the concrete. His contemporary Joseph Schumpeter criticized him for offering 'in the garb of general scientific truth, advice which . . . carries meaning only with reference to the practical exigencies of [a] unique historical situation'. In Schumpeter's view, he constructed 'special cases which in the author's own mind and in his exposition are invested with a treacherous generality'. His Cambridge colleague Dennis Robertson called his 'general theory' the 'theory of a very deep slump'. Kurt Singer also wondered whether it was 'not in fact tailored to fit a very particular situation dominated by the political vicissitudes and their psychological consequences of that uneasy weekend between the two world wars, and whether [Keynes] was not in fact dealing with a phenomenon not likely to recur'.[6]

Keynes replied effectively to these charges by saying that the world constructed by classical economics happened not to be the world we actually live in. The debate between what is 'normal' and what is 'abnormal', and whether any epoch has a special claim to be considered one or the other, still lies at the heart of economic theorizing, and has paralysed the ability of economics to be useful to the policymaker.

In my biography of Keynes I called him an 'unusual economist'. I would now go further. Deep down, he was not an economist at all. Of course, he could 'do' economics – and with the best. He put on the mask of an economist to gain authority, just as he put on dark suits and homburgs for life in the City. But he did not believe in the system of ideas by which economists lived, and still live; he did not worship at the temple; he was a heretic who learned how to play the game. In former times he would have been forced to recant, perhaps burnt at the stake. As it was, the freedoms and the exigencies of his times enabled him to force himself on his church. Only a person of colossal self-confidence, outstanding intellect and passionate concern for his countrymen and humankind could have set himself the task of rewriting a large chunk of the Western intellectual tradition. Yet this is what Keynes set out to do. One can only marvel that he got as far as he did. He mesmerized and fascinated his contemporaries; for thirty years after his death they lived in his intellectual and moral afterglow. But to the technicians who inherited his mantle his ideas seemed strangely alien to the main themes of their subject. They tried to assimilate them, but found it difficult and made a mess of it; and the next generation gave them up altogether. Orthodoxy won out; the economic temple was shaken, but still stood.

KEYNES IN THE MARKET

Keynes's theories of economics were drawn to a large extent from his own experience of business life: chiefly as a speculator and investor, to a lesser extent as a government official. Apart from a brief involvement, in the 1920s, in a market-sharing plan to handle surplus capacity in the Lancashire textile industry, his knowledge of the business of 'making things' rather than 'making money' was slight. This is by no means a disqualification in a world so dominated by finance as today's. 'It was his understanding of the speculative instinct which made Keynes such a great economist,' noted his friend and fellow financier Nicholas Davenport.[7] His success in business gave Keynes authority to pronounce on economic issues. Practical men respect theorists who show they can make money. Today Soros and Buffett command attention because they have made billions. Keynes was always at or near the centre of the great financial convulsions of his lifetime; and his monetary theory which led to his 'general theory' was always highly informed by what was happening in the financial world. He ended up as a director of the Bank of England.

His first, and only, personal experience of a British 'credit crunch' was in the early days of the First World War, when, aged thirty-one, he was summoned from Cambridge University to the British Treasury to help deal with a banking crisis. Basically, the retail banks found themselves with a load of bad debts. This was not the result of reckless lending on their part, but because the exchange controls imposed by all belligerents on the outbreak of war prevented foreign buyers of British goods and stock-market securities from remitting money to pay the financial intermediaries which had financed their purchases with money borrowed from the retail banks. The City acceptance houses (merchant banks) could not pay back the discount houses from which they had borrowed money, and the discount houses (the then equivalent of the wholesale market) could not pay back their own advances from the retail banks. Assets which the banks had regarded as liquid had suddenly become illiquid, and the banks stopped lending; for a few days they even refused to pay out to depositors. The government closed the Stock Exchange; there was talk of Britain having to suspend the gold standard. As Keynes explained in his account of the crisis: 'If A owes B money, and B owes it to C, and C to D, and so on, the failure of A may involve the failure of the whole series.'[8]

Keynes argued in the Treasury that all that was necessary was to declare a moratorium on old bills and guarantee new bills, leaving the banks and discount houses to hold some bad debts for the time being. However, the government instead instituted a package of rescue operations which he considered grossly extravagant. Guaranteed against loss by the government, the Bank of England bought up £100 million of old debt itself (about £8.6 billion today) and the Treasury printed £70 million (or £6 billion) of new notes, which it placed at the disposal of the banks at the Bank of England, without collateral. The City was thus relieved of its obligations at the expense of the taxpayer.

In his published account of the crisis in the *Economic Journal*,[9] Keynes criticized the joint-stock banks for 'hoarding' public money in their shareholders' interest, rather than lending it out to industry. In retrospect, it is clear that what averted a recession was not the increase in the money supply, but the hugely expanded government spending on war purchases – i.e. fiscal, not monetary, policy – the new money simply providing a first tranche of the (inflationary) finance for it. There was also a personal side to the banking crisis. Keynes had personally lent money to the discount market. Like others in the same position, he feared a default. In urging the government not to guarantee the bills held by the discount houses, he was giving advice directly contrary to his own interests.

Keynes had started speculating in a small way, on his own and his friends' behalf, before the war. One motive seems to have been to test his new theory of probability. 'I lie in bed for hours in the morning', he wrote to his father in 1908, 'reading treatises on the philosophy of probability by members of the Stock Exchange. The soundest treatment so far is by the owner of a bucket shop.'

'The investor', he wrote in 1910,

will be affected, as is obvious, not by the net income which he will actually receive from his investment in the long run, but by his expectations. These will often depend upon fashion, upon advertisement, or upon purely irrational waves of optimism or pessimism. Similarly by risk we mean, not the real risk as measured by the actual average of the class of investment over the period of years to which the expectation refers, but the risk as it is estimated, wisely or foolishly, by the investor.[10]

If Keynes's important innovation was to introduce 'expectations' into economic theory, one can see that the idea was dancing around in his mind long before he wrote his big treatises.

Keynes was a hedge-fund manager a generation before Alfred Jones, acknowledged inventor of the hedge fund. Investing in the most difficult and volatile markets of his time, he made his money between 1920 and 1940. He was almost cleaned out three times.

In 1919 he created what was in effect a hedge fund with his friend the stockbroker Oswald 'Foxy' Falk, to take advantage of the floating currencies which followed the war. Most of the investors were his Bloomsbury friends. The fund started operations on 1 January 1920, going long in US dollars, but shorting the mark, franc and lira. By the end of February the fund was up by more than 20%. In March/April performance stalled as Keynes's gains on other positions were offset by a bet on the pound going down against the dollar. This turned out wrong when the Bank of England unexpectedly raised its interest rate.

In April, the European currencies rallied against sterling, and, though the rally was short, it lasted long enough to wipe out Keynes's highly leveraged fund. He had lost the whole of his group's capital, and owed Falk £5,000 (£170,000, $280,000, €200,000 in today's value). His Bloomsbury friends did not redeem, and so he claimed he was still solvent. Keynes paid off his debt to Falk with a £5,000 loan from the financier Sir Ernest Cassell, and immediately formed a new syndicate, convinced that 'it must be right to sell marks, francs, and lire forward' if one could stand the racket for a couple of months. This time he was right. 'My finances have been prospering pretty well lately,' he told his father on 13 September. By the end of 1920 he had repaid his new borrowings and had a small profit. By the end of 1922 the debts to his Bloomsbury friends had been cleared and Keynes had a modest profit of between £25,000 and £30,000 (in today's value £1.1–1.3 million, $1.8–2.1 million, €1.3–1.5 million) for himself.

'Speculation', wrote Nicholas Davenport, 'improved [Keynes's] economics and economics improved his speculation.'[11] Gambling on currencies and commodities in the early 1920s produced an expert account of the theory of forward exchanges in his *A Tract on Monetary Reform* (1923), in which he described how traders and investors could use forward markets to insure themselves against currency risk.

Keynes's personal losses coincided with the collapse of the British post-war boom and with the onset of depression, followed by stagnation, which lasted for the rest of the 1920s. Keynes learned from this experience too. Most economists at the time believed that economies reacted to shocks like alert individuals, rapid losses being followed by quick recoveries, with agents switching into new lines of business just as Keynes had switched currencies and commodities. The great lesson of the first post-war depression was that economies are much more sluggish than individuals. Once prices started to fall, after July 1920, uncertainty about how far they would fall caused everyone to act in ways to ensure that they continued falling. Dealers unloaded their stocks; owners sold their property and businesses as banks called in mortgages; manufacturers laid off workers; workers resisted employers' attempts to cut their wages, so profits fell further as real wages went up. The cumulative effect of all this was to pull economic activity down, not push it up. In *A Tract on Monetary Reform* Keynes offered a theoretical explanation. 'The *fact* of falling prices injures entrepreneurs, consequently the *fear* of falling prices causes them to protect themselves by curtailing their operations.'[12] Evidently, the economy was not like a central-heating system, producing a thermo-statically controlled temperature. When the temperature dropped, the economists looked for the automatic adjustment and discovered there was none – or that it was much feebler than they had supposed.

In the 1920s Keynes followed a 'credit-cycle' investment strategy based on a newfangled 'barometer', worked out at the London School of Economics and the Economic Research Department of Harvard University, which claimed to be able to predict changes in the relative prices of different classes of stocks (for example, growth stocks relative to value stocks) over the business cycle. The very moderate results he achieved by this method may have convinced him that we simply do not know enough about the causes and character of business fluctuations to make such predictions feasible.

Keynes's business experience expanded when, in 1921, he was appointed chairman of the National Mutual Life Assurance Society, and acquired several directorships and consultancies. He was by now also bursar of his Cambridge college, King's, with exclusive control over the College Chest. Having read Edgar Lawrence Smith's *Common Stocks as Long-Term Investment* (1925), he started extol-ling the virtues of equities, calling them 'compound interest machines'; he urged an 'active' investment policy. He persuaded the National Mutual to hold three times as much of its funds in ordinary shares as the average of other life-assurance companies, and the King's College Chest to shift from investment in land and fixed-interest shares to equities. Convincing investment-company boards and college bursars to change course was hard, as most financial institutions judged equities riskier than bonds. A typically shocking piece of Keynes advice to fellow college bursars was not to set aside large sums against depreciation of assets. 'In fifty years a million things might happen ... You might as well put by a definite fund against smallpox or an earthquake.' Any reserve fund should be invested in 'whatever seemed best'.[13] There was a subtle theoretical point here which was to be made explicit in the *General Theory*: setting aside reserves or sinking funds against depreciation before the expenditure on new plant falls due diminishes current spending and thus requires a higher volume of net investment to absorb. Reserve accumulation by US companies before 1929 for plant which did not need replacement was on 'so huge a scale' that it was 'alone probably sufficient to cause a slump'.[14]

THE EFFECT OF THE GREAT DEPRESSION

Keynes's scientific imagination was powerfully roused by the Great Depression of 1929–32. On a personal level, the depression cost him his second fortune and changed his investment philosophy. In public terms, it changed his economic philosophy and sharpened his moral critique of capitalism. Keynes abandoned for good the belief that markets were automatically self-correcting. In a notable shift in moral perspective, he started to place less emphasis on efficiency, more on duty.

In the 1920s, Keynes had been speculating with mixed success in the commodity markets. By the end of 1927 his net assets totalled £44,000 (or about £2.1 million today; $3.4 million; €2.5 million). But in 1928 he was long on rubber, wheat, cotton and tin when their prices started to fall. His losses on commodities forced him to sell American securities to cover his position, so he was not invested on Wall Street when the crash came in 1929. The stock-market collapses left him with a security portfolio dominated by 10,000 shares in the Austin Motor Company, whose value fell from £1.10 per share in January 1928 to 25p by the end of 1929. By that date, his net worth had slumped from £44,000 to £7,815 (in today's value from £2.1 million to £380,000; $3.4 million to $620,000, €2.5 million to €445,000) – a fall of more than 80% – and it fell even more in 1930. He was so strapped for cash that he tried to sell his best pictures, but withdrew because bids were so pitiful.

The Great Depression was the worst contraction in modern history. As in today's slump, the United States was at the heart of it. Between 1929 and 1932 the value of US goods and services fell almost by a half. The volume of production fell by a third. Unemployment rose to 25% of the labour force (about 13 million). And investment stopped completely. Similar magnitudes were recorded all over the world, with Germany, where unemployment rose to 6 million, particularly disastrously hit. Limited recovery started at the end of 1932 or early 1933, after twelve quarters of decline, but there was no complete global recovery till the Second World War.

As now, the depression itself was triggered off by a financial crisis, though this was initially in the stock markets rather than the banks. In September 1929 the Dow Jones index peaked at 381. The pricking of the hugely inflated stock-market bubble on 24 October brought an uncontrollable urge to sell. Two ruined financiers jumped off the hundredth floor of the Empire State Building hand in hand. By 1932 the Dow stood at 41.2, a drop of 90 per cent. It did not recover its 1929 level till 1954. The wiping-out of paper wealth, the foreclosing of loans and mortgages, and pressure on the banking system led to rapid cutback in production, which fell by 10 per cent between October and December 1929.* The main banking crisis came only in 1931. In February 1932 Keynes observed that 'we are now in the phase where the risk of carrying assets with borrowed money is so great that there is a competitive panic to get liquid. And each individual who succeeds in getting more liquid forces down the price of assets in the process, with the result that the margins of other individuals are impaired and their courage undermined.'[15]

Immediately after the Wall Street crash, Keynes anticipated that a 'cheap-money' policy would soon revive enterprise throughout the world. By May 1930, however, he recognized that 'we are now in the depth of a very severe international slump, a slump which will take its place in history as amongst the most acute ever experienced. It will require not merely passive movements of bank rates to lift us out of a depression of this order, but a very active and determined policy.'[16] The New York Reserve Bank's discount rate did come down, to 2% in December 1930. Unfortunately, prices were falling even faster than interest rates, raising the real cost of debt. This demonstrates that, in a massive bear market in both real and financial assets, there is no escape through interest-rate policy. The Bank of Japan and the

---

*Indices of US production had started to turn down before the stock-market crash. But it was the crash itself which turned the prospect of a mild recession into a deep depression.

Japanese Ministry of Finance had to learn this lesson all over again in the 1990s.

Keynes's analysis of the crisis was also influenced by his business experience. There was a persistent tendency to excess supply in primary products. Savings were being absorbed in speculating in stocks. When savings were switched to the New York bull market in 1928, the cost of holding stocks rose, the stocks were unloaded, and commodity prices started to fall. It was this fall which wiped out Keynes's long positions.

Thus Keynes's public and personal experience both fed his explanation of the Great Depression in *A Treatise on Money* (1930). Savings had been 'running ahead' of investment. Instead of being used to buy new capital equipment, they were fuelling speculation. The high degree of leverage allowed on the stock markets of that time – investors had to put down only 15% up front – increased the speculative frenzy. The result was a 'profit inflation' for a narrow class of rich investors as stock prices soared; but, since no new real assets were being created, the bubble was bound to burst sooner or later.

It is commonly believed that Keynes failed to predict the slump, as though Black Swans are predictable. As a matter of fact, both Keynes and Hayek thought a big crash was likely in 1928–9, though for completely opposite reasons: Hayek because interest rates were too low, Keynes because they were too high. The test of inflation, Keynes insisted, was the test of prices. Judged by the commodity price index, there was no danger of inflation in 1927. Hence, by raising its funds rate from 3.5% to 5% in July 1928 to choke off Wall Street speculation, the Fed was imposing an act of deflation on a thriving US economy. 'The difficulty will be', Keynes argued in September 1928, 'to find an outlet for the vast investment funds coming forward – particularly if central banks resist the tendency of the rate of interest to fall.'[17] And he wrote again in October 1928, 'I cannot help feeling that the risk just now is all on the side of a business depression . . . If too prolonged an attempt is made to check the speculative position by dear money, it may well be that the dear money, by checking new investments, will bring about a general business depression.'[18] Once the slump had started, Keynes conceded that the stability of the price index in 1927–8 had concealed a 'profit inflation'. He now argued that speculation in real estate and stocks had masked a more general tendency to underinvestment in relation to corporate savings. Once these markets had collapsed, what he called 'psychological' poverty set in and people stopped spending.[19]

Hayek's 'prediction' was based on a completely different theory, which was standard among conservative bankers and businessmen at the time. The Fed had kept money too cheap for too long and had thus allowed an unsustainable credit boom to build up. To prevent booms and busts, Hayek would never allow any credit 'injections' from the banking system, and he acknowledged the logic of this position by rejecting fractional reserve banking – the banking practice requiring banks only to keep a fraction of their deposits in reserves. Hayek implied that equilibrium in the late 1920s required the price level to fall – in line with increases in productivity – and an asset inflation was being stoked up by keeping it stable. The credit boom had led to 'overinvestment'. The economy was bound to collapse as investment increasingly ran ahead of 'genuine' savings. This remains the basis of the 'Austrian' criticism of Greenspan's cheap-money policy today.[20]

The causes of the Great Depression are still disputed between the 'money-glut' and the Keynesian 'saving-glut' views.

Keynes conceded that trying to curtail a boom by higher interest rates before the slump occurred might be the only remedy against inflation if there was no other policy in place for managing aggregate demand. But this, he thought, was 'dangerously and unnecessarily defeatist'. The way to keep economies booming was by maintaining a high volume of investment and increasing the propensity to consume 'by the redistribution of incomes . . . so that a given level of employment would require a smaller volume of current investment to support it'.[21] 'Austerity at the Treasury, not high interest rates, should be the method for controlling inflation,' he wrote in 1937.[22]

The other strand in the orthodox explanation of the Great Depression concentrates on policy mistakes made during the downturn, which had the effect of deepening and prolonging it. In a classic work,[23] Friedman and Schwartz argued that the Federal Reserve Board failed to pump money into the banking system after October 1930 to offset 'hoarding' by the banks and the public. This was due to weak and divided leadership, the Fed's strongman, Benjamin Strong, having died in 1928. They admit that the fall of production by 27%, of wholesale prices by 13.5% and of personal incomes by 17% between October 1929 and October 1930 would still have ranked as 'one of the most severe contractions on record'. But in October 1930 came the first banking crisis. Widespread bank failures in rural areas led the public to convert their deposits into currency and banks to accumulate excess reserves as both sought to protect their assets against panic. This led to a collapse in the money supply. According to Friedman and Schwartz, then, the downward shift in the supply curve of money led to downward pressure on real income and prices. The world depression intensified the American one through the pressure on the dollar after the collapse of the gold standard in 1931.

The nub of Friedman's 'monetarist' explanation is that the quantity of money fell not because there were no willing borrowers, but because the Fed allowed the quantity of money to fall. By contrast, most Keynesians have followed Keynes's own lead in explaining the depression in terms of failure to maintain aggregate demand. It was the fall in spending which led to the fall in the money stock, not the other way round.[24]

Later Keynesian analysis would emphasize more than Keynes did the role played by unequal income distribution in causing the crisis. In the US, the top 24,000 families received three times as much income as the 6 million at the bottom. As a result, credit had been channelled from the wider economy into financial speculation and conspicuous consumption. While easy money stoked the inferno, farmers and other primary producers struggled with poor prices and mounting debts.[25] Much the same was true in post-Reagan America and post-Thatcher Britain.

A final explanation concentrates on the breakdown of the international system.

The explanation of this book [writes economic historian Charles Kindleberger in *The World in Depression 1929–1939*] is that . . . the 1929 Depression was so wide, so deep, and so long because the international system was rendered unstable by the British inability and United States unwillingness to assume responsibility for stabilizing it in three particulars: (a) maintaining a relatively open market for distress goods; (b) providing counter-cyclical long-term lending; and (c) discounting in crisis ... The world economic system was unstable unless some country stabilized it as Britain had done in the nineteenth century and up to 1913. In 1929, the British couldn't and the United States wouldn't. When every country turned to protect its national private interest, the world public interest went down the drain, and with it the private interests of all.[26]

The key events in this return to 'private interest' were the US's gigantic Hawley–Smoot tariff of 1930, which restricted the international market and accelerated the fall in world commodity prices, and Britain's departure from the gold standard in 1931, which disorganized the world's monetary system.

It is now generally admitted that the recovery policies pursued by governments in the 1930s – except for those in Hitler's Germany under semi-militarized conditions, backed by terror – were patchy and insufficient to bring about full recovery. Roosevelt's New Deal achieved long-lasting improvements in the US banking system and transport infrastructure, but the amount of 'stimulus' was actually quite small. Keynes attacked the President's National Recovery Act of 1933 for putting reform before recovery, and reckoned (in 1934) that loan-financed spending of $4.8 billion a year (amounting to close to $76.5 billion today: £46.6 billion; €54.6 billion), or 11 per cent of then US national income, was needed to set America firmly on the road to recovery.[27] In fact spending never reached anything like this. In Britain, governments balanced their budgets. Cheap money (with bank rate at 2% and long-term interest falling to 3.5%) brought about a housing-boom-led recovery, but it was seriously incomplete. In 1937–8 both economies collapsed once more into sharp recessions from which they were rescued only by growing spending on rearmament.

FROM PROMISCUITY TO
FAITHFULNESS

The shift in Keynes's investment philosophy from 'promiscuity' to 'faithfulness' is signalled in a memo he wrote on 3 September 1931, close to the bottom of the great bear market, discussing future investment policy for the National Mutual Life Assurance Society. Some members of the board favoured dumping stocks, but he argued that 'a drastic clearance would be a mistake'. His memo confronts some of the classic dilemmas of institutional portfolio management:

- The tendency of deflation will be sooner or later towards very cheap money.
- Shares are undervalued for 'panic reasons bred out of uncertainty'.
- 'Most things one would pick out to sell are not saleable at all on any reasonable terms.'
- It is difficult to predict what is ahead, 'though there might be a complete turn-about for reasons at present quite unforeseeable'.
- 'Some of the things which I vaguely apprehend are, like end of world, uninsurable risks, and it's useless to worry about them.'
- 'If we get out, our mentality being what it is, we shall never get in again until much too late and will assuredly be left behind when the recovery does come. If the recovery never comes, nothing matters.'
- 'We must keep up our income yield.'
- 'From the point of view of our credit etc, a recovery which we failed to share would be the worst thing conceivable.'
- Institutions should not aggravate the bear tendency 'by hurrying each to be in front of others in clearing out, when a general clearing out is in the nature of things impossible . . . [and] would bring the whole system down'. There are times when one has to remain in the procession and not try to cut out.[28]

Two points stand out. First, the impossibility of predicting which way the market will go means that 'playing the cycle' is not rational. This marks the end of Keynes's career as a 'scientific' gambler: he became a 'buy-and-hold' investor. In his 'credit-cycling' days, Keynes claimed that market efficiency could be assured by there being merely enough discerning investors to countervail the actions of those less sophisticated. After the stock-market crash of 1929 he abandoned the hypothesis that skilled investors act as kind of 'market makers', keeping the markets 'orderly'. In *A Treatise on Money*, he wrote, 'it may often profit the wisest [stock-market professional] to anticipate mob psychology rather than the real trend of events and to ape unreason proleptically.' The reason is that he really knows very little more than the crowd, though he pretends to.[29] So his best strategy will generally be 'to anticipate the basis of conventional valuation a few months hence, rather than the prospective yield of an investment over a long term of years.[30] This being the case, the successful long-term investor needs to be a 'contrarian'.

Second, the investor should have a sense of responsibility. An investing institution has a duty not just to its shareholders, but to the public interest. When Oswald Falk suggested in 1931 that the Independent Investment Trust, of which they were both directors, should replace a dollar loan with a sterling loan, Keynes wrote back, 'What you suggest amounts in the present circumstances to a frank bear speculation against sterling. I admit that I am not clear that this would be against the national interest . . . All the same I am clear that an institution has no business to do such a thing at the present time.' As a result the trust lost £40,000 – £2 million, $3.3 million, €2.3 million in today's value – when sterling was devalued a month later.[31]

Keynes's new investment philosophy can be summed up as fidelity to a few carefully chosen stocks – his 'pets' as he called them. As does Warren Buffett, Keynes believed that the investor should buy, not sell, on a falling market, the expectation of picking up bargains being more rational than yielding to the panic psychology of the crowd. Thus his personal investment philosophy came into line with his increasing theoretical emphasis on the social need to stabilize investment. The investor, like the government, should fight the mania for liquidity. In the *General Theory* he toyed with the idea of making the purchase of investments 'permanent and indissoluble, like marriage', as a way of forcing the investor to think seriously about the investment's long-term prospects, but recognized its impracticability and inefficiency.[32] The realization that, as he put in 1938, 'civilization is a thin and precarious crust'[33] also pointed to the investor's rational interest in social stability. A new form of the equation between long-run self-interest and the public good had formed in Keynes's mind.

He acted on his principles, despite frequent attacks of 'nerves'. In 1932 he started buying preferred shares of the big American public utility holding companies, which his analysis showed to be depressed far below their intrinsic worth. He also took advantage of depressed prices to buy pictures, manuscripts and rare books. His 'contrarian' approach was well expressed in a letter to a French friend: 'Is not the rule [for an investor] to be in the minority? It is the only sphere of life and activity where victory, security is always to the minority and never to the majority. When you find anyone agreeing with you, change your mind. When I can persuade the Board of my Insurance Company to buy a share, that, I am learning from experience, is the right moment for selling it.'[34]

He never quite renounced the joy of the chase, of gambling on borrowed money. As he wrote in the *General Theory*, 'the game of professional investment is intolerably boring and over-exacting to anyone who is entirely exempt from the gambling instinct; whilst he who has it must pay this propensity the appropriate toll.'[35] Once, in 1936, he even had to take delivery of a month's supply of wheat from Argentina on a falling market. He planned to store it in the crypt of King's College Chapel, but found this was too small. Eventually, he worked out a scheme to object to its quality knowing that cleaning would take a month. Fortunately, by then the price had recovered and he was safe. There were loud cries that 'infernal speculators' had cornered the market. His considered view was that gambling should best be left to 'frivolous activities'. He had a theory that, because grass wouldn't grow in the United States (*sic*), America's gambling instinct had been channelled into stock-market speculation rather than the tote, so that American industry had become the 'by-product of a casino.'[36] There's probably nothing in the theory that Wall Street was America's substitute for grass, but with Keynes one can never be sure.

By 1936 he was worth over £500,000 or £27 million in today's value ($44 million, €32 million). His net worth had appreciated 23 times, when the US stock market tripled and the London market did very little. The portfolios he oversaw for various college endowments and insurance companies also outperformed the indexes. The more control he had, the better the funds performed.

The third big collapse of his investment career came in the sharp recession of 1937–8. The 1937 stock-market collapse found Keynes heavily leveraged and committed in both New York and London. 'I've not gotten to the point of being a bear, but I am much more disinclined to be a bull on borrowed money. And to bring down some loans is a necessarily tedious and difficult process.' By March 1938, with prices drifting lower, he thought it only prudent to reduce his debt, even if it meant selling blue-chip stocks. One analyst considers the main fault in Keynes's investment strategy to be an inability to dispose of overpriced stocks.[37] By the end of 1938 his capital had shrunk to £140,000 – down 72% from the end of 1936 – and, since markets had already rallied, his losses must have been deeper at the bottom. At his death, in 1946, he had an investment portfolio of £400,000 (today, £12 million, $20 million, €14 million), and an art and book collection worth £80,000 (£2.5 million, $4.1 million, €2.9 million).

He was unrepentant at being caught out by the crash. As he told a fellow director of the National Mutual in 1938, to hold on in a falling market was more than self-interest, it was a duty:

I find no shame at being found still owning a share when the bottom of the market comes. I do not think it is the business of . . . [a serious] investor to cut and run on a falling market . . . I would go much further than that. I should say that it is from time to time the duty of a serious investor to accept the depreciation of his holdings with equanimity and without reproaching himself. Any other policy is anti-social, destructive of confidence, and incompatible with the working of the economic system. An investor . . . should be aiming primarily at long-period results and should be solely judged by these.[38]

4

Keynes's Economics

In Keynes's economics, the logic of choice under uncertainty confronts the classical logic of choice under scarcity. Both are logics of rational people; the difference is in the state of knowledge which market participants are assumed to have. Classical economists believed implicitly, New Classical economists believe explicitly, that market participants have complete knowledge of all probability distributions over future events. This is equivalent to saying that they face only measurable risks. In making investments, they are in exactly the same position as life insurers: they know the odds. Keynes believed that in many situations market participants face irreducible uncertainty. They have no basis on which to calculate the risks they face in making an investment. They are plunging into the unknown. That is why, he wrote, wealth is 'a peculiarly unsuitable subject for the methods of the classical economic theory'.[1] From this follows the crucial role of money in Keynes's theory as a 'store of value'. Money is one of the 'conventions' which human societies have adopted to guard themselves against uncertainty, by allowing people to postpone decisions about whether and what to buy. It plays a crucial role in Keynes's explanation of the development of financial crises and economic depression. The chief role of economic management should be to reduce the scope of irreducible uncertainty.

Keynes was convinced that economics had taken a decisively wrong turn with the economist David Ricardo (1772–1823). 'The extraordinary achievement of the classical theory was to overcome the beliefs of the "natural man" and, at the same time, to be wrong.'[2] Ricardo's turn to abstraction was thus a momentous event in human history. Keynes's own policy proposals were directly influenced by his theories.

'Naturally', he wrote, 'I am interested not only in the diagnosis, but also the cure.' But he considered his cures 'were on a different plane from the diagnosis. They are not meant to be definitive; they are subject to all sorts of special assumptions and are necessarily related to the particular conditions of the time.'[3] So how Keynes would have diagnosed the present crisis is as interesting as how he would have reacted to it – perhaps more so, though the two are obviously connected.

THE PRE-KEYNESIAN MINDSET

Four concepts dominated pre-Keynesian economics, and they still largely dominate economics, despite Keynes's efforts. They are scarcity, the neutrality of money, equilibrium thinking, and unrealism of assumptions. Progress in economics since Adam Smith (1723–90) has consisted in making explicit – mainly by using mathematics – assumptions, arguments and methods which were implicit from the start. The foundations of the discipline, laid in the eighteenth century, have proved almost impervious to assault. The question is, What does this undeniably impressive intellectual edifice, one of the pinnacles of Enlightenment thought, have to tell us about our world today?

Scarcity

Pre-Keynesian economics, dating from Adam Smith, was based on the compelling logic of scarcity. Resources were scarce relative to wants. This being so, there could never be a shortage of 'demand' for the products of 'industry'; there will be as much demanded as is supplied. Equally, there could never be unemployment. People had to produce food and other necessaries to live. If they did not produce, they would not eat. If they did not eat, they would die. As Ricardo put it, 'demand is only limited by production', or, in the (amended) words of the French economist J. B. Say (1767–1832), 'supply creates its own demand.' In a world of scarcity, the economic problem was how to produce enough of things, not that there might be lack of demand for them. So economics became the study of the 'laws' governing the allocation of production between different uses. Lionel Robbins's definition of 1932 would still be accepted by most economists: economics is 'the science that studies human behaviour as a relationship between ends and scarce means which have alternative uses'.[4]

The ubiquity of scarcity led to a prescription: the task of good economic organization was to ensure that production was carried out as efficiently – that is, as cheaply – as possible.

Following the publication of Adam Smith's *The Wealth of Nations* in 1776, it was increasingly accepted that the most efficient organization was that of competitive markets. The 'invisible hand' of the market would force producers, in promoting their own self-interest, to promote the interests of all. The wider the market, the more opportunities for the division of labour and increased production: this was the economic basis for free trade. Under the powerful influence of this theologically inspired metaphor, government interferences in the free market came to be condemned as impious impediments to the growth of wealth. The government's role should be limited to defence and providing a framework of law and order.

The scarcity perspective continued to dominate economics even as output started to outstrip population, bringing plenty and choice to an increasing proportion of the people, at least in rich countries. The Industrial Revolution brought with it the possibility, and the goal, of poverty reduction. 'Needs' became 'wants', and goods were said to be acquired to satisfy 'utility', which included needs (e.g. for food, shelter and so on) but went beyond them. The increase in the margin of comfort over necessity, the development of stock markets for investment, the divorce between the saving and entrepreneurial classes, and the growing number of crises which had their origin in financial collapses did not alter the basic scarcity perspective of economic theory. For the fear remained that, if people consumed too freely, the growth of population would outstrip the accumulation of capital, dousing the vistas of happiness in the sheer growth of numbers. Hence the emphasis the Victorians put on 'postponing satisfaction'.

In direct contrast, the Keynesian revolution sprang from the perception that, in circumstances so frequent as to be called normal, demand could fall short of supply; that there was no guarantee that all that was earned in a period would be spent; and that saving could be a subtraction from, not a part of, spending.

During the Great Depression, economists gave advice appropriate to the age of scarcity. But, as Keynes remarked in 1932, this was not a crisis of poverty, but a crisis of abundance. 'The voices which – in such a conjuncture – tell us that the path of escape is to be found in strict economy and in refraining, wherever possible, from utilizing the world's potential production, are the voices of fools and madmen.'[5]

The Neutrality of Money

Classical theory was the theory of a 'real-exchange economy'. Prices were the ratios at which quantities of goods exchanged with each other. Economics was the study of how these prices were established (laws of supply and demand), and how the prices of particular products formed part of a general system of prices. Money was simply a means of facilitating exchange. It improved on barter (the exchange of goods for goods) by avoiding the need to find a 'double coincidence of wants' for each exchange. A money-using economy was a more convenient form of barter economy. True to the scarcity perspective, economists assumed that people acquired money only to get rid of it as quickly as possible, either by buying consumption goods or by making investments in machines, since money had no 'utility' in itself. Because people acquired money only in order to buy goods, changes in the quantity of money had no effect on the *ratios* at which goods exchanged against each other, only on the general price level of all goods. If you doubled the quantity of money, everything was twice as expensive, but nothing else changed. This was the famous quantity theory of money.

For Keynes, money was a 'store of value' as well as means of transactions; it was 'above all, a subtle device for linking the present to the future'.[6]

Equilibrium Thinking

Classical economics was the illegitimate offspring of Newtonian physics. It pictured the economy as a world of independent atomic particles (human beings), whose actions and reactions keep it in a state of balance or equilibrium. Adam Smith believed that the economic analogue to the force of gravity was rational self-interest operating in an environment of free competition. Under the influence of self-interest and free markets, economies naturally gravitate to a position of optimum equilibrium, the competing agents acting so as to neutralize each other's errors. 'Economies' were thought of as having a gravitational pull either to a state of rest (the stationary state of classical economics) or to a steady state of growth, in both of which resources were fully employed in accord with the logic of scarcity. The nineteenth-century French mathematician Leon Walras pictured the economy as a system of simultaneous equations. This picture of the economy as a mechanism has remained the basis of economic 'modelling'. Robert Lucas tells us that he set out to construct 'a mechanical, artificial world, populated by the interacting robots that economics typically studies'.[7] According to Benôit Mandelbrot, a large part of economic theory is just physics with the words changed.

Economists did not deny that there could be 'disturbances' akin to Newtonian 'unbalanced forces', but dealt with this objection by arguing that full-employment 'equilibrium' was to be conceived of as a 'normal' condition to which the economy tended to return after a 'shock', rather like a disturbed pendulum returning to its stationary point. As Keynes put it, it was held to be self-adjusting in the long run, 'though with creaks and groans and jerks, and interrupted by time lags, outside interference and mistakes'.[8] It was the 'persistent' forces making for equilibrium which should be the subject of economic theory, not the temporary forces making for disturbance to the equilibrium.

The point at issue emerged in an exchange between two nineteenth-century economists which Keynes liked to cite as a fork in the road. In 1817 David Ricardo wrote to his friend Thomas Malthus:

It appears to me that one great cause of our differences ... is that you have always in your mind the immediate and temporary effects of particular changes, whereas I put these immediate and temporary effects quite aside, and fix my whole attention on the permanent state of things which will result from them.

To this Malthus replied:

I certainly am disposed to refer frequently to things as they are, as the only way of making one's writing practically useful to society ... Besides I really do think that the progress of society consists of irregular movements, and that to omit the consideration of causes which for eight or ten years will give a great *stimulus* to production and population or a great *check* to them is to omit the causes of the wealth and poverty of nations.[9]

Keynes sided with Malthus. His first major impact on economics was to switch the focus of economic reasoning from the long run to the short term – i.e. to pick up Malthus's baton. It was surely the Ricardo–Malthus exchange he had in mind when penning his best-known aphorism: 'But this *long* run is a misleading guide to affairs. *In the long run* we are all dead. Economists set themselves too easy, too useless a task if in tempestuous seasons they can only tell us that when the storm is long past the ocean is flat again.'[10]

Business-cycle theory grew up to fill the short-run 'gap' in classical theory. Bouts of overexcitement – generated by, say, a bunching of new inventions – leading to overinvestment would be followed by collapses. Keynes's contemporary Joseph Schumpeter saw these boom–bust cycles, which involved both the creation of new capital and the destruction of old capital, as inseparable from progress. Fed chairman Alan Greenspan subscribed to Schumpeter's doctrine of 'creative destruction', which is perhaps why he did little to curb what he called the 'irrational exuberance' which accompanied the dot-com revolution of the 1990s.

Another short-period type of analysis was the 'monetary-disequilibrium' approach. Money, it started to be said, was 'neutral' only in the long run: the American economist Irving Fisher argued in 1911 that, because of rigid contracts, changes in the value of money could temporarily disturb the adjustment of relative prices, leading to bouts of unemployment. In 1923 Keynes himself took this up in *A Tract on Monetary Reform*, arguing that changes in the quantity of money can unsettle business expectations. The Swedish economist Knut Wicksell (1851–1926) showed how changes in the speed with which money circulates can produce an oscillation of boom and slump around a (notional) full-employment equilibrium. But later economists retrieved the intellectual position by arguing that sluggishness of adjustment to monetary shocks depended on 'money illusion', which would disappear after repeated experience.

The business-cycle theorists raised a crucial question about the role of institutions and policy in keeping market economies stable. To what extent did the so-called self-adjustment of the market depend on institutions and policies? For example, Milton Friedman argued, as we have seen, that the Great Depression might have been avoided by the correct monetary policy. Hayek believed, as do many economists today, that it is excessive credit creation by the central bank which causes unsustainable booms. But if equilibrium depends on what the government or central bank does or does not do, does not the whole notion of the self-adjusting market dissolve?

In time, Keynes came to reject the whole Newtonian schema, with its notion of mechanical equilibria interrupted by 'disturbances' or 'shocks'. He denied that human beings were like billiard balls whose position and speed could be accurately plotted. Economics was a

moral science . . . it deals with introspection and with values . . . it deals with motives, expectations, psychological uncertainties. One has to be constantly on guard against treating the material as constant and homogeneous. It is as though the fall of the apple to the ground depended on the apple's motives, on whether it is worthwhile falling to the ground, and whether the ground wanted the apple to fall, and on mistaken calculations on the part of the apple as to how far it was from the centre of the earth.[11]*

---

*As anomalies in the classical paradigm multiplied, refinements to the Ricardian picture were added. By Keynes's time it was no longer controversial to allow that full employment was, as Axel Leijonhufvud has put it, a 'point attractor' rather than a realized condition, since market processes took place in time, and there was always bound to be some sluggishness in the adjustment of relative prices to changes in demand – especially if existing jobs and wages were protected by legislation, trade unions, and contracts. Keynes's teacher Alfred Marshall identified 'time' as the most

Unrealism of Assumptions

Economists have always argued about how to 'do' economics. This debate has centred round 'realism of assumptions'. From Ricardo's time, economists adopted the strategy of building 'parsimonious' models, incorporating only a limited number of variables, to distinguish the main drivers of the system from mere description. But there always remained the question of how realistic the assumptions driving the logic should be. On the whole, economists have opted for an 'ideal-type' approach. Their assumptions are not arbitrary (they claim to be derived from the facts of experience), but they are not realistic either. They deal in 'pure' cases, which should not be confused with average cases. The most famous 'ideal' construct is that of '*Homo economicus*', super-rational, self-interested, perfectly informed, relentlessly engaged in 'maximizing his utilities'. Economics has constructed a Platonic world of ideal forms to show up the imperfections of the actual world. From this point of view the *unrealism* of the assumptions is the hallmark of good model-building.

Like any other economist, Keynes used models, but he rejected the ideal-type approach to model-building. Economic theorizing, he said, should conform to what the world is like, not invent a perfect world. Unlike Friedman, and the New Classical economists, he attached enormous importance to realism of assumptions. He was not prepared to sacrifice realism to mathematics, because he thought this would make economics useless for policy. For Keynes, 'vigilant observation' was required to see facts without preconceived theories – that is, from a disconfirming rather than a confirming standpoint. Economics had to be able to explain the facts in a way which appealed to the intuition or common sense of the ordinary person. What he called 'scholasticism' was a useful check on the logic of one's explanations, not a substitute for observation.[12]

Keynes's particular criticism of the classical school was that it used

difficult problem in economics, and divided different speeds of adjustment to change into 'periods' of different lengths, most famously distinguishing the 'short period' from Ricardo's 'long period'. But his own *Principles of Economics* (1890) were concerned with the long run – the state of the economy after the 'adjustments' had taken place.

models which assumed certain things which did not occur in the real world: perfect flexibility of wages and prices, perfect competition, perfect information, and absence of contractual debt – equivalent to absence of money. He rejected the type of reasoning which started with the absence of money (the real-exchange economy) and then 'added on' money as a disturbing or complicating factor. Keynes was the first major economist to make money an integral part of economic analysis. It was the primary hedge against uncertainty. His own *General Theory of Employment, Interest and Money* offered the world a 'monetary theory of production'. 'A monetary economy', he wrote in his preface to that book, 'is one in which changing views about the future are capable of influencing the quantity of employment and not merely its direction.'[13] In that pregnant sentence is the core of the Keynesian revolution.

KEYNES'S ECONOMICS

In Keynes's economics, the invisible thread of convention took the place of Smith's invisible hand of the market in shaping systemic outcomes, setting deep parameters within which the intentional behaviour of rational human beings takes place. This allowed him to provide a more realistic account of human behaviour than the 'ideal-type' theorizing of classical economics. The main consequence of this 'top-down' approach was to cut the direct link between individual behaviour and the physical conditions of scarcity which had underpinned classical economics. The link between them is now powerfully, and inescapably, mediated through institutions. Keynes did not abandon the notion of equilibrium, but his equilibria are in the nature of 'bootstraps equilibria' – states of rest given by the state of expectations rather than by the 'fundamental forces' of productivity and thrift. The practical conclusion of this approach was a denial that a competitive, free-market economy has a 'normal' tendency towards full employment. There are many possible 'equilibria', no one more 'natural' than another.

Uncertainty

Uncertainty pervades Keynes's picture of economic life. It explains why people hold savings in liquid forms, why investment is volatile, and why the rate of interest doesn't adjust savings and investment. It also explains why economic progress throughout history has been so slow and fitful. All the actors in his drama are motivated to a greater or less extent by uncertainty about the future, and regard the possession of money, or money contracts, as an important way of coping with it. Uncertainty loosens all the 'tight' relationships assumed by the classical theory which produce a smooth flow of demand into supply and validate Say's Law. It also explains why a state of poor expectations can persist and dampen business activity long after goods, services and investments are available at 'bargain prices'. This feeling of uncertainty waxes and wanes: sometimes people are more confident than at others. When confidence is high, the economy thrives; when it is low, it sickens.

It is important to emphasize that Keynes did not think the whole of economic life was uncertain. Uncertainty becomes an issue for economics only when our livelihood or prosperity depends on our taking a view of the future. If the only demand was for necessaries, economics would not have to bother with uncertainty: the only sources of uncertainty would arise from outside events like the weather or war. Under capitalism, uncertainty is generated by the system itself, because it is an engine for accumulating capital goods whose rewards come not now but later. The engine of wealth creation is at the same time the source of economic and social instability.

Keynes's obsession with the problem of uncertainty went all the way back to his student days, when he started work on the theory of probability. His *A Treatise on Probability* (1921) was an exploration of what it means to hold rational beliefs about the future under varying conditions of knowledge. His main contention was that probability is not statistical, but logical. Its distinctive ingredient was the appeal to reason rather than observation as the source of knowledge. His 'logical theory of probability' stuck as closely as possible to the way people used terms like 'probably', 'likely', 'I don't know'.

In *A Treatise on Probability* Keynes considers three types of probability. The first is cardinal or measurable probability, according to which all probabilities can be compared by distances between numbers and their absolute values. For example, the statement 'There is a one in six chance of your house catching fire in the next year' means that the chance of fire is 16.7%. This is the domain of *risk* proper. Without this risk being known, fire insurance would be impossible. For risks to be known they must be uncorrelated: there should be no reason to believe that your house burning down will change the risk of my house burning down. 'In actual reasoning . . . exact measures [of this kind] will occur comparatively seldom,' Keynes wrote.[14] Yet the whole of efficient financial market theory, and its derived risk-management apparatus, presumes that this is the normal condition. That is the meaning of the bell-curve view of the universe described in Chapter 2. The efficient market theory assumes, in other words, that financial markets are equivalent to insurance markets.

The second type of probability is ordinal probability, where the only information to be had is that of the relative position of the event in a ranking. One can say that X is more likely to pass the exam than Y, without being able to say that he is twice as likely to pass. Keynes thought this was by far the largest class of probability. We reason that some events, based on our evidence, are more likely to occur than others, but not how much more likely, because we don't have enough observations to make a proper statistical inference. We have entered the domain of uncertainty. Ordinal probabilities fall between statistical frequency and irreducible uncertainty and represent what one might call 'vague knowledge'. The difference between this and cardinal probability is between qualitative and quantitative judgements of probability. Most of the estimates of risk in business risk-control systems are qualitative judgements disguised as quantitative measurements. For instance, on 30 January 2009 Bloomberg reported that NIBC Bank ran a 70% risk of defaulting. Keynes would have insisted that all that could be said was that it was more likely to default than not. Such spurious precision gives the investor the false impression that he can insure against default by paying the appropriate insurance premium. This is the function of the credit-default swaps.

The third type of probability in Keynes's universe of probabilities is unknown probability. This is the domain of irreducible uncertainty.

It arises from non-comparable premises. The stock market is experiencing a bounce, but the OECD projects continuing output decline. What are the chances of the rally continuing? Keynes would say (like most investors at this moment) we simply don't know. In this situation we cannot assign any probability whatsoever, cardinal or ordinal. The disasters which bring down banks and companies are usually unforeseen: Keynes would have said that most of them are unforeseeable.

He gave the following example in *A Treatise on Probability*:

Is our expectation of rain, when we start out for a walk, always *more* likely than not, or *less* likely than not, or *as* likely as not? I am prepared to argue that on some occasions *none* of these alternatives hold, and that it will be an arbitrary matter to decide for or against the umbrella. If the barometer is high, but the clouds are black, it is not always necessary that one should prevail over another in our minds, or even that we should balance them – though it will be rational to allow caprice to determine us and waste no time on the debate.[15]

'Caprice' here is not irrational: it is rational to act on caprice when we have no way of telling what the future will hold. Keynes treated individuals as rational, not irrational. Only he held a more general theory of rationality than the classical and New Classical economists. Rational belief is not to be identified with true belief. 'Realism of assumptions' is not tantamount to assuming that human behaviour is irrational. The 'caprice' of *A Treatise on Probability*, which became 'animal spirits' in the *General Theory*, is depicted as *rational*, or at least *reasonable*, given the state of knowledge. It is consistent with Keynes's view that *luck* plays a much greater role in success or failure than explicable causes which we invent afterwards.*

In the *General Theory*, Keynes dropped the category of ordinal probabilities to sharpen the contrast between the classical economists' implicit identification of probability with statistical frequency and his own theory of unknown probabilities:

---

*'When reason has arrived at its limits, arbitrary or conventional behaviour will be consistent with, and not opposed to, reason.' (See O'Donnell, *Keynes: Philosophy, Economics and Politics*, pp. 43, 44, 59.)

By 'uncertain' knowledge [he explained a year later, in 1937] I do not mean merely to distinguish what is known for certain from what is only probable ... The sense in which I am using the term is that in which the prospect of a European war is uncertain, or the price of copper and the rate of interest twenty years hence, or the obsolescence of invention, or the position of private wealth owners in the social system in 1970. About these matters there is no scientific basis on which to form any calculable probability whatever. We simply do not know.[16]

Notice that Keynes's 'uncertainty' is consistent with holding either optimistic or pessimistic beliefs about the future. Someone contemplating an investment in Russia may think the chances of another revolution are either very low or very high, and may even attach a range of probabilities to its occurrence. The point Keynes was making is that neither belief will be well grounded, and therefore each will be liable to sudden upset with any change in the news, however trivial.

Keynes argued that, faced with varying degrees of uncertainty, it is rational to fall back on conventions, stories, rules of thumb, habits, traditions in forming our expectations and deciding how to act. Their function is partly psychological – designed to give a feeling of security, like magic spells or incantations to ward off evil spirits. Talking about 'risk' when one should be talking about 'uncertainty' is a typical 'convention', ubiquitous in company boardroom discussion. We also construct explanations of past events to give us a sense of security in facing the future, which equip us with wrong maps. Generals, as is often said, always fight the last war. Governments fight the last recession. However, some updating does take place. Conventions and rules also reflect human learning experience. Without such learning, it would be impossible to make any progress in human affairs. But Keynes emphasized two things. First, learning makes only very slow inroads into ignorance and uncertainty. Second, the process is erratic, since the material of learning is subject to unexpected changes. What was learned in one period might become useless in the next.

In *A Treatise on Probability* Keynes made a crucial distinction between our expectations about the future and the *confidence* with which we hold them, something that would be irrelevant if we had statistical probabilities for all expectations. The greater the amount of evidence supporting an expectation, the more confident we will be in having it. In the *General Theory* Keynes would say that business expectation depends not just on 'the most probable forecast we can make. It also depends on the *confidence* with which we make this forecast – on how likely we rate the likelihood of our best forecast turning out quite wrong.' He added, 'The *state of confidence*, as they term it, is a matter to which practical men always pay the closest attention. But economists have not analysed it carefully.'[17] The 'liquidity premium' commanded by money was a payment for the increased sense of comfort and confidence which its possession gave the possessor.

Keynes talks of some probabilities being unknown because of lack of information. Are they also unknowable? In other words, is Keynes talking about epistemological uncertainty or ontological indeterminacy? It is not clear. In the first case, one might expect that more information and computing power will in time reduce uncertainty to the status of calculable risk. In the second case, uncertainty is genuinely irreducible. The future is not out there waiting to be learned: we create it ourselves.

The Limits of Econometrics

In a stream of letters and articles criticizing the use of econometrics, dating from the late 1930s, Keynes seemed to veer away from the view that there is a map of the future which we can't yet read to the view that human beings make their own map. He makes four main points.[18] First, he argues that employing regression analysis* to get parameters and then treat them as if they were constant is fundamentally flawed. 'There is no reason at all why they should not be different

---

*Regression analysis is a quantitative method of exploring how changes in factors which you have reason to think are relevant (independent variables) explain changes in your variable of interest (dependent variable). For instance, how does your prospective lifetime income change as your education level changes? By using a form of sophisticated averaging, the results are given as so-called regression coefficients which you attach to the independent variables. These might tell you that, for instance, each additional year of schooling increases income by 5%. Regression analysis is empirical, and therefore uses data which obviously has to come from the past.

every year,' since we know that many economic relations are 'non-homogeneous through time'.

Second, Keynes criticizes the *ad hoc* character of much quantitative modelling. 'With a free hand to choose coefficients and time lags, one can, with enough industry, always cook a formula to fit moderately well a limited range of past facts. But what does this prove?' Too much is expected of the data, he continues. It often is not detailed enough to even 'support one-tenth of the burden which is placed on [it]'.

Third, in sharp contrast to modern economics, Keynes argues that, rather than assuming that quantitative analysis is appropriate when investigating a problem, the default assumption should be the opposite: assume that you cannot use it, and justify the instances when you do. There are simply 'such important influences which cannot be reduced to statistical form'.

This view underlies his fourth point: there are areas in which statistical analysis can be very useful, but they are limited to simpler, less abstract, relations. 'The notion of testing the quantitative influence of factors suggested by a theory as being important is very useful and to the point. The question to be answered, however, is whether the complicated method . . . does not result in a false precision beyond what the method . . . can support.' Thus, although credit cycles might be too complex to analyse statistically, Keynes gives the example of the relation between the volume of traffic and the operating costs of a railway system as a case where econometric analysis might warrant some valid conclusions.

The main conclusion to deduce from these points is that Keynes viewed economics as a 'moral' science, not a natural science. Although some aspects could be reduced to numbers, much could not. In particular, innovation – a human achievement – destroys regularities. Keynes would have said that it was absurd to rely on risk models based on past data at the moment when bankers were creating complex new products every week.

Keynes's emphasis on uncertainty colours his whole view of the human drama. It imposes a kind of permanent fearfulness about the future which puts a damper on economic progress. Economic activity requires the stimulus of exciting events to lift it out of its normal rut.

It is impossible to say whether Keynes would have regarded the amount of uncertainty as having increased or decreased over time. Clearly natural disasters, disorder, disease, pillage, arbitrary confiscations of property played a much larger part in earlier economic life than they do today. Economic life has become more orderly and predictable. On the other hand, the increased importance of investment, the interconnectedness of today's economies, the global reach of financial trading, technology-driven innovation, and the surfeit of distracting information produced by the media may well have rendered the scale and frequency of collapses generated by economic activities themselves, rather than by outside events, much greater than in the past.

Effective Demand

The Great Depression saw the collapse of demand for products which industry was well capable of producing. Keynes wrote the *General Theory* to explain not why this had happened, but how it could happen. People's freedom in a monetary economy not to spend money is the crux of his denial of Say's Law, that production creates its own demand. He broke up the 'aggregate demand function' into two components: consumption demand and investment demand. Together these determine the volume of output and employment. Consumption was the stable element in demand, investment the unstable element.

In the short run, the 'propensity to consume' is a 'fairly stable' proportion of current income. It does not fluctuate much. This is because it depends largely on habits – in contrast to investment, which depends on expectations. According to Keynes's 'psychological law', when income increases, consumption rises by less than income, and when income decreases consumption falls by less. The fact that consumption is more stable than income gives the system a certain measure of stability. But it also sets it a problem. In a growing economy, the gap between consumption and production must be filled by investment if full employment is to be maintained. The classical school claimed that people wanted to save only in order to invest. So changes in saving habits did not affect the level of aggregate demand, but only the composition of demand between present and future consumption. In contrast, Keynes treated saving as a subtraction from consumption demand, but not an addition to investment demand. This is for a good theoretical reason. A great deal of saving is a demand for cash, not a demand for capital goods. And the demand for cash increases the more uncertain the prospects for investment become.

Keynes insisted that a decision to save is not equivalent to placing an order for future consumption. His 'liquidity-preference' theory of saving is set out in his 'paradox of thrift'. If everyone wants to save more, firms will sell less and therefore output will fall, unless the inducement to invest is increasing at the same time. So the more 'thrifty' a society is, the more difficulty it will have in maintaining full employment.[19] Moreover, since recoveries increase the amount saved, simply as a consequence of incomes rising, saving and investment may well be equalized before full employment is regained. This was the basis of Keynes's view that, under laissez-faire, recoveries are liable to peter out. It is spending, not saving, which creates output and employment; and when spending falls short of earnings, unemployment results.

The Inducement to Invest

Given a community's 'propensity to consume', the amount of employment depends on the rate at which it is adding to its capital stock. There is an 'inducement to invest' whenever the expected rate of return on the investment is higher than the 'cost of capital'. The rate of investment thus depends jointly 'on the investment demand-schedule and . . . on the rate of interest'.[20] The difficulty of maintaining continuous full employment arises from the 'association of a conventional and fairly stable long-term rate of interest with a fickle and highly unstable marginal efficiency of capital'.[21] 'Marginal efficiency of capital' is Keynes's technical term for the expected rate of profit.

It had long been recognized that investment was the volatile element in the capitalist economy. Keynes's understanding of the part played by expectations, ignorance and uncertainty in decisions to invest long antedated the account of the investment process he gave in the *General Theory*. But the acknowledged volatility of investment was absent from the 'long-run' theorizing favoured by Ricardo and his followers, as revealed in Ricardo's exchange with Malthus. It was seen as a 'short-run' phenomenon, not considered of great practical significance, since the 'errors' investors made were considered to be minor – and random – deviations from the path given by the fundamental forces governing the productivity of investment.

The main point Keynes wanted to make is that the 'expected yield' of different classes of investment depends on estimates of risk which, despite the precision with which they were made, have very little basis. His starting point was the 'extreme precariousness of the basis of knowledge on which our estimates of prospective yield have to be made'.[22] It was a 'tacit' axiom of the classical theory of the self-regulating economy that economic actors had statistical probabilities concerning the outcome of their investments. 'Risks', as he put it, 'were supposed to be capable of an exact actuarial computation.' But we 'simply do not know' what the price of oil will be in ten, or even five, years' time, or whether there will be a war or revolution, or a dot-com revolution, somewhere in the next few years. Investments which promised returns 'at a comparatively distant, and sometimes an indefinitely distant, date' were acts of faith. And in that fact lay the possibility of huge mistakes.[23]

How, under such circumstances, do we save our faces as rational actors? Keynes's answer is that we adopt certain conventions or 'rules of thumb'. Of these the most important are:

- 'We assume that the present is a much more serviceable guide to the future than a candid examination of past experience would show it to have been hitherto. In other words, we largely ignore the prospect of future changes about the actual character of which we know nothing.'
- 'We assume that the *existing* state of opinion, as expressed in prices . . . is based on a *correct* summing up of future prospects.'
- 'Knowing that our own individual judgement is worthless, we endeavour to fall back on the judgement of the rest of the world, which is perhaps better informed. That is, we endeavour to conform

with the behaviour of the majority or the average. The psychology of a society of individuals each of whom is endeavouring to copy the other leads to what we may strictly term a *conventional* judgement.'[24]

Although Keynes did not use the term, he was advancing a theory of *conventional* expectations in contrast to the New Classical theory, implicit in the old classical theory of *rational* expectations. Conventional expectations are perfectly rational – or perhaps one should say reasonable – given that we know so little about what the future will bring. They afford an assurance of stability as long as no one questions them. If everyone agrees house prices should be going up, they will continue to go up. But any view of the future based on 'so flimsy a foundation' is liable to 'sudden and violent changes' when the news changes, since there is no basis of real knowledge to hold it steady. 'The market will be subject to waves of optimistic and pessimistic sentiment, which are unreasoning, yet in a sense legitimate, where no solid basis exists for a reasonable calculation.'[25]

Not only is this a recognizable account of the generation of a financial panic and collapse, but it makes the deep epistemological point that prices are set by conventional judgements only indirectly related to what economists call the 'fundamental' forces of productivity and thrift which are supposed to govern supply and demand in investment markets. Or, rather, the conventions *are* the fundamentals. They may be compatible with full employment; just as likely they will not be.

Keynes's argument in Chapter 12 of the *General Theory* – by far the most sparkling chapter in that complicated book – is that the uncertainty attaching to the future yield of investment has given rise to a peculiar institution through which most investment is channelled in a capitalist society: the stock market. The stock market reduces the riskiness of investment by making investments which are 'fixed' for the community 'liquid' for the individual, at the same time supplying the investor with conventional share valuations (stock-market prices) in which he can place some reliance as measuring the productivity of different pieces of capital. The 'convention' promises that 'the existing state of affairs will continue indefinitely, except insofar as we have specific reasons to expect a change', thus limiting the risk to 'that of a genuine change in the news over the *near future*'. But a conventional valuation thus established will have 'no strong roots of conviction' to hold it steady in face of transient changes in the news. Suddenly everyone wants to become 'liquid', but 'there is no such thing as liquidity for the community as a whole.' Chapter 12 of the *General Theory* is the best account in the literature of the psychology of panics. It also illustrates, with unerring precision, the contradictory character of financial innovation: by making investment more 'liquid', the stock market reduces the proportion of their resources that people will want to hold in cash; but by the same token it enlarges the scope for speculation and thus makes economic life more volatile. This has been exactly the effect of 'securitization' in the last few years.

Keynes was here anticipating something which has been subsequently developed by behavioural psychologists: that our tendency to follow the crowd may be 'hard-wired'. The demand for 'social proof' – if people behave in a certain way they must have a reason for doing so – may be a survival instinct.[26] Similarly, the psychologists emphasize the importance of institutions which build trust and secure greater stability of expectations. Keynes's insight was to explain this kind of behaviour by the existence of uncertainty. Trust would not be necessary if all agents had statistically based expectations of others' behaviour. He placed so much stress on this point precisely because economists ignored the influence of uncertainty in shaping human behaviour and social institutions.

A major theme of Chapter 12 of the *General Theory* is the inherently speculative character of stock-market investment. Keynes wrote, 'Speculators may do no harm as bubbles on a steady stream of enterprise. But the position is serious when enterprise becomes the bubble on a whirlpool of speculation. When the capital development of a country becomes a by-product of the activities of a casino, the job is likely to be ill-done.'[27]

Although the financial markets through which today's crisis have been transmitted have spread far beyond the stock and bond markets which Keynes encountered, his account of the psychology of those markets remains extremely relevant – and his attack on classical theory more impressive. For to have a theory of investment which assumes that the present value of the expected future cash flow produced by a machine over many years can be accurately calculated makes even less sense when most of the capital of companies consists of intangible assets like brand names.

The Rate of Interest

The other influence on the inducement to investment is the rate of interest. What then determines the rate of interest (or, more accurately, the structure of interest rates)? The classical belief that the economy was self-correcting rested on the view that the rate of interest was the equilibrating or balancing element in the economic system. It was the adjustment of this 'price' to shifts in the supply of saving and the demand for investment which was supposed to maintain the balance between the two. When the desire to save ran ahead of the inducement to invest, the rate of interest would fall. (This was the basis of the classical prescription that people should save more in a slump.) By contrast, Keynes argued that the rate of interest has little effect on saving (which depended on the level of income), but a big effect on investment. For any given state of profit expectations, the continued expansion of investment depends on a corresponding reduction in the cost of borrowing.

'The rate of interest', Keynes writes, 'is the price which equilibrates the desire to hold wealth in the form of cash with the available quantity of cash.'[28] The greater people's liquidity preference, the higher the rate of interest they will charge for parting with money. A collapse in the expected profitability of investment tends to lead to an increase in liquidity preference, thus pushing interest rates up, when they need to come down. The logic of the *General Theory* is thus completed by showing that the rate of interest can remain above the expected rate of return to capital necessary to secure full employment.

Why, Keynes asks, should anyone outside a lunatic asylum want to hold money. 'What an insane use to which to put it! For it is a recognized characteristic of money as a store of wealth that it is barren; whereas practically every other form of storing wealth yields some interest or profit.'[29]

The answer was that

partly on reasonable and partly on instinctive grounds, our desire to hold money as a store of wealth is a barometer of the degree of our distrust of our own calculations and conventions concerning the future . . . It operates, so to speak, at a deeper level of our motivation. It takes charge at the moments when the higher, more precarious conventions have weakened. The possession of actual money lulls our disquietude; and the premium which we require to make us part with money is the measure of the degree of our disquietude.[30]

In short, Keynes distinguished between the *risk premium*, which is expected to be rewarded by greater wealth, and the *liquidity premium*, which is compensation for a decreased sense of comfort.[31]

Again, this is a completely recognizable picture of today's 'credit crunch'. Keynes did not deal explicitly with the behaviour of banks. His account of how changing expectations cause people to switch the composition of their portfolios between cash, bonds and shares referred to individual investors rather than institutions. But it applies equally to banks. Because of their bad loans, all the major lending institutions are now trying to increase their cash balances, and have therefore either stopped lending to customers or put up the rates, or are refraining from reducing the rates, at which they are willing to lend.

Wages and Prices

Although post-war American Keynesians adopted 'sticky wages' as their main explanation of why economies failed to adjust quickly to external shocks, wage rigidity had only a supporting role in Keynes's play. Even if wages were perfectly flexible, the economy could still collapse. His explanation for this was undeveloped, but it centred round the view that a decline in money wages would cause aggregate money demand to decline by almost as much. Keynes also accepted that wage rigidity was likely to exist in the real world. Uncertainty comes into this too: workers bargain for relative shares with other workers, so no group will be the *first* to accept a wage cut which might leave them worse off than others; forward contracts also suit both employers and workers, because they are a way of hedging against the uncertainty of future selling prices for labour and goods.[32]

All the major propositions of Keynes's *General Theory* depended on the uncertainty principle, and the consequent role of money as a store of wealth. In his picture of economic life, a world inhabited by atomic individuals each of whom knows what he wants and how to get it gives way to a world in which people act within a framework of rules and conventions designed to cope with an uncertain future.

The Outcome

The *General Theory* advanced one main proposition: that a decentralized market economy lacks any gravitational pull towards full employment. Consequently, it is as likely as to be in a state of under-unemployment as of full employment.[33] This proposition combines two claims which probably coexisted in Keynes's own mind. The first is that an unmanaged capitalist economy is inherently unstable. Neither profit expectations nor the rate of interest are solidly anchored in the underlying forces of productivity and thrift. They are driven by uncertain and fluctuating expectations about the future. The second claim is that when demand falls off, it is the fall in output, not the movement of relative prices, which restores equilibrium. The collapse of optimistic expectations causes the economy to collapse; once established, pessimistic expectations cause unemployment to persist. This is Keynes's famous 'underemployment equilibrium'. Government should manage demand to limit fluctuations to the smallest feasible amount.

Keynes's original insight was that contraction in one part of the system doesn't stimulate expansion in another part, unless relative prices change instantaneously. Otherwise output effects in any sector swamp or obliterate price effects, and excess supply – or deficient demand – spreads from one market to another through the multiplier process. The economy is not a see-saw, but a leaky balloon.[34]

Keynes conceded that relative price adjustments might come into play in the 'long period', but only as a result of the decline in output, not as an alternative to it.[35] Consequently, the full adjustment of supply to demand takes place within a shrunken economy. In the absence of an external stimulus – technological or political – to revive profit expectations, the Keynesian economy oscillates round a suboptimal level with no marked tendency to recovery or collapse.*

When investment starts to fail, what stops the economy from running down all the way? The brief answer is that the impoverishment of the community tends to eliminate the 'excess saving' relative to investment which caused the downturn in the first place. If the propensity to consume is known – say it is 90% of current income – it is possible to demonstrate by a simple arithmetical calculation known as the income multiplier that expansions and contractions of income converge to a fixed point in which saving and investment are equal. As Austin Robinson put it, 'In equilibrium . . . saving must equal investment . . . If these two tend to be unequal, the level of activity will be changed until they are restored to equality.' The income multiplier established output adjustment as the main mechanism by which the economy reaches a new position of equilibrium.

According to one leading student, the demonstration that it is 'quantities, not prices' which adjust is the 'major novel feature' of the *General Theory*.[36] It is certainly the part of the theory most useful for policy, because it makes possible the calculation of output and inflation 'gaps', a potential fulfilled by the later development of national income and expenditure statistics.

Keynes first made use of the income multiplier in his pamphlet *The Means to Prosperity*, published in 1933. To obtain its magnitude 'we have simply to estimate . . . what proportion of typical expenditure becomes someone else's income and what proportion of this income is spent. For these two proportions, multiplied together, give us the ratio of the first repercussion to the primary effect . . . We can then sum up the whole series of repercussions.'[37] The income multiplier is also a treacherous instrument, for in this part of his theory Keynes is assuming *certain* expectations concerning the effects of government policy, whereas he was assuming that *uncertain* expectations cause

---

*The formal difference between Keynes's long-run equilibrium and the classical long-run equilibrium may be more apparent than real. If prolonged depression leads to an actual destruction of supply – through manufacturing capacity closing down, or discouraged workers leaving the labour market – then the two become formally equivalent.

the economy's collapse. As we have seen on pp. 21–2, the magnitude of the income multiplier depends on expectations of government policy.

The concept of 'underemployment equilibrium' should not be taken too literally. It encapsulates the idea of the lack of an efficacious mechanism for righting economies after a major capsize. It also expresses Keynes's belief that suboptimal performance is normal, because the growth of economies takes place in the twilight world of uncertainty. But in some periods, following a major collapse, economies can fare worse than normal. The existence of such prolonged periods of stagnation is not just a theory: even in a world with government circuit breakers available, Japan experienced such a period in the 1990s. It was Keynes's eagerness for mankind to escape from the economic problem and move on to higher values that explains his eagerness for running economies, for a period, at full blast. Finally, Keynes saw his underemployment equilibrium much as the classicals did: as a point of attraction, with oscillations round it, rather than as a point of rest. Business cycles were still possible in a world of 'underemployment equilibrium' – there would still be 'moments of excitement', and moments of collapse. This describes the US economy following the collapse of the dot-com bubble in 2000, on to which has now been superimposed the much bigger credit crisis of 2007–8.

For those who regard the notion of equilibrium as a possibly useful reference point, but not otherwise important, the 'equilibrium' aspect of Keynes's theory cannot be seen as the most fertile or essential part of his contribution. Most Keynesians thought it crucial that Keynes had 'proved' the possibility of 'multiple equilibria', as this killed off the idea of the optimally self-regulating economy. The notion of a 'determinate' equilibrium was also taken up by those chiefly interested in policy, as essential in calculating the size of the 'output gaps' and the value of the income multiplier. In their remedial actions they were often led astray by over-reliance on short-term forecasts. However, for most purposes it is more important to understand why the crashes of the economy occur, can be severe, last a long time, and should be prevented.

Policy

Keynes's chief domestic prophylactic against uncertainty was what he called 'cheap money, wise spending'. To offset fluctuations in private investment demand, money should be kept permanently cheap, and the state's capital budget, which consists of all public, or publicly influenced, investment programmes, should be used to keep total spending at a high level. By contrast, the government's 'ordinary' budget for current spending should normally be in surplus. As Keynes put it in 1942, 'If two-thirds of or three-quarters of total investment is carried out or can be influenced by public or semi-public bodies, a long-term programme of a stable character should be capable of reducing the range of fluctuation to much narrower limits than formerly ... If this is successful it should not be too difficult to offset small fluctuations by expediting or retarding some items in this longer-term programme.' He was just as keen to keep global demand at a continuously high level. One of the main causes of the Great Depression, he believed, had been a global 'saving glut' originating in the United States. The US's accumulation of gold through its current-account surplus had forced all other countries on the gold standard to deflate their economies. It was to avoid a repetition of this deflationary pressure that Keynes worked out his Clearing Union plan in 1941, which was designed to prevent countries from accumulating, or hoarding, reserves.

As the returns from investment fell, the domestic aim of policy should switch to reducing income inequalities (thus raising the 'propensity to consume') and increasing leisure time, with shorter working hours and more frequent holidays. In the golden age of capital saturation, with the economic problem solved, people would learn to live 'wisely, agreeably, and well'. This was Keynes's answer to the question: What is economic growth for?[38]

5

The Keynesian Revolution:
Success or Failure?

THE KEYNESIAN WORLD

For roughly a quarter of a century after the Second World War, Keynesian economics ruled triumphantly. No one wanted to go back to the 1930s. Nationally, governments accepted responsibility for maintaining high and stable levels of employment. Internationally, institutions, collectively known as the Bretton Woods system, were set up to prevent depressive forces from being transmitted through the international payments and trading system. It was also a period of remarkable growth, not confined to the war-damaged economies of Europe and Japan. Many economies that had largely avoided physical destruction – like the American, the Australian and the Swedish – recorded stunning performance. Latin America and the Soviet Union experienced high economic growth.

From the late 1960s this dispensation started to unravel; by the 1980s both theory and policy had swung back to pre-Keynesian ideas. Government was seen once more as part of the problem, not the solution. Expansionary government policies were accused of fuelling inflation and crowding out better-informed private investment without reducing unemployment in the long run. With the coming to power of Margaret Thatcher and Ronald Reagan in 1979 and 1980 respectively, markets were deregulated, taxes were lowered, trade unions were bashed, and the international institutions were emasculated. The Bretton Woods philosophy of managed global capitalism was replaced by the Washington Consensus – a term coined by John Williamson in 1989 to denote the neoliberal policies advocated for developing countries by the US administration: free trade, privatization, deregulation, balanced budgets, inflation targeting, floating exchange rates. What defined the new world view was the classical belief in efficient and self-regulating markets. Free markets would deliver *better* results than fettered ones.

The unravelling of the Keynesian revolution can be explored along two dimensions: intellectual and practical. There was a counter-revolution in economic theory, and a counter-revolution in economic policy. The relationship between the two is neither simple nor direct. The ideas of economists and philosophers may be ultimately determinative of policy, for good or ill, as Keynes thought, but they always enter the public arena mixed up with politics, ideology, vested interests and national circumstances. This was true of the Keynesian revolution itself. The Keynesianism attacked by the intellectual counter-revolutionaries was not the Keynesianism left by Keynes. So in some ways they were punching a straw man. Nor were the policies pursued by governments in the Keynesian era pure distillations of Keynesian theory or advice. Some doubt whether the Keynesian golden age owed much to Keynes at all. Nor were the ideas of the New Classical economists completely embodied in the policies of the Reagan–Thatcher era. Nevertheless, I believe we are justified in treating the policies pursued in both the Keynesian and the post-Keynesian eras as in some sense the practical expression of the dominant ideas of the two periods. The first part of this chapter will trace the counter-revolution in ideas; the second section will compare the economic records of the Keynesian and the post-Keynesian ages.

THE THEORETICAL UNRAVELLING

Uncertainty dominates Keynes's economics. The future is a twilight zone; it is full of unexpected, unpredictable events. It resembles the past in the way that children resemble their parents and forebears: the genetic ingredients are the same, but the possible combinations are unlimited. Tiny differences in initial arrangement can make for huge differences in outcome. To cope with uncertainty, human beings fall back on conventions. These allay anxiety, give them confidence. The conventions allow for considerable diversity of opinion, as in bulls and bears in a stock market, or competition between parties in politics. When some shock causes the conventions to break down, herd behaviour takes over: everyone rushes for the entrance or exit. In finance, everyone becomes either a bull or a bear. In politics, the masses flock to a leader offering salvation.

There was something about this picture which stuck in the gullet of the power-holders in economics and in politics. This was particularly so in the United States, the cradle of economic individualism, which had always prided itself on being exempt from the conventional expectations of the Old World. Keynesianism was accepted largely on sufferance: by economists as a pragmatic accommodation to reality; by businessmen as a barrier to socialist agitation; by politicians of the right as providing additional arguments for tax cuts or large defence expenditures, and by those of the left as justifying more social spending. Intellectual conviction was always less important than practical usefulness. The Keynesian revolution as it took root in the United States was to a large extent a policy revolution without a theory. This theoretical void was waiting to be filled by old theory in new mathematical clothes; the New Classical macroeconomics was ready to succeed to the old classical economics as soon as receding memories of the Great Depression, policy mistakes of the Keynesian managers, and changing technological and social structures had created fertile political soil.

Joan Robinson described American Keynesianism as 'bastard Keynesianism'. The flavour of what became known as the 'neoclassical synthesis' is given by the remark of its main author, Nobel laureate Paul Samuelson: 'Had Keynes begun his first few chapters with the simple statement that he found it realistic to assume that modern capitalistic societies had money wage rates that were sticky and resistant to downward movements, most of his insights would have remained just as valid.'[1] So, despite his faulty theory, Keynes's conclusions were valid: the use of Keynesian policy tools was justified on practical, not theoretical, grounds. This interpretation fitted American pragmatism, and the urgent political imperative to counter the appeal of Communism. The first-generation Keynesian economists were fervent Keynesians. They passionately believed in anti-depression policies. But the way they interpreted Keynes implied that he was a theoretical charlatan.[2] For classical economists of Keynes's generation like Arthur Pigou had also explained lapses from full employment by the 'stickiness' of prices, and had advocated 'Keynesian' anti-depression policies for exactly this reason. Yet Keynes relied on uncertainty, not sticky wages or prices, to explain how slumps occur and why they were likely to last a long time.

It has to be admitted that Keynes himself sanctioned most of this 'bastardization'. Having written the *General Theory*, he was much more concerned to get activist policy going than to insist on precise adherence to his theory. And there was sufficient technical satisfaction to be had out of macroeconomic theory itself to satisfy most economists and statisticians, especially as it gave them a much greater role in making policy. The needs of Keynesian macroeconomic policy spawned vast quantities of national-income statistics which were fed into huge computer-forecasting models set up to capture the significant short-term trends of the macroeconomy. The Keynesian age was the golden age of macroeconomics: the famous economists of the time were all macroeconomists; most of them worked for or advised government at least some of the time. The study of markets and how they worked, or even failed to, was distinctly unfashionable: certainly it was not the royal road to promotion and influence. Chicago bided its time.

For the fact was that the neoclassical synthesis was intellectually unstable. It left the relationship between macroeconomics and microeconomics in a mess. There seemed no logical way of getting from the optimizing behaviour which microeconomics attributed to the individual to the perverse outcomes in the macro sphere which justified the theory of counter-cyclical policy. If workers were rational, why were they so inefficient in adjusting wages to the appropriate levels? Keynes would have answered that the assumption of individual optimization is not a realistic way of modelling states of the world with uncertain expectations. But this was precisely what was rejected.

There were two possible escape routes for the profession: either macroeconomic theory could be adjusted to fit classical micro theory or microeconomic theory could be adapted to fit Keynesian macroeconomic policy. The first was the dominant strategy. It was pursued by monetarists, New Classical economists, and real business cycle theorists (broadly the Chicago boys, or freshwater economists, of

Chapter 2). The second, minority, strategy was adopted by the 'New Keynesians' (the saltwater economists of Chapter 2).

Enter Milton Friedman

Keynes explicitly introduced expectations into economics. But he had little to say about how expectations were formed. What he did have to say seemed to leave out learning from experience or making efficient use of available information. If agents were truly 'rational' they wouldn't go on making the same mistakes. The conventions or 'rules of thumb' he equipped them with seemed invariant to changes in conditions or policy. It seemed more reasonable to assume that recurrent events would cause them to regard the structure of the future as probabilistic rather than uncertain. The reduction of uncertainty to certainty or calculable risk, the attribution of economic fluctuations to efficient responses to 'real' shocks, the denial that governments could ever improve on the performance of unimpeded markets – these were the weapons used by the New Classical economics to reinstate the classical theory of the self-regulating economy, destroy the Keynesian revolution, and limit the economic functions of government to maintaining sound money and open markets.*

The high priest of the classical counter-attack was Milton Friedman, the gnome of Chicago. Coming out of the monetary-disequilibrium tradition (see p. 81), Friedman argued that, whereas in the long run changes in the money stock affect the level of prices rather than the level of output, in the short run 'changes in the rate of growth of the money stock are capable of exerting a sizeable influence on the rate of growth of output as well.'[3] Since discretionary monetary and fiscal policy is itself a potent source of instability – being subject to 'long and variable lags' – governments should follow a monetary rule which aims to keep the money supply growing steadily at a rate equal to

*There were important neo-Keynesian attempts, like those of James Tobin and Franco Modigliani, to work out optimizing principles for the Keynesian portfolio, consumption and investment functions. Similarly, Robert Clower and Axel Leijonhufvud analysed effective demand failures in terms of the failure of the price system to coordinate the plans of individuals, households and firms in face of demand shocks. For a succinct account of these efforts to ground Keynesian aggregates in micro-rationality, see Klamer, *The New Classical Macroeconomics*, pp. 4, 10–11.

the long-run increase in national output. This would simultaneously achieve price stability (or more precisely an equilibrium path of the price level) and keep the economy fully employed. A predictable policy regime, rather than policy changes to match changing conditions, was what was needed for stability.

Friedman's most influential contribution was his analysis of rising post-war inflation in terms of the growth of inflationary expectations. Keynes had admitted that the quantity theory of money was valid at full employment: an increase in effective demand beyond full employment would only raise prices, not output. Friedman agreed, but with a crucial modification. By full employment he meant not the absence of any spare capacity in the economy, but an equilibrium level of unemployment which he called the 'natural' rate. This was that rate which established itself under conditions of stable inflation or 'neutral' money.

The post-war Keynesians refused to accept price behaviour as a measure of full employment. Short of an absolute limit on labour supply, the expansion of aggregate demand could always produce output gains, even if these were a declining fraction of price increases. This amounted to the view that labour was nearly always off its supply curve.* The Keynesians of the 1960s believed in a stable trade-off between inflation and unemployment, giving policymakers a 'menu of choice' between different mixes of the two. Friedman claimed that the trade-off was temporary, and existed only because workers were fooled into accepting lower real wages than they wanted by not taking into account the rise in prices. But if governments repeatedly resorted to monetary expansion in an attempt to reduce unemployment below its 'natural' or 'wanted' rate, money illusion would disappear and workers would put in increased wage demands to match the expected

*In the General Theory (CW, vii, pp. 6–8) Keynes did distinguish between 'voluntary' and 'involuntary' unemployment, but he never formalized the former as the 'equilibrium' rate, and post-war Keynesians ignored the distinction. They never doubted, that is, that more labour would be willing to work at the existing money wage if it were demanded. There is no theory of inflationary expectations in 'The Theory of Prices', Chapter 21 of the General Theory, especially on pp. 301–3. However, during the Second World War, Keynes became convinced that workers had become 'index conscious', so that a policy of raising the price level to reduce civilian consumption would not work (Skidelsky, Keynes vol. 3, p. 53). But this was forgotten when Keynesian economics reverted to depression thinking after the Second World War.

rise in prices. This would render the unemployment-reducing policies ineffective. In Friedman's interpretation, the phenomenon of cost push – trade unions pushing up wages ahead of productivity – was not an autonomous source of inflationary pressure, but an induced response to excessive money creation.

Milton Friedman predicted the coming of simultaneous increases in inflation and unemployment – so-called stagflation – as early as 1962. His prediction seemed borne out by the 'stagflationary' data of the late 1960s and early 1970s. The natural rate of unemployment, it could be said, was rising owing to growing structural rigidities in the labour market; inflation, temporarily controlled by socially disruptive pay policies which soon broke down, was also rising owing to repeated injections of demand into the economy to reduce unemployment to a socially acceptable level. British prime minister James Callaghan was expounding pure Friedmanite doctrine when he said in 1976 that the option of 'spending our way out of recession' no longer existed, and had worked in the past only by 'injecting bigger and bigger doses of inflation into the economy'. This statement is widely seen as marking the end of the Keynesian age.

Friedman held a fundamentally different interpretation of history from the Keynesians. 'The Great Depression,' he argued, 'like most other periods of severe unemployment, was produced by government mismanagement rather than by any inherent instability of the private economy.' Thus history as well as theory called for the unfettering of private enterprise from government: lighter taxes, less regulation. Friedman declared himself to be in favour of 'cutting taxes under any circumstances and for any excuse, for any reason, whenever it's possible'. As the Keynesian age slipped into crisis, Friedman became the new prophet of the free market.

Friedman's theories marked a return to the classical method of deducing macroeconomic outcomes from the logic of individual choice. Rational self-interested agents were forward-looking. They learned by experience to change their strategies when governments attempted to force unwanted outcomes on them. Like Keynes's own 'general theory', Friedman's monetarism was a decisive challenge to orthodox policymaking – now Keynesian – at a time of crisis. Just as Keynes succeeded politically because unemployment was the problem of the 1930s, Friedman succeeded politically because inflation was the problem of the 1970s. Friedman's defence of free markets also came at the moment when big business, alarmed by the growing social expenditures needed to finance President Johnson's Great Society programme, started to swing against 'big government'. From the late 1960s to the early 1980s there was a halting but eventually decisive swing back of the political pendulum towards conservative economic and social policy. Thus the intellectual and political logics started to coincide, with each feeding the other.

The New Classical Economics

However, Friedman's theory of 'adaptive expectations' did not go far enough for a new generation of mathematically trained economists like his former student Robert Lucas. Friedman has agents learning from, and adapting their behaviour to, changing market signals, but with an inevitable lag since market processes take place in time. But rational agents should be able to do better than that. They should already have learned from past experience (their own and everyone else's) that certain types of event will bring about certain results. In that case, Friedman's distinction between the short period in which agents can be fooled and the long period in which they know what to expect becomes superfluous. Adaptive behaviour is a description of *irrational* behaviour if agents know what to expect already.

So, in the 1980s, the theory of adaptive expectations was followed by the theory of rational expectations. Rational expectations theorists have carried Friedman's scepticism about managing the business cycle to its logical conclusion. If monetary policy is systematically operated according to Keynesian principles, it will be anticipated, and have no real effects even in the short run! Stabilization policy would then be possible only if governments had better information than private agents. By abolishing the 'short period', the New Classical macroeconomics abolished the narrow interval of time that Friedman's monetarism had left for Keynesian policy to work in. In Robert Solow's words, the rational expectations revolution swept away 'all of the loopholes that provided some fuzziness in the vertical long-run Phillips Curve'.[4]

Real business cycle theory was invented to close any remaining loophole for government intervention. The economy is constantly at full employment, since the observed fluctuations in output are fluctuations in Friedman's 'natural rate' of unemployment and not deviations from it. Thus, government interference to reduce instability will *always* result in a reduction in welfare.

It is hard to know whether real business cycle theorists actually believed in their models, or whether they just found it more mathematically elegant to do their economics in this way. The political comfort their theory gave to those clamouring to reduce taxes and 'get Washington off our backs' was clear enough. Nothing a government could do to stimulate the economy would work; in fact it was bound to make things worse. So government might as well cut taxes, deregulate economic life, and let businessmen get on with the job of producing wealth, not least for themselves.

The New Keynesians

New Keynesianism arose in the 1980s to challenge the newly dominant Chicago school of Robert Lucas and his followers. It started with the fact that the Reagan–Thatcher revolutions had left a heavy and persisting legacy of unemployment in their wake, contrary to real business cycle teaching. As has been pointed out, belief in rational expectations does not entail belief in instantaneous market clearing, as it takes time to change contracts, and not all prices convey new information. Thus New Keynesians were able to explain sticky prices in a rational expectations framework. Yes, agents can be assumed to have rational expectations, but not instantaneous adjustment capacities, since it might be costly for them to update their information. New Keynesian models allowed for both supply and demand-side shocks which cause involuntary unemployment. Incorporating the rational expectations hypothesis and Friedman's natural rate hypothesis – two distinctly classical assumptions – along with the Keynesian assumption that markets do not always clear, New Keynesian theories justified limited government intervention since they implied that economies fail rapidly to self-equilibrate and the actual rate of unemployment can remain above the natural rate for a long time.

This attempt to refloat Keynesian theory on a sea of market imperfections did not please post-Keynesians like Paul Davidson, who accused New Keynesians like Joe Stiglitz of being traitors to the cause, since they had abandoned Keynes's central postulate of uncertainty. However, the post-Keynesians were even more isolated than the New Keynesians, and mostly failed to obtain tenured positions in prestigious universities.

The New Neoclassical Synthesis

By the end of the twentieth century, commentators were talking about the emergence of the 'New Neoclassical Synthesis', which incorporates both New Classical and New Keynesian elements. It adheres to the rational expectations hypothesis; at the same time it recognizes the importance of imperfect competition, and it incorporates the costliness of price adjustments. This new synthesis allows for monetary policy to have real effects in the short run while dismissing any long-run trade-off between inflation and real activity. However, this synthesis is possible only because of the large number of assumptions the New Keynesians share with the New Classicals. As Krugman recognizes, the New Keynesians have not yet mined the 'deep foundations' of real-world disorders (see above, p. 50).

Public Choice Theory

Running parallel with developments in macroeconomics proper, a branch of economics known as public choice theory has grown up which analyses the interactions between politics and economics. Whereas the conventional (normative) approach simply regards the policymaker as a 'benevolent social planner', public choice theory views the government as an inside actor in economic life. The former is concerned with how policymakers should act; the latter looks at how they actually do act.

Public choice theory claims that public policies are motivated not by a concern for the public interest, but by the private interests of politicians, bureaucrats and 'rent-seeking' lobbies. This theory of 'government failure' constituted another powerful argument for the limited state, and one in which politicians were constrained by rules. What the rational expectations and public choice theories share is the methodology of modelling public policies as the solution to individual maximization problems.[5] In doing so, they revive the original eighteenth-century inspiration of economics, which juxtaposed the efficiency of markets with the failures of government.

To Bring the Story Up to Date

Mainstream economics today, by improving on the maths, and abandoning common sense, is further away from Keynes's economics than ever before. Eight differences stand out:

(1) Keynes's distinction between uncertainty and risk has been abolished. All uncertainty about future events can be reduced to a probability calculus – that is, to the presumption that the probability distributions of the past and present are also valid in the future. This amounts to saying that economic agents have perfect information about future events or, in weaker versions, that perfect information is available, though costly to obtain. Keynes's marvellous insights into the psychology of financial markets, the variability of investment, and the role of money as a store of value are irrelevant.

(2) New Classical economics has abolished time. Events do not have to happen in a sequence: they happen simultaneously. Equipped with continuously updated information, economic agents adjust instantly and efficiently to all external 'shocks'. The New Keynesian economists inhabit the same mental universe, but, by 'relaxing the assumptions', they allow for situations in which markets may misbehave in the short run. Although real GDP fluctuates around a rising long-term trend, there may be short-run fluctuations primarily caused by 'stickiness' of prices in face of demand shocks, and they have investigated the microeconomic sources of this stickiness. Even so, their models cannot explain the sources of aggregate demand failure, which require a recognition of uncertainty. Keynes said that people *cannot* possess the information required to validate the theory that markets are

self-equilibrating at full employment either in the long run or in the short run.

(3) While the simple aggregate equations of Keynes's macroeconomic model are still taught, there has been a return to neoclassical standards of method. No longer is it acceptable to posit *ad hoc* supply and demand functions. Macroeconomics is best seen as an application of microeconomics, in the sense that macroeconomic models *should* be based on optimization by firms and consumers. This is contrary to Keynes, who believed that individual behaviour is structured by aggregate psychological data ('propensity to consume', 'state of confidence', 'liquidity preference') arising from inescapable uncertainty about the future.

(4) Mainstream macroeconomics today is based on supply, not demand. It has reasserted some version of Say's Law – that supply creates its own demand – which Keynes repudiated. Thus, both New Classicals and New Keynesians believe that the growth of real GDP in the long run depends on an increase in the supply of factor inputs and technological progress. Further, many economists only accept sticky contracts as contingent, not inescapable. The 'supply-side' school of economists has been busily advocating their dissolution by weakening trade unions and fixed-wage contracts and stiffening conditions for receipt of unemployment and welfare benefits. They look forward to a world in which all contracts are instantly renegotiable.

(5) Contemporary mainstream economists have reasserted the quantity theory of money – the view that the rate of growth of the money supply determines the rate of inflation – completely in line with Friedman's argument, but contrary to Keynes, who asserted that this is true only at full employment.

(6) In modelling economies, contemporary macroeconomists are not fazed by the unrealism of their assumptions; indeed, they regard this as a strength of their models. Fortified by maths, they have reverted more completely than their ancestor classical economists to 'ideal-type', or Platonic, theorizing, sacrificing truth for mathematical elegance. This is in direct contrast to Keynes, who insisted on 'realism of assumptions'.

(7) In contrast to the Keynesian consensus during the 'golden age', it

is now widely thought that governments should not attempt to fine-tune the economy. Instead, stabilization policy should merely aim to assist the market's self-correcting capabilities, chiefly by keeping prices stable.

(8) Whereas in the 1950s and 1960s stabilization was seen as a control-theory problem, it is now modelled as a strategic game between the authorities and private agents, whose expectations the authorities need to 'manage' by means of clear rules. This follows the normative prescription that governments should aim to provide agents with a consistent model of the economy. This is expected to make real variables more stable.

The cumulative effect of these theoretical developments has been to narrow the scope of macro policy and change its explicit aim. With acceptance of the 'natural rate' doctrine, much of macro policy's earlier unemployment-reducing function is now assigned to supply-side reforms, leaving macroeconomic policy with the single aim of maintaining price stability. This is turn tends to re-establish the so-called classical dichotomy between money and the 'real' economy, leaving the quantity theory of money as the only relevant macro-economic theory. That amounts to the theoretical abolition of the Keynesian revolution.

Having said this, most politicians, being deficient in mathematics, and more keenly alive to political needs, remain understandably sceptical of the New Classical and even the New Keynesian claims. There is little acceptance by policymakers that 'shocked' economies rapidly recover to full-employment equilibrium, even if this is defined as the 'natural rate'. They certainly do not act on this assumption. This is only sensible in view of the prolonged periods of unemployment, underemployment and stagnation which have characterized most economies since the collapse of the golden age.

What we have described in the last two chapters is a long passage from classical to New Classical economics, with the Keynesian revolution as an intermission of common sense. The question is how far the New Keynesian strategy of 'relaxing the assumptions' of New Classical macroeconomics can proceed without inducing a 'paradigm shift'. In his influential *Structure of Scientific Revolutions* (1962), the historian of science Thomas Kuhn argued that the dominant scientific theories of the day are overthrown by the accumulation of 'anomalies' – the occurrence of events unpredicted by the theory, which have to be given *ad hoc* explanations. Thus Ptolemaic astronomy was overthrown by the Copernican revolution, Newton's physics by Einstein's revolution, and so on. A similar accumulation of anomalies has occurred within the New Classical macroeconomic paradigm, of which the present crisis is the latest, and most egregious, example. The time is ripe for a new 'paradigm shift', which needs to build on Keynes's original insight into the nature of behaviour under conditions of uncertainty.

Ideas Versus Vested Interests

So far, I have treated the 'rise and fall' of Keynesian economics as a contest of ideas, but the political context in which ideas are generated, gain acceptance, and fall into disuse should certainly not be ignored. The Keynesian full-employment policy was adopted by the leading capitalist powers after the Second World War as a consensus-building strategy and to put capitalism in a stronger position to withstand revolutionary assaults, both domestic and international. But the political work it did in the different countries varied. In the US it was the tax-cutting aspect of Keynesianism which was most in evidence; in Britain, spending on the social services; on the European continent, public investment programmes. All had their particular justifications, but all could invoke the general rationale of maintaining high levels of demand.

The United States is a particularly interesting example of how the 'new economics', as it was known to avoid calling it Keynesian, had to be mixed up with domestic ingredients before it could become acceptable. Initially, it offered a way of carrying on FDR's New Deal in a way acceptable to the business community.[6] Having enjoyed, in war, the benefits of high profits, businessmen were determined not to fall back into recession. In the tax cut, they now had the ideal instrument for avoiding it. The 'new economics' could, after all, be married to one of the constants of business thinking – reducing taxes – while simultaneously winning the support of labour. Budget deficits – sometimes relying on the automatic stabilizers, sometimes promoted by vigorous tax cutting – remained the basis of 'pragmatic' macro policy American style from Kennedy and Johnson in the 1960s to Reagan in the 1980s to Bush in the 2000s. (The Clinton surplus of the late 1990s represents an intermission of virtue.) It is hard to avoid the conclusion that the quasi-permanent deficit has been, for a long time, the mainstay of the American consensus. It enabled high employment to be maintained by methods which did not alarm the business community. In fact it was associated with two big tax-cutting bouts (under Reagan and George W. Bush), a gradual whittling down of social programmes, and a huge increase in inequality. Keynesians could argue in favour of the tax cuts on employment-boosting grounds, anti-Keynesians on incentive-improving grounds. None of this had any connection with Keynes's own fiscal policy, which required current spending to be balanced by tax revenues.

There is also a political context for the fall of Keynesianism – one that has recently been emphasized by Paul Krugman.[7] Krugman's main argument is that, from the 1980s, Keynesian economics and, more generally, social-democratic reform were derailed by 'a vast right-wing conspiracy', which duped the poor-white voter into neglecting his material interests by playing on his fear of racial swamping. Race is Krugman's main explanation for America's lack of universal health care: whites did not want integrated hospitals. This is the 'vested-interest' argument, which Keynes himself minimized. Marxists have long argued that Keynes's ideas were taken up because they served the interests of the bourgeoisie in the 1930s, and were dropped when they started to endanger capitalist profits in the 1970s. Friedman and Hayek, Marxists say, became popular in the 1980s because they legitimized the re-creation of the 'reserve army of the unemployed'. Freeing up markets also provided ideological cover for the use of state power to promote financial interests. But the heavy unemployment in the 1980s also provided the political setting for the birth of New Keynesianism, just as it is bringing Keynes back into fashion again today.

All this raises the old question of whether ideas are part of the base or the superstructure of social life – society's building blocks or weapons in the struggle for power. I know of no way of answering this question except in terms that Keynes himself would have given:

that, whatever the short-run fate of ideas, the ideas that survive are those that answer to what is universal in human nature or experience, and not just to the interests of particular groups.

THE KEYNESIAN AND POST-KEYNESIAN ERAS COMPARED

The persistent criticism of Keynes's economics has been that, if applied, it would reduce the natural dynamism of the capitalist system, which thrives on 'irrational exuberance'. Keynes believed that capitalism suffered not from a surfeit of dynamism, but from a surfeit of fear, which allowed dynamism to break out only sporadically. So, as he saw it, a reduction in uncertainty would make the economy more dynamic over time, though more steadily. Events since his death have provided some test of both theories.

All policies are bound to be imperfect reflections of their intellectual aspirations. However, it is still interesting to consider which of the two imperfect global regimes – the 'Keynesian' Bretton Woods system and the 'New Classical' Washington Consensus system which succeeded it – delivered the better performance.

The structures of the two systems can be depicted in the following tables.

Bretton Wood ('Golden Age') System

Objective	Instrument(s)	Responsible authority
Full employment	Demand management (mainly fiscal)	National governments
Balance-of-payments adjustment	Pegged but adjustable exchange rates (capital controls)	IMF
Promotion of international trade	Tariff reductions etc.	GATT
Economic development	Official assistance	World Bank

This is a rough outline of the system which was set up for remedying the deficiencies of the interwar years. It was consciously intended to codify and improve the rules and practices of a liberal world economy which had grown up fitfully, and in an *ad hoc* way, in the nineteenth century, and which had failed so conspicuously between the wars. It lasted till the 1970s. First to go was the fixed-exchange-rate system, which collapsed between 1971 and 1973. The full-employment commitment was abandoned from the late 1970s onward. Capital controls were dismantled in the 1980s and early 1990s. The system which replaced it can be represented as follows:

Washington Consensus System

Objective	Instrument(s)	Responsible authority
Price stability	Interest-rate policy	National central bank, ECB for Eurozone
Balance-of-payments adjustment	Floating exchange rates	
Promotion of international trade	Tariff reductions etc.	ITO, WTO (since 1995)
Economic development	Loans	Private lending, World Bank

The two regimes were shaped by two different philosophies. The Bretton Woods system broadly reflected the Keynesian view that an international economy needed strong political and institutional supports if it was to be acceptably stable. The Washington Consensus regime was shaped by the theory of the self-regulating market. Of course, neither system embodied its underlying philosophy in pure form. The Bretton Woods institutions fell far short of Keynes's plan for an 'economic government of the world'. And the Washington Consensus system only to a limited extent realized the New Classical insistence on floating exchange rates. Nevertheless, the spirits of the two systems are sufficiently different for some test of the 'fruits' of the two philosophies to be possible.

The Bretton Woods period is defined as the twenty-two years from

1951 to 1973. The starting point was chosen to allow the economies involved to have put a few years behind them after the end of the war. The end date corresponds to the first OPEC shock of 1973 – a convention adhered to by economic historians such as Alec Cairncross in *The Legacy of the Golden Age*.[8] The Washington Consensus era ranges from the start of the 1980s until today. Many comparisons simply compare pre-1973 with post-1973. However, to allow Reagan and Thatcher to come into power, and to create two roughly equally long periods, 1980 has been chosen as the starting date. The future will determine whether the crash in September–October 2008 marked the end of the Washington Consensus period.

It is easy enough to compare outcomes in different periods, much harder to explain the causes of those outcomes. Did a football team's performance over successive periods improve because it had a better coach or because of other factors? We lack a counter-factual comparison – a comparison between what happened and what would have happened under different conditions. Our comparison between the Bretton Woods and Washington Consensus eras is a comparison of outcomes. And the outcomes differed significantly. Later we shall ask how much difference the old coach (Keynes) made to the performance of the Bretton Woods era.

The graph below shows the growth of global real GDP from 1951 to 2009 (estimated). The growth rate during the Bretton Woods years was on average higher than during the Washington Consensus period – at 4.8% as compared to the 3.2% growth rate after 1980. These averages are indicated by the horizontal lines in the graph. A 1.6 percentage point difference might not seem very big. However, had the world economy grown at 4.8% rather than at 3.2% from 1980 until today, it would have been more than 50% larger, something we shall achieve only in 2022 with the 1980–2009 average rate. (This calculation excludes the impact of the present economic downturn.)

The lightly shaded areas represent global economic recessions. The IMF defines a global economic recession as a year with less than 3% growth. This might seem like an odd definition. Surely 3% still signifies positive growth, and should therefore hardly count as a recession. However, while this is true of rich countries, the IMF argues that

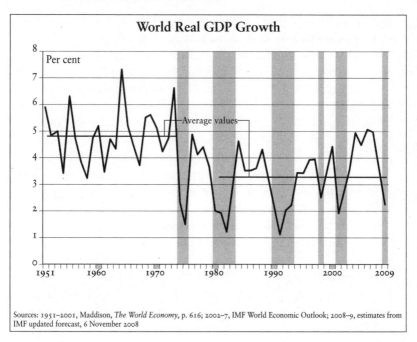

Sources: 1951–2001, Maddison, *The World Economy*, p. 616; 2002–7, IMF World Economic Outlook; 2008–9, estimates from IMF updated forecast, 6 November 2008

many developing countries – particularly the emerging-market econo-mies – have much higher 'normal' growth rates. China has been growing by at least 9% over the last decade. If growth were to fall to say 6% even, the impact would be similar to a recession in advanced countries. By this definition, then, there were no global recessions in the Bretton Woods age, whereas there were five recessions in the Washington Consensus period. This contrast is made even more remarkable by the fact that the Western dominance of the global economy was much stronger in the 1950s and 1960s than in the last few decades of the century. In other words, the global economy could rely less on strong emerging-market growth rates to maintain a high average in the Bretton Woods age than in the Washington Consensus age. Even so, the world did not record a single year with less than 3% growth between 1951 and 1973.

The growth in per-capita GDP slowed down, too, in all major economies. During the Bretton Woods age, France and Germany saw their GDP per capita grow by on average 4.0% and 4.9% respectively. In Japan the rate was a full 8% annually. The UK and the US also experienced high growth rates in GDP per capita, but the large influx of immigrants to these economies limited the growth to 2.5% and 2.2% respectively.[9] In the Washington Consensus era these numbers had shrunk to 1.6% for France, 1.8% for Germany, 2.0% for Japan, 2.1% for the UK and 1.9% for the US – decreases across the board.[10] Even in the US, where the difference is merely 0.3 percentage points, this slowing-down of growth has had a significant impact. The average American would have been 10% richer had the US GDP per capita grown as quickly between 1980 and 2007 as it did between 1950 and 1973.

In terms of unemployment, the contrast between the Keynesian and post-Keynesian periods is also large. Disregarding the American experience, the Bretton Woods decades were a period of record low unemployment rates. In the UK, for instance, merely 1.6% of the workforce was unemployed on average. In France, the percentage was even lower, at 1.2%, whereas in Germany – partly owing to the immigration of 12 million Germans from eastern Europe after the war – average unemployment was slightly higher, but still only 3.1%. This was called the European Miracle by observers at the time, and was contrasted with the persistently high unemployment figures in the US (1950–73 average of 4.8%). This might seem odd to us today, considering how often the 'flexible' American labour market has been praised for its ability to keep unemployment down over the last few decades.

After 1980, however, the labour market looks very different. In the UK, average unemployment went up from 1.6% to 7.4%; in Germany it rose from 3.1% to 7.5%. In the US the rate went up from 4.8% to 6.1%.

Another important measure is volatility. Volatility describes the relative rate of change of a variable of interest. In other words, it answers the question of how much – in this case – the growth rate of real GDP varies over time. There are two main reasons why volatility is important. First, high volatility normally implies great uncertainty. If real GDP growth is prone to sudden and significant changes, you are less likely to know what growth in the next period will be. This

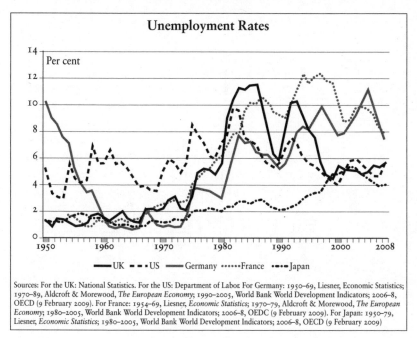

Unemployment Rates

Sources: For the UK: National Statistics. For the US: Department of Labor. For Germany: 1950–69, Liesner, *Economic Statistics*; 1970–89, Aldcroft & Morewood, *The European Economy*; 1990–2005, World Bank World Development Indicators; 2006–8, OECD (9 February 2009). For France: 1954–69, Liesner, *Economic Statistics*; 1970–79, Aldcroft & Morewood, *The European Economy*; 1980–2005, World Bank World Development Indicators; 2006–8, OEDC (9 February 2009). For Japan: 1950–79, Liesner, *Economic Statistics*; 1980–2005, World Bank World Development Indicators; 2006–8, OECD (9 February 2009)

in turn means that it is harder to plan ahead. So, if you are the government and you are uncertain about the growth of the economy next year, it will be harder to present a forward-looking budget which appropriately responds to levels of output and tax revenue. The second reason for looking at economic volatility is that there is evidence suggesting that higher volatility leads to lower growth. Viktoria Hnatkovska at Georgetown University and Norman Loayza at the World Bank analysed the relationship between volatility and growth between 1960 and 2000 and found not only that 'macroeconomic volatility and long-run economic growth are negatively related', but, more importantly, that 'the negative global relationship between macroeconomic volatility and long-run growth actually reflects an even stronger, harmful effect *from volatility to growth*.'[11] This link, they claim, is particularly strong for low and middle-income countries, but holds true across the board. Thus, keeping volatility low can have important benefits for the economy.

Using a definition for volatility employed by Michael Bordo, the

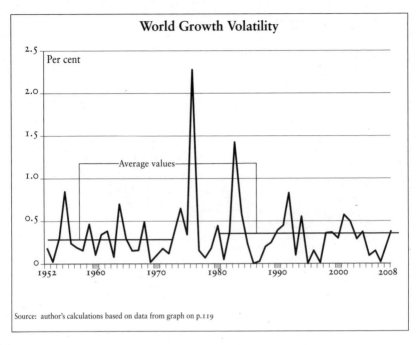

Source: author's calculations based on data from graph on p.119

graph above shows growth volatility as the absolute rate of change of the natural logarithm of the growth rate.[12] The average values for the two periods are represented by the horizontal lines.

Contrary to a widely held view, there has been hardly any change in the level of volatility between the Bretton Woods and the Washington Consensus periods. The perception that economic growth has been more volatile in recent decades is largely a misinterpretation of the fact that there have been so many recessions. But a larger number of recessions does not necessarily mean more growth volatility: lower average growth rates imply that volatility more easily brings economies into the red. Hnatkovska and Loayza conclude, 'The world is not more volatile now than 30 years ago, but volatility is taking a larger toll on growth.'[13] And this toll frequently results in recession at current average growth rates.

Another type of volatility of interest is exchange-rate volatility. Under the Bretton Woods system, currencies were pegged to the dollar; in the Washington Consensus era they were allowed to float freely.

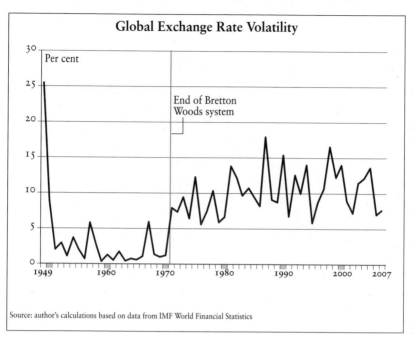

Global Exchange Rate Volatility

Source: author's calculations based on data from IMF World Financial Statistics

The graph above shows the increase in volatility ensuing from the collapse of Bretton Woods. The vertical line marks the end of the Bretton Woods system. Since then, liberalization of international capital flows and an enormous increase in the scale of cross-border financial transactions have contributed even further to large exchange-rate movements – and this at a time when a host of countries, predominantly in eastern and central Europe, joined the global capitalist system.

Intuitively, one expects exchange-rate volatility to disrupt trade flows. However, according to an IMF report from 2004,[14] the effect of exchange-rate volatility on trade was, at most, marginal. On the other hand, the report concedes that major fluctuations in times of currency crises could have serious repercussions. These occurred in the late 1980s and late 1990s.

One of the myths of post-war economic history is that the Keynesian age was one of high inflation brought to an end only by a salutary dose of monetarism. In fact there was no significant difference in the

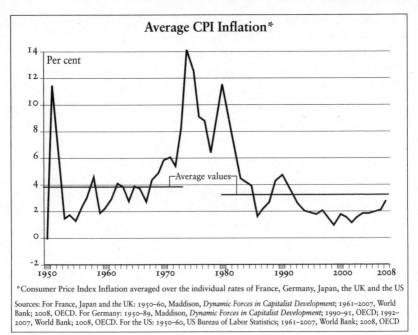

Average CPI Inflation*

*Consumer Price Index Inflation averaged over the individual rates of France, Germany, Japan, the UK and the US

Sources: For France, Japan and the UK: 1950–60, Maddison, *Dynamic Forces in Capitalist Development*; 1961–2007, World Bank; 2008, OECD. For Germany: 1950–89, Maddison, *Dynamic Forces in Capitalist Development*; 1990–91, OECD; 1992–2007, World Bank; 2008, OECD. For the US: 1950–60, US Bureau of Labor Statistics; 1961–2007, World Bank; 2008, OECD

inflation rates of the two periods – the 1950–73 average being 3.9%, the 1980–2008 average 3.2%. There was no inflation 'price' paid for the higher employment and faster growth of the Keynesian age. Its policy success was if anything more impressive because global competition was weaker. In the first period it was fixed exchange rates which provided the anti-inflationary anchor; in the second period, inflation targeting by central banks. There was a large upsurge in inflation in the intervening 1970s, brought about largely by the collapse of the fixed-exchange-rate system in 1971.

What about inequality? Has the gap between the richest and the poorest widened? The mixed economies of the earlier period, unlike the free-market economies of the Washington Consensus years, emphasized moderate redistribution and the creation of the welfare state. This would suggest that inequality should have increased in the Washington Consensus years. And this turns out to be the case.

James Galbraith is leading the University of Texas Inequality Project (UTIP), which is pioneering inequality measurement. It replaces the

Gini coefficient, which is used to measure income inequality between individuals, with the Theil index, which measures inequality between groups and regions. Galbraith finds that, among the OECD countries, all but Denmark saw an increase in inequality from the beginning of the 1960s.[15] Among the non-OECD countries the trend was similar. In the US, inequality of *pay* has fallen, whereas inequality of *income* has risen. The best-off have been getting relatively richer on the back of 'extra income' like stock options and bonuses rather than their base salary. Globally, inequality was stable in the Bretton Woods age, but it rose sharply in the Washington Consensus years from 1982 and all the way into the new millennium. A rather surprising exception to this trend is South America. UTIP has recorded decreases in inequality in the southern part of the continent since the financial crises in the late 1990s and the early 2000s. This, Galbraith argues, is the result of 'that region's retreat from neoliberal orthodoxy'.[16] The financial collapse in Argentina led to a downsizing of the previously disproportionately dominant financial sector and an increase in public-sector employment.

The increase in inequality matters for two reasons. First, many regard equality as an intrinsic good. The welfare state is widely regarded as a constitutive aspect of the identity of an advanced economy. The second reason is political. Throughout history, large discrepancies in wealth have produced political instability. And today it is not simply a coincidence that three of the countries with the largest income inequalities – Brazil, Mexico and South Africa – also suffer from some of the highest crime rates on earth. We have also seen a massive increase in inequality *between* countries. Paul Collier talks about the 'Bottom Billion' – the sixth of the global population, predominantly in Africa, which is becoming poorer in both absolute and relative terms while the rest of the world is either developed or developing. Although moral considerations matter, Collier argues that the key reason why the West should do everything it can to reduce this inequality is because of the effects on our own economies in terms of mass migration and transnational violence.

To sum up, then, the comparison between the Bretton Woods and Washington Consensus years shows that the former had less unemployment, higher growth, lower exchange-rate volatility and lower inequality. The Washington Consensus era was not, as often assumed, more volatile in terms of GDP growth, although it has now suffered from five global recessions – the latest being the largest and deepest since the Great Depression. Before we can answer the question of whether the absence of the old coach made a difference, we must at least try to answer the question whether the Bretton Woods golden age was really a Keynesian golden age. How far was it due to Keynesian ideas and policies, and how far due to other factors? This is a good test of the importance of ideas.

THE INFLUENCE OF IDEAS ON PERFORMANCE

As we saw above, unemployment in the Bretton Woods age was much lower than in the Washington Consensus years. Full employment had become a 'realistic' objective for the macro economy. Keynesian activism took root in Canada, the UK and Scandinavia. It was written into law in the US (the Full Employment Act of 1946, not fully implemented until the 1960s) and in Germany (the Stabilization Law of 1967). And even in countries which were more supply-side focused, like France, full resource utilization became the normative standard to which to aspire. Some governments had unemployment targets, but the targets were revised downward as actual unemployment fell below targeted unemployment. Low unemployment, it could be argued, was not caused by setting low unemployment targets: the targets were set because unemployment was low. The argument that golden-age full-employment performance was not the result of full-employment policy was most famously made by R. C. O. Matthews in 1968. His case was based on British evidence, but applies more generally. Matthews pointed out that 'throughout the post-war period the Government, so far from injecting demand into the system, has persistently had a large current account surplus . . . Fiscal policy as such therefore appears on the face of it to have been . . . quite strongly deflationary.'[17] Why, then, did Britain have such a prolonged period of full employment? Matthews suggested a combination of 'Keynesian' and 'non-Keynesian' factors. The 'Keynesian' factor was a 'gigantic cyclical' private-investment boom based on the huge back-log of investment opportunities left over from the interwar and war years; the non-Keynesian factor was an increase in the scarcity of labour relative to capital, which 'provided a measure of protection to labour from the effects of fluctuation in the demand for the final product'. However, the 'Keynesian' factor – increased investment demand – was not due to Keynesian policy. It was due to a conjuncture of favourable factors, of which the big increase in export demand compared to the inter-war years was important.

The weakness in Matthews's argument is that he uses deficit spend-ing as the test of Keynesian policy. This is a mistake: budget surpluses were as much a part of the Keynesian technique for restraining demand as were budget deficits for stimulating demand. The use of Keynesian policy to *restrain* demand started in the Second World War, and continued for many years afterwards. It was an important factor in allowing the boom to continue.

What, then, caused the long 'quasi-boom' of the 1950s and the 1960s? A Keynesian growth theory is one that makes economic growth a function of investment demand. Evidently, if Matthews is right, Keynesian growth policy cannot have had much responsibility for the high growth rates of OECD countries in the golden age, since the investment ratio was largely determined by private-sector decisions. As the story is currently told, the fast post-war growth of the European countries was generated on the supply side of the econ-omy by technological 'catch-up'. According to Moses Abramovitz, 'the countries of the industrialized "West" were able to bring into production a large backlog of unexploited technology . . . The princi-pal part of this backlog . . . consisted of methods of production and of commerical and industrial organization already in use in the United States.'[18] The opportunities for technological catch-up gave capital a high marginal productivity, leading to high private-investment demand. This explanation begs the question of why the opportunities for technological catch-up – which had existed since the start of the last century – were seized only in the post-war years.

Intuitively, the answer must lie in the greater *confidence* generated by the post-war institutions, notably the IMF, the World Bank and the GATT (General Agreement on Tariffs and Trade). The IMF fell far short of Keynes's hopes for a world central bank which would be able to create credit to finance trade expansion. GATT also fell short of many hopes for an International Trade Organization to provide agreed rules for a liberal trading system. Nevertheless, fragments of the Keynesian grand design for a better world were put into place, and they certainly represented a great improvement on the institutional disorder of the interwar years. A leading historian of the Bretton Woods system wrote in 1978 that 'during a quarter of a century' it had stood as the 'foundation upon which world trade, production, employment and investment were gradually built'.[19]

The role of the United States in maintaining global demand was crucial, but it was not played out as a result of the obligations it had assumed under the Bretton Woods system. Because Keynes's own specific doctrine of 'creditor adjustment' was not accepted at Bretton Woods, the agreement provided no mechanism for dealing with the post-war 'dollar gap': lack of dollars to buy US exports. This gap was filled by the United States providing the world with dollars. The dollar outflows led to a rundown in US and a build-up of European and Japanese reserves, which in turn enabled the leading exchange rates to be stabilized and currency convertibility to be established. This promoted trade liberalization between the three partners – carried out partly to cement political cohesion – and trade liberalization sustained the post-war investment boom. In effect, the US Treasury substituted for the absent Keynesian central bank as global macro-manager, injecting a steady stream of demand into the world economy.

It is not denied that the outflow of dollars had Keynesian effects, but it is often claimed that it was done for Cold War, rather than Keynesian, reasons. However, the intellectual background to American policy was not just anti-Communism, but recognition that the flourishing of the free-enterprise system could not just be left to the market. This was the work of Keynes.

As we have seen, the monetarists attributed the collapse of the long boom to the build-up of inflationary expectations under Keynesian demand-management policies. Naturally, Keynesian demand-managers of this epoch don't accept this. Some emphasize the inflationary financing by the United States of the Vietnam War, contrary to the advice of the Keynesian policy advisers. This spilled out into global inflation through the mechanism of the gold-exchange standard. Others stress an inflationary bias in the wage and price-setting institutions. All agree that the OPEC oil-price shock of 1973–4 converted an already sizeable inflationary problem into a full-blown inflationary recession. Some admit that Keynesian economics, with its focus on preventing demand shocks, was slow to develop a convincing analysis of, and response to, a major supply shock. This was the conceptual and policy gap into which monetarism stepped.

Keynesian policy advice cannot be held responsible for the inflationary financing of the Vietnam War. But it cannot be absolved from the charge of letting inflation build up without taking effective corrective action on the supply side of the economy. The result was that, except in Japan, the quadrupling of oil prices in 1973–4 hit inflexible labour markets. This made both the inflation and the recession worse than they need have been. Some Keynesians believe that nothing could have been done about supply: wage-push short of full employment was made inevitable by the institutions of the mixed economy. The truth is that tackling supply-side rigidities and inefficiencies was never a priority for the Keynesian establishment, which believed that unemployment could always be reduced if there was enough demand. This was to apply an attitude of mind built on mass unemployment in the 1930s – when supply did not matter – to a situation of full or even over-full employment. So Keynesianism was at least partly responsible for the institutions which led to inflation.

Keynesianism was more to blame for the eventual mishandling of fiscal policy. I have suggested that an important contribution of Keynesian fiscal policy to the golden age was to keep inflation under control by methods which did not bring about the collapse of the boom, exactly as Keynes himself would have advocated.

However, US fiscal restraint was overwhelmed in the 1960s by a wave of Keynesian hubris. This was not the moment when Keynesianism 'came of age' in the United States: it was the prelude to its downfall. The mindset of the new generation of Keynesian economists was that there were virtually no supply constraints, and that macro policy could be timed, and its effects predicted, with scientific precision. A large package of tax cuts and increased military and social spending was enacted between 1964 and 1966 – to get the economy moving, to counter an alleged Soviet arms build-up, and to alleviate poverty and black alienation. Keynesian and non-Keynesian motives were jumbled up together in this fiscal stimulus. But it resulted in a widening budget deficit and rising inflation before the much greater spending on the Vietnam War came on stream. This was the high period of government activism, in Britain and Europe as much as in the United States. The breakdown of most of these activist policies marked the start of the conservative counter-attack in both politics and economics, whose fruit was the triumph of Reagan and Thatcher in the 1980s.

The question remains: To what extent were the successes and failures of the golden age the result of Keynesian theory, however bastardized? The quick answer is: To a much greater extent in the former than in the latter. Keynesianism provided an analytical framework for organizing policy choices. It also provided *ad hoc* rationalizations for what governments wanted to do for other reasons. At the rhetorical level, these were important. They created the expectation that full employment would be maintained by policy. This reinforced the favourable background for business investment. To a more limited extent, Keynesian policy as practised in the 1960s brought the golden age into crisis: but there were more profound reasons relating to the drift of social policy (sometimes called the 'revolution in entitlements'), the role of the United States in the world, and the weakness of the Bretton Woods system of international institutions. So the old coach did make a difference.

PART III

The Return of Keynes

6

Keynes and the Ethics of Capitalism

THE MORALS OF CAPITALISM

'The key thing that went wrong was that a culture was allowed to develop over the last fifteen years or so where the relationship between what people did and what they got went way out of alignment, especially at the top end.'[1] There is a typical politician's ambiguity in this observation by Alastair Darling. It could mean that people spent more than they earned, which is true. In addition to stretched mortgaging, Britain has half the total of European credit-card debt. But reference to 'at the top end' suggests that Darling had something else in mind: that people especially 'at the top end' were being paid too much for what they did. Whichever way his remark is taken, he seemed to be saying that the fault lay in a money-obsessed culture – one in which money had become the measure of all things. And this is right. But this is a moral judgement. And, being a politician, Darling left out the premise on which his argument rested, as too offensive to the culture which he represented: that there was something wrong with the morals of contemporary Britain. Being an intellectual, Keynes had no such inhibition. He was a philosopher and moralist as well as an economist. And he never ceased to question the purposes of economic activity. Briefly stated, his conclusion was that the pursuit of money – what he called 'love of money' – was justified only to the extent that it led to a 'good life'. And a good life was not what made people better off: it was what made them good. To make the world ethically better was the only justifiable purpose of economic striving.

This doctrine sounds utterly alien to all but the religious, since there is now no generally accepted idea of the good life in this sense. We can still talk about the duties of wealth. There is also a long tradition, which still resonates, that people should not be treated as commodities, and that therefore the scope of market exchange should be limited. But on wealth as an object of desire we have nothing to say: if that's what people want, then that's what they should have. Moreover, the accumulation of wealth has behind it one powerfully resonant 'moral' argument: it lifts people out of poverty. And this is universally acknowledged to be good, even though traditional religious teaching tended rather to the opposite view: for example, Jesus Christ said, 'It is harder for a camel to go through the eye of a needle, than for a rich man to enter the kingdom of God' – one of his teachings that has been universally ignored since the advent of Protestantism. The only questions that economists and moralists feel they can ask about wealth are second-order ones: Does its increase in fact make people happier? Has it been justly acquired? Is it fairly distributed? But the relation of wealth to ethical ends is left silent.

Today, wealth increase is the only goal that Western society has to offer. The two previous great competing objects of striving – military glory and eternal bliss – are radically out of favour. This was Francis Fukuyama's problem in *The End of History*: what was the last man to do? Capitalism is everywhere triumphant, but its moral basis is just as shaky as it was in Keynes's day. Criticism has found a much stronger voice with the current economic meltdown. Because its only goal is to make societies richer, capitalism has to be more successful than any rival economic system in order to survive. Any large-scale collapse – or succession of collapses – challenges its claim to be the most *efficient* mechanism for increasing material wealth. But the moral critique of capitalism owes as much to its successes as to its failures. A single-minded concentration on boosting average living standards is now seen to carry increasingly heavy social costs. Current denunciation has come to centre on market-led globalization. Celebrated and promoted by all devotees of the market system as carrying economic freedom and efficiency to new heights, globalization has been attacked for destroying communities, wrecking the environment, undermining democracy, and generating growing inequalities of wealth and income. As societies get further away from poverty, the costs of the wealth-producing treadmill become clearer: 'welfare' as measured by economists and 'well-being' as it has been understood by practically everyone else come into sharper conflict. Researchers have noticed that, beyond a certain point, increased wealth does not make people happier, so the dream of bliss attached to the accumulation of riches is a delusion.

In this and the next chapter I insert Keynes into this discussion, in both its ethical and its political aspects. He was not a socialist, but nor was he an uncritical admirer of capitalism. He saw it as a necessary stage to get societies from poverty to abundance, after which its usefulness would disappear. This brings him close to the Karl Marx of the *Communist Manifesto* of 1848. But, unlike Marx, he did not look forward to capitalism's violent overthrow, nor did he think it was inevitable: his criticisms of Soviet Communism were devastating, and he appreciated the value of private property and decentralized decision-making as requirements for economic efficiency and political liberty. So he wanted to preserve capitalism from its wreckers on both the extreme right and the extreme left. This aim underpinned his politics of the 'middle way'. In line with his evolutionary perspective, he rejected the notion of a sharp break between capitalist and post-capitalist societies. Capitalism was evolving new forms of public–private partnership which blurred the traditional separation of state and market and weakened the emphasis on maximizing profit. At the same time, it was continually expanding the possibilities of civiliz-ation, or what Keynes called 'the good life'. But for these possibilities to be grasped it was essential to keep alive the traditional religious strictures on the unlimited pursuit of wealth. Keynes stood secularism on its head: a religious attitude to life becomes more, not less, neces-sary as society approaches abundance. Long before people started to discern any 'natural' limits to economic growth from the exhaustion of non-renewable resources or climate change, Keynes suggested that there should be 'moral' limits to growth, based on a proper under-standing of the ends of life and of the role of economic motives and economic growth in relation to those ends. The empire of greed should be progressively retracted as its job neared completion.

Keynes's reflections on ethics and economics can be considered under four headings: the relationship between wealth and goodness, the psychology of wealth creation, the role of justice in economics, and the place of religion in economic life.

Wealth and Goodness

Keynes was neither a Christian nor a socialist, so his conception of the good life made no explicit appeal to either of these traditions. Rather, the appeal he made was to rationality. His ethics seems very old-fashioned, because he attached rationality to ends as well as to means. His philosophical education came before the logical-positivist revolution of the 1930s, which dubbed ethical beliefs irrational, a mere expression of private preference. The key to Keynes's ethics is that, although he was an atheist, he was close enough to the 'believing' generation to feel the need for 'true' beliefs.

The ethical framework within which Keynes thought about economic problems was provided by the Cambridge philosopher G. E. Moore, whose *Principia Ethica* was published in 1902, Keynes's first year as a Cambridge undergraduate. This work provided him with his ethical criteria. Moore made a sharp distinction between ethics and morals, and subordinated the latter to the former. For Moore, the primary ethical question is 'What is good?' or 'What sort of things ought to exist for their own sake?' The moral question 'What ought I to do?', 'How ought I to behave?', can be answered only by reference to the primary question as well as to the probable consequences of action.

Moore's doctrine is both startling and austere:

By far the most valuable things we know or can imagine are certain states of consciousness which may be roughly described as the pleasures of human intercourse and the enjoyment of beautiful objects . . . It is only for the sake of these things – in order that as much of them as possible may at some time exist – that one can be justified in performing any public or private duty . . . It is they . . . that form the rational ultimate end of human action and the sole criterion of social progress.[2]

Things 'good in themselves' are states of mind. Actions are good only as means – only if they contribute to bring about good states of mind. The following comments are in order:

(1) Moore's list of intrinsically valuable goods is very short; for example, it leaves out justice. Keynes added 'love of knowledge' to this list. The most ethically valuable goods for Keynes were states of consciousness described by such phrases as 'being in love', 'experiencing aesthetic emotions' and 'the pursuit of knowledge'.

(2) These ethical goods are not to be construed as statements of personal preference. Good is an objective, indefinable quality of things, intuitively *known* to be present or absent, in much the same way as we perceive an object to be green or yellow without being able to define 'green' or 'yellow'. Rational people know what is good. There is a strong connection between ethics and truth. It is this belief more than any other which distances Keynes from the economics (and indeed the ethical philosophy) of today. It aligns him with the tradition of Platonic philosophy and Christian religion, in which all rational people held unanalysed notions of what is good.

(3) Moore's ethical doctrine may be described as 'ideal' (as distinguished from hedonistic) utilitarianism, because that which is to be maximized is not happiness or pleasure, but goodness. The ethicist is enjoined to ask, To what extent and in what way do wealth-producing activities increase or retard the production of the greatest possible amount of goodness in the universe? The link between wealth and goodness is far more problematic for Moore and Keynes than it was for Bentham. A sensationalist psychology combined with the greatest-happiness principle yields the straightforward conclusion that any desired increase in the aggregate of pleasure-producing goods is ethically desirable. This is not so in Moore's system. The connection between pleasure and goodness is indirect, and always has to be argued. Keynes follows Moore in treating pleasure as extrinsic to goodness. Being in love is a source of both pleasure and pain, and the same is true of intense aesthetic and intellectual experiences.

(4) In place of Bentham's 'felicific calculus', Moore offers the principle of 'organic unity', not as a way of measuring, but as a way of judging the quantity of goodness in any state of affairs. In other words, you can't sum up the quantity of goodness in the universe simply by adding up individual states of consciousness. Good

states of affairs are 'complex organic unities'; their ethical value could be more or less than the sum of their parts. Acceptance of the doctrine of organic unities is incompatible with methodological individualism – the idea that any 'whole' is simply the sum of the individual parts. Keynes rejected methodological individualism in both ethics and economics.

(5) Moore's utilitarianism shares with Bentham's the characteristic of treating instrumentally ('as means') all values not specified as being intrinsically good. Capitalism is merely an instrument. Liberty and justice, for example, are not 'good in themselves', but means to the realization of intrinsic goods. Duty falls out of the picture except as a means to the good.

(6) In general, Keynes accepted the Benthamite conclusion that egoism is superior to altruism as a maximizing principle. This is because we have no direct knowledge of any state of mind but our own. This is Keynes's main justification for the system of political and economic liberty.

There is a moral prescriptivism in Moore lacking in Bentham, which arises from the central issue which Moore's ethics raises concerning the connection between happiness and goodness. It cannot be readily assumed that what we desire is desirable. Here Keynes, like Moore, was captive to the eighteenth-century philosopher-economist David Hume's distinction between 'is' and 'ought'. The solution urged by many ethicists (including John Stuart Mill) is to improve the quality of our desires to the point that they become desirable. Keynes would have been interested in Daniel Kahneman's 'hedonic psychology', the study of what makes experiences pleasant or unpleasant, but, while he would have recognized its usefulness for social and economic policy (see Chapter 7), he would have regarded it as partly irrelevant for ethics, because of any feeling deemed pleasant one can always ask, Is it good?

Keynes thought that the goodness of states of mind could be increased or diminished by what he called the 'fitness' of states of affairs. This opened up a wide justification for business, political and philanthropic endeavours as *means* to ethical goodness. Keynes made the common-sense judgement that it is easier for people to be good – in the sense that he and Moore thought of good – if they have a certain level of material comfort. In this way, economic and political action to improve material conditions could be accommodated within Moore's doctrine. Keynes also followed Moore in treating enjoyment of beauty as an integral part of the good life, and acted on it in a personal capacity as a patron of the arts and theatre-builder, by public advocacy of the beautification of cities and the preservation of the countryside, and most notably by setting up the Arts Council of Great Britain at the end of his life. A follower of Moore might also interest himself, without contradiction, in raising standards of education and health, insofar as these improve the knowledge, sensibility and comeliness of the population.

However, Keynes never fell into the trap of believing that there was an automatic connection between pleasure and goodness. He recognized the possibility of trade-offs. Here are three examples of his hesitating line of argument. The first is an argument he used to have with his Cambridge friends:

As time wore on towards the nineteen-tens, I fancy we weakened a bit about pleasure. But in our prime pleasure was nowhere. I would faintly urge that if two states of mind were similar in all other respects except that one was pleasurable and the other painful there *might* be a little to be said for the former . . . but it was the general view that pleasure had nothing to do with the case and, on the whole, a pleasant state of mind lay under grave suspicion of lacking intensity and passion.[3]

The second comes from a paper on tragedy which he read to the Apostles, the famous (and selective) Cambridge philosophical society, in 1921:

I am not certain that all tragic states of affairs are bad on the whole, when everything has been taken into account, or that the goodness of the states of mind, if it is very great, may not outweigh the badness of states of affairs . . . [But] it is possible, I think, to imagine two states of affairs, one of which is tragic or unjust, and the other not, such that the states of mind in each are exactly of equal value, and to believe that the tragic state of affairs is less desirable than the others.[4]

This line of thought led, thirdly, to a quasi-Aristotelian argument for the importance of the dramatic arts in an ethically progressive civilization:

In actual life many of the feelings which we deem noblest and most worth having are apt to be associated with troubles, misfortunes, and disasters. In itself we generally judge the state of mind of the hero going into battle as good – but it is such a pity that he should be killed . . . If, on the other hand, it were possible to sympathize with, enjoy at second hand, or admire the noble feelings *without* the evil happenings which generally accompany them in real life, we would get the best of both worlds. Now, as it seems to me, the object of Tragedy is precisely to secure for us a conjuncture in which this comes about. We come into contact with noble feelings and escape the bad practical consequences.[5]

The cost of heroism, or pity, in other words, can be reduced to the price of a theatre ticket: a good bargain for the social reformer. With notable twentieth-century exceptions, the price of goodness – in the sense in which Keynes is using the term – has been continually falling, as revolutions and wars become theatrical spectacles, with few casualties, but mass television audiences.

Today we would say that the Moore–Keynes goal of maximizing the quantity of goodness in the universe cannot provide an agreed criterion for economic action, because rational people disagree about what is good. Economics therefore is bound to take wants as data and treat the maximization problem in terms of want satisfaction. This is a problem for any attempt to marry ethics and economics. We can ease it, but not remove it entirely, by constructing indexes of 'well-being' which contain 'quality-of-life' measures.

Keynes was touching here on an issue which has always baffled economists with a philosophical bent: the relationship between quantity and quality. The problem does not arise if goodness is thought of in numerical terms – for example, if maximizing the quantity of motor cars in the universe is the ethical task, it is perfectly straightforward to measure the amount of goodness being produced. Keynes's partial solution was to let quantitative measures rule till abundance reigned, when ethical or 'quality-of-life' values could come to the fore. On the way, though, public investment in the arts, architecture, sport and other leisure activities should remind society of what economic growth was for. In particular, there was no need to trade quantity for quality while resources were unemployed.

However, the contemporary retreat from ethical judgement is also a sign of the weakness of ethics today in the face of science. In believing that good and bad were intuitively known, Moore and Keynes were heirs to a philosophical and religious tradition which was collapsing. Today, society has 'morals' but not 'ethics'. Morals tells us how to behave in carrying out our activities, but not whether those activities are worth doing. The philosopher Alastair MacIntyre calls these 'secondary virtues', those attaching to processes, rather than to ends – rules of behaviour like honesty, tolerance, loyalty, fairness, and the types of character needed for their exercise. Liberal society is essentially a process or transactions society: its values are second-order values, to do with the arrangement of relationships, political and social, so as to minimize conflict between competing values, religions, ethnicities. Much of this goes under the label of 'virtue ethics'. But it leaves untouched the question: What is life for?

Similarly, the task of checking the unrestrained pursuit of wealth is transferred from ethics to politics, which supposedly establishes patterns of income distribution, property rights, regulation and so on which voters prefer. These social arrangements take the place of ends in our moral universe. But they are unanchored to any more general view of life's purposes. We attack greed, but have no answer to the question: How much is enough? It is perfectly possible for virtues to attach to destructive ends, as the history of Nazism, Communism and contemporary nationalist violence amply shows.

Love of Money

Moore's focus on states of mind as the sole criterion of goodness gave rise to what Keynes called his 'favourite dilemma': the conflict between 'being good' and 'doing good'. Briefly, the conflict is between the states of mind required for the enjoyment of ethical goods and those required for practical life, and especially for success in making money. What if any ethical value, Keynes often asked, was to be attached to a life of 'moneymaking and bridge'? Business life was at best only good as a means, but even as a means Keynes ranked it below public service, which at least was concerned with the public good. This was because business life overturned the correct hierarchy of values, teaching society to value 'love of money' above love of goodness. Keynes's characterization – and condemnation – of capitalism as based on 'love of money' echoes the biblical statement 'the love of money is the root of all evil' (1 Timothy 6:10).

In 1925 Keynes wrote some 'philosophical pages' on 'love of money'. He followed Max Weber in defining capitalism not as a particular structure of property relations, as Marx did, but as a spiritual or psychological disposition towards abstract gain. In placing money rather than production at the heart of his picture of modern capitalism, Keynes was being prescient, for its later dominance was only potential in his own lifetime. Neither warrior nor priest had left the scene, and manufacture was still the main economic activity in advanced capitalist countries.

By 'love of money' Keynes meant two things, between which he did not always distinguish. The first was the objectless pursuit of wealth. The second was a specific subset of the first, which was the disposition to 'hoard' or not spend money – the psychology of the miser. The first was the engine which drove capitalism; the second was the brake on its progress, which related particularly to uncertainty. He would have said the first was morally inefficient, the second economically inefficient. But the two somehow merged in his critique of the outsize role of money values in modern civilization. His speculations on love of money are in a well-established philosophical tradition which includes Aristotle, who saw that the good life is endangered when acquisition of money comes to be seen as intrinsically valuable, and Karl Marx, who distinguished between 'use value' and 'exchange value'.

Keynes's point of departure was the economist's standard view that money has no utility in itself, but is simply the means to acquire goods which possess utility. People want goods, not money. Keynes, however, saw the capitalism of his day not so much as a goods-generating machine as a cash-generating machine: people acquired money to get more money. What should have been a means had become an end. This disposition to value money above the things it could buy was true of both the moneymaker and the money-hoarder, but the pleasure in the possession of money took different forms in the two cases.

The overvaluation of monetary gain could be seen in the fetish of cheapness. Keynes suggested that standardization, stimulated by advertising, had 'raised the price of idiosyncrasy'. If we all consumed exactly the same thing, prices would be much lower and we would all be 'better off'. But variety is a good in itself. It was not good to know what everything cost. It was right to weigh concrete things against concrete things, not against abstract money, 'the ultimate object of which is vaguely conceived or not conceived at all'.

The test of money measurement constantly tends to widen the area where we weigh concrete goods against abstract money. Our imaginations are too weak for the choice; abstract money outweighs them. The sanctification of saving tends dangerously on the side of abstract money. The growth of individual wealth does the same . . .

It is not right to sacrifice the present to the future unless we can conceive the probabilities of the future in sufficiently concrete terms, in terms approximately as concrete as the present sacrifice, to be sure that the exchange was worth while.

We ought more often to be in a state of mind, as it were, of not counting the money cost at all . . . We want to diminish, rather than increase, the area of monetary comparisons.[6]

Since Keynes's day, the tendency has been the opposite of what he wanted: financial innovation has made stocks and shares increasingly 'abstract', disembodied from the businesses they represent.[7]

Keynes's fascination with the hoarding aspect of 'love of money' comes out in his brief discussion of Freud's association of hoarding with the anal-sadistic character. (One of the sections of *A Treatise on Money* is headed 'Aura Sacra Fames' – 'Hunger for Sacred Gold'.)[8] His interest in the Freudian mechanism of sublimation tempted him into the unwise hypothesis that the Jews had 'sublimated immortality into compound interest' – which brought the crushing rejoinder from a Jewish scholar that civic insecurity had made many Jews 'extremely extravagant' and prone to 'reckless gambling rather than painful accumulation'.[9]

For a brief moment Keynes toyed with the idea that the Soviet Union might have discovered the antidote to 'love of money'. Although he found Communism in many ways detestable, after a visit to Russia in

1925 he thought it just possible that Soviet Communism might represent 'the first confused stirrings of a great religion'. The significance of Bolshevism, he thought, lay not in its economics, which was rubbish, but in its attempt to construct a social system which condemned personal enrichment as an end and made it legally impossible for anyone to pursue it seriously. After a further visit, in 1928, Keynes reluctantly concluded that the price for the creed was too high. One could not enjoy good states of mind if nothing worked.

It was to show how capitalism, despite its faults, might be evolving the conditions of the good life that in 1930 Keynes wrote a futuristic essay, 'Economic Possibilities for our Grandchildren.' His thesis was that the engine of capitalism was driven by a neurosis which he called 'love of money', but this neurosis was also the means to the good, because it was the means to the abundance which would make it unnecessary. Keynes reckoned that if capital increased at 2% per annum, population growth levelled off, and productivity rose at 1% a year, in three generations – roughly in a hundred years – the prospective population of the civilized world would have a standard of living between four and eight times as high as in the 1920s, obtainable at a small fraction of current effort. With the economic problem solved, mankind would face its permanent problem, how to live 'wisely, agreeably, and well', by which Keynes meant that people would be able to shed their pathological 'purposefulness' and 'love of money' and trade even higher incomes for more leisure and enjoyment of life.[10]

With the coming of abundance, 'love of money' would be regarded as a 'somewhat disgusting morbidity . . . which one hands over with a shudder to specialists in mental disease'. People would be free to adopt once more the 'sure and certain principles of religion and traditional virtue', valuing today over tomorrow, ends over means, the good over the useful, and living like 'lilies in the field'. But for the time being we must go on pretending that 'fair is foul and foul is fair; for foul is useful and fair is not. Avarice and usury and precaution must be our gods for a little longer still. For only they can lead us out of the tunnel of economic necessity into the daylight.'[11] One can see here that Keynes was not much of a Promethean, or a believer in technological progress for its own sake.

Consider what Keynes was saying. Good states of mind depend on people not having to work for a living. This was a generalization of the aristocratic ideal, derived from the classical Greeks, and also from the Christian vision of Paradise Regained: in expelling Adam and Eve from the Garden of Eden, God condemned them to work. Keynes looked forward to the saturation of wants. But he saw this not as a natural but as an ethical terminus. Wants were to be controlled not by the size of the stomach, but by a generally accepted conception of 'sufficiency' for the good life.

In terms of arithmetic, he was almost spot on in his predictions of growing wealth, but attitudes have changed less than he expected. Although real incomes in rich countries have doubled in the last thirty years, the populations of these countries work harder than ever and are no happier.[12] This raises the question of why they are still on the growth treadmill. Is it because capitalism needs constantly to expand markets, and ensnare by advertising more and more people into useless consumption? Is it because economists have ignored the fact that, as societies become wealthier, positional goods – goods which satisfy not our needs, but our longing for status – become more and more desirable? Is it because globalization has made affluence too insecure and too uneven in its spread for most people in wealthy societies to ease off work? Or is it because we lack any agreed idea of the good life in the name of which we can say 'enough is enough'?

One answer to the question does suggest itself. An economy devoted to the manufacture of goods may be said to have a natural terminus when wants are satisfied. Advertising may postpone the day of fulfilment, but it cannot remove it. But an economy which treats money as goods has no such cut-off point, because, as Keynes said, abstract money will always seem more attractive than concrete goods. Our imaginations race ahead of our senses, filling us with unsatisfied desires, and money is the continual stimulator of our imagination, creating a perpetual sense of dissatisfaction with what we already have.

In one passage, Keynes comes close to anticipating the Green agenda. The system of economic calculation, he declared in a speech in Dublin on 17 April 1933, made 'the whole conduct of life . . . into a sort of parody of an accountant's nightmare': 'We destroy the beauty of the countryside because the unappropriated splendours of nature have no economic value. We are capable of shutting off the sun and the stars because they do not pay a dividend.'[13]

Keynes's speculations on the theme of 'love of money' are the nexus that binds together his ethical theory and his economic theory. But the coherence is only partial. His economic theory attacks the hoarding aspect of 'love of money', but not the priority given to moneymaking. The problem for him is that Moore's ethics requires him to treat capitalism purely instrumentally – as a mechanism for getting from scarcity to abundance as quickly as possible. This leads him to understate the possibilities of improving the ethical and moral conditions of capitalism itself, no doubt for fear that it would slow down the progress towards his ethical utopia. So one has put up with what is 'foul' to get quickly to 'fair'. But a life dedicated to a 'foul' set of values cannot be an entry ticket to a life with a 'fair' set. Nor does Keynes really suppose that it should be. But all he can suggest as a bridge between the two is that we make preparations for the good life even while tainted with economic striving. Even here consistency eludes him. To point the way to civilization was, or should have been, the role of a *rentier* bourgeoisie like the Bloomsbury Group. Yet Keynes looked forward to the 'euthanasia of the *rentier*'. He also ignored the possibility that ignoring economic calculation now would delay rather than speed up the time when we could ignore it permanently. He wrestled with these tensions, but failed to resolve them.

Justice

Justice was not an end in Moore's philosophy, and Keynes does not treat it as one. It is a means to the good life. Nor did he try to derive a theory of justice from a hypothetical social contract, as for example did John Rawls. Rather he treated justice instrumentally, as contributing to a 'contented' society. In this respect, he comes closest to the idea of justice as 'fairness'. By 'fairness' he usually meant the social arrangements generally accepted as fair in the society he best knew, Britain. His fragmentary observations on this theme encompassed the rights and duties of different classes in society, as well as the duties of the state. The most important strand to draw out is his revival of the idea of the 'just price'.

The notion of the 'just price' has long been banished to the attics of economics. Prices are to be set in the market, not by any consideration of what is just or fair. Yet the idea of justice in exchange is a very old one, and is far from dead in the popular mind – as shown in the outbreak of anger at the excessive salaries, bonuses and pensions earned by top executives. The public attitude is not as crass as is sometimes made out. There is no hostility to large rewards as such – we do not hear outcries against the gigantic earnings of entertainers or footballers. Nor is there any resentment against money gained through luck: anyone might win the Lottery or Tote. Popular anger is largely directed against rewarding what is seen as doing harm: bankers who bankrupt their institutions, business executives whose 'restructuring' schemes involve sacking large numbers of workers. In a rough-and-ready way, people expect to see a link between reward and benefit to themselves. They are also concerned – much more in Keynes's day than now – with relative pay, which fixes the position of the classes in the social hierarchy.

What did Keynes mean by a 'just' economic system? He accepted the classic view of justice that reward should be proportioned to merit or contribution, with its Aristotelian corollary that 'nothing is more unjust than to treat unequals equally.' He was not, therefore, an egalitarian. Justice is a matter of equity, not equality, and just prices are those which correctly reward talents and efforts. He was a meritocratic elitist. It was 'most unjust and most unwise', he wrote, 'to put on an appearance of being against anyone who is more successful, more skilful, and more industrious, more thrifty than the average', and elsewhere he declared, 'I do not want to level down individuals, I want to give encouragement to all exceptional effort, ability, courage, character.'[14] None of these positions distinguished Keynes from the classical liberals of his day. Nevertheless, while he thought there was 'social and psychological justification for significant inequalities of incomes and wealth', he did not think the game needed to be played for 'such high stakes as at present'.[15] As one would expect, he preferred inheritance taxes to income taxes. He started to pay more attention to income redistribution after the Great Depression – not for socialistic reasons, but as a method of reducing the propensity to save.[16]

In today's weightless economy it has become much harder to

establish a connection between effort and reward. Taleb distinguishes between work subject to gravity (making things) and those activities (such as derivatives trading) which just add zeroes to balance sheets without extra effort. He calls the first non-scalable, and the second scalable.[17] Our economies are increasingly dominated by the latter, which, by separating efforts from rewards, are far more random in their results. Similarly, Keynes's idea of the just price depends on being able to measure effort in terms of things produced rather than money produced. One cannot have a just society in Keynes's sense if the main purpose of economic activity is the manufacture of money.

Keynes held two distinctive positions which have almost vanished from economics today. The first was to keep the rate of interest continually low, which would end 'the cumulative oppressive power of the capitalist to exploit the scarcity-value of capital'. The ground for this is set out as follows: 'Interest today rewards no genuine sacrifice, any more than does the rent of land. The owner of capital can thus obtain interest because capital is scarce, just as the owner of land can obtain rent because land is scarce. But whilst there may be intrinsic reasons for the scarcity of land, there are no intrinsic reasons for the scarcity of capital.'[18]

As capital became steadily abundant the rate of interest would fall naturally, but Keynes also relied on policy to keep it low. Keynes regarded the rate of interest set by the market as the foremost 'unjust price' in the economic system, and he did not hesitate to use the medieval term 'usury' to condemn it. The essence of his view was that the premium commanded by liquidity as such, due to a combination of an objectively uncertain future and the psychological disposition to hoard (or avarice), allowed the lender to charge a reward for parting with money greater than his contribution to the production of goods. It was 'usury', he wrote to a correspondent, to 'extract from the borrower some amount additional to the true sacrifice of the lender which the weakness of the borrower's bargaining position or his extremity of need . . . make[s] feasible . . . I find it interesting to put it this way because it really amounts to exactly the same thing as my theory of liquidity preference.'[19] Thus slumps were the wages of sin, after all – but not the sin of extravagance, as the classical economists taught, but the sin of usury. His policy of keeping money permanently cheap is simply a modern way of applying the medieval anti-usury laws.

Second, Keynes identifies justice with price stability; injustice with fluctuations in the price level. Good behaviour, it will be recalled, should have reference not only to what is good, but also to the probable consequences of action. But people cannot be expected to take proper account of the consequences of their economic acts if the standard of value is constantly fluctuating. 'Unemployment, the precarious life of the worker, the disappointment of expectation, the sudden loss of savings, the excessive windfalls of individuals, the speculator, the profiteer – all these proceed, in large measure from the instability of the standard of value.'[20]

Changes in the price level had distributional effects which soured class relations. Keynes regarded as unjust the 'arbitrary' shifts of wealth and incomes caused by avoidable business fluctuations – shifts unrelated to effort and beyond the control of ordinary prudence. The insight that what groups of workers really cared about was the loss of *relative* position informed his discussion of wage behaviour in the *General Theory*. Justice was a matter of contractual predictability. For Keynes, then, a stable general price level was a necessary condition for the justice of relative prices.

This goes against contemporary economic thinking. The New Classical economists argue that the unemployment problem arises only if workers suffer from 'money illusion'. With rational expectations, there would be instantaneous recontracting, and no involuntary unemployment. New Keynesians have explained why recontracting is not feasible – 'menu costs' are too high. So unemployment is possible while wages and prices slowly adapt to shocks. Keynes took a different view: completely flexible wages and prices are not desirable, even if feasible, because '*binding* nominal contractual commitments are a sensible method for dealing with true uncertainty regarding future outcomes.'[21] Keynes would say that if full employment were continually maintained by policy there would be greater wage and price flexibility than there is now, because there would be less uncertainty.

Keynes and Christianity

Writing to William Temple, archbishop of Canterbury, on 3 December 1941, Keynes explained that most eighteenth-century writers on economics were churchmen. 'Marshall always used to insist that it was through ethics that he arrived at political economy and I would claim myself in this, as in no other respect, to be a pupil of his.' Such a claim might seem paradoxical from someone who was an atheist, and who later said about himself and his Cambridge and Bloomsbury circle, 'We repudiated entirely customary morals, conventions and traditional wisdom. We were, that is to say, in the strict sense of the term, immoralists.'[22] Keynes's penchant for iconoclastic utterance has been grist to the mill of anti-Keynesians. His most famous remark, 'In the long run we are all dead', was interpreted by Schumpeter as a 'childless' – he might have added godless – perspective.[23] Childless became homosexual in William Rees-Mogg's suggestion that Keynes's rejection of moral rules led him to reject the gold standard 'which provided an automatic control of monetary inflation'.[24]

This view of Keynes's economics as product of the closet rather than the cloister is profoundly false. It rests on the superficial association of Bloomsbury with levity and immorality, and ignores the fact that Bloomsbury, while adopting modes of expression designed to shock its Victorian elders, subscribed to, and tried to live by, exacting ethical principles. Keynes's target was not morality, but *conventional* morality; as a young man, he believed that individuals were sufficiently evolved to be safely released from the 'outward restraints of convention and traditional standards' to pursue their own '*pure motives and reliable intuitions of the good*' (italics added). In short, his belief was that, given freedom, human behaviour would be both ethically and morally better, certainly less hypocritical, than conventional morality allowed. (The same belief underlay the permissive legislation of the 1960s.)

As he grew older – and grew up – Keynes realized that he had been wrong. In 1938, looking back at his 'early beliefs', he admitted to having had a 'disastrously mistaken' view of human nature: he and his friends had ignored the 'insane and irrational springs of wickedness in most men', and the dependence of civilization on 'rules and conventions skilfully put across and guilefully preserved'.[25] On another aspect of those early beliefs, the rejection of the 'Benthamite calculus', he remained unrepentant. Benthamism was 'the worm which has been gnawing at the insides of modern civilization and is responsible for its present moral decay'.[26]

By 'Benthamism' he meant roughly the calculating spirit applied to areas of life where it had no place. It was fundamental to Keynes's outlook that we do not have sufficient knowledge of the future to play the 'game of consequences' to any effect, except in certain specified cases. As a young man, he argued the case for direct individual judgement of right and wrong against both Christianity and Benthamism. As he grow older he came to understand the value of conventional behaviour, not just as a protection against wickedness and madness, but also as, in many situations, the only rational way of behaving in face of the unknown. In particular, he came to understand the dependence of morals on conventions. He did not foresee the extent to which economics would take over moral language, replacing the older idea of duty by the notion of providing 'incentives' for good behaviour. With its model of the maximizing individual, economics was virtually bound to assume that people would cheat unless given incentives not to; when cheating did occur, it would be explained in terms of 'misaligned' incentives. A great deal of financial innovation like stock options has been designed to 'align' the interests of managers and shareholders, as though managers are bound to defraud their owners without such incentives. Keynes would have argued against much of this language that it completely missed the point: we rarely know enough about the consequences of our actions even to have a probable assurance that 'honesty pays.' If we rely on incentives alone to secure good behaviour, we will get bad behaviour.

In 1934 Keynes told T. S. Eliot that he 'would be inclined not to demolish Xty [Christianity] if it were proved that without it morality is impossible'. He told Virginia Woolf, 'I begin to see that our generation – yours & mine – owed a great deal to our fathers' religion . . . We destroyed Xty & yet had its benefits.'[27] This was not a conversion, but it was a recognition of 'one of the great primal questions': Was morality possible in the long run without religion?

Most of Keynes's thinking on ethics and morals revolved round the problem of knowledge. That is why he attached so much importance to intuitive or *a priori* judgement, concerning both ends and means. He thought most problems of behaviour were problems of knowledge at one remove. If everyone knew the outcome of wars for certain, there would never be any wars. Those who knew they would lose would never fight. This seems to be refuted by martyrs and suicide bombers – but perhaps they are convinced that they will win in the afterlife. With a long enough time horizon, all defeats can be turned into victories. However, the more usual problem is one of beliefs based on the illusion of knowledge. The 'Benthamite calculus' seemed to provide a secular answer, by promising knowledge of consequences, but it was fraudulent, simply a convention. Religion was perhaps another. But Keynes came to see at least certain kinds of religious belief as superior to Benthamism, because they were unconditional. Immortality was a state of being, innocent of calculation, with no connection with the 'before' and 'after'.

Keynes's ethical approach offers considerations which have acquired a fresh importance in the context of the present 'crisis of capitalism'.

First, and most important, it keeps alive the importance of having an idea of the good life. Without it, economic activity is bound to be simply an envious striving for relative advantage, without any natural terminus.

Second, it brings out the relevance of philosophy for economics. Keynes was not an economic liberal, in today's sense, but a philosophical liberal: he constantly pondered on the relationship between economic and non-economic aims and behaviour. One of the greatest defects of economics today is that it has become a branch of applied mathematics. This is reflected in the way students are taught. Keynes thought of economics as part of the human discourse. He had, as he put it, been 'properly brought up' to do so. This is connected with the question of the language of economics. He wanted to bring economic analysis closer to 'ordinary' or 'common-sense' language, which reflected the existence of a mass of non-quantifiable, vague, but nevertheless useful knowledge of how to think and how to behave.

Third, Keynes forces us to consider the question of what economic activity is for. Broadly speaking, he believed in an ethical Pareto optimum: material progress will increase the welfare of the universe up to the point when it starts to diminish the quantity of ethical goodness. When it does so is a matter of judgement. In advocating state sponsorship of the arts and the beautification of cities, he provided an ethically based argument for public action to influence the composition as well as the level of demand.

Fourth, Keynes kept alive the idea of the 'just price'.

Finally, he raised the question whether morals can survive in the long run without religion.

Having said this, it is easy to see that he might have been deluding himself. He envisaged a modern capitalist economy governed by a Platonic ideal, and gentlemanly codes of behaviour. But once the capitalist genie is let out of the bottle it cannot be pressed into the service of a pre-modern ethics of the good life and pre-modern codes of behaviour. The good life in the classical sense presupposes that human desire has some ultimate end, or *telos*, whereas modern economic theory and life presuppose that it is insatiable. As regards behaviour, he took for granted a class-based system of values which economic progress was undermining. These were contradictions which Keynes never fully faced.

7

Keynes's Politics

In ethics Keynes was a Platonist, in politics he was an Aristotelian. His ethics pointed him towards the ideal; his politics towards moderation. This chapter does not aim to give a complete account of Keynes's political beliefs, but to highlight those aspects of his statesmanship which might seem most useful today.

KEYNES'S NEW WAY

Keynes offered both a New Way and a Middle Way. The New Way was his macroeconomic theory dating from the 1930s, which followed on from the Great Depression, and in which insufficiency of aggregate demand was identified as the main economic problem. This was his great achievement in 'thinking out of the box'. At a stroke, he transferred the reform agenda of politics from the task of reforming the microeconomy to that of stabilizing the macroeconomy. The problem was insufficient demand, not inefficient supply. This overturned the whole trend of his Middle Way thinking in the 1920s, which had focused on what economists would call 'market failures'. The Middle Way arose from the attempt of a group of liberals, of whom Keynes was one, to equip the Liberal Party with a social philosophy which would be a compromise between capital and labour. This philosophy was based on the idea of public–private partnership. Keynes thought of this as part of a social evolution modifying the dependence of economic progress on the profit motive. The Keynesian revolution did not abolish these earlier discussions, but for thirty years it took the heat out of them. When they returned, in the 1980s, it was in muted form.

The New Way was signalled in the *General Theory*. It was in its failure to secure full employment, not in its inability to allocate labour efficiently, that the existing system had broken down. Thus, if 'our central controls succeed in establishing an aggregate volume of output corresponding to full employment as nearly as is practicable', the market system could be left free to handle the problem of allocation. His aim, Keynes wrote, was not to dispose of the market system, but to 'indicate the nature of the environment which the free play of economic forces requires if it is to realize the full potentialities of production'.[1] The Keynesian revolution, in short, aimed to control demand, not to interfere with supply. With demand controlled, supply could be left to look after itself, subject to the usual qualification that competition should be free enough to prevent monopoly.

By the same token, 'supply-side' or 'structural' explanations for the depression, whether they came from left or right, were wrong. The crisis of capitalism had nothing to do with monopoly power in business or in the supply of labour. There was no need to nationalize the economy or smash the unions or curtail democracy in order to get rid of mass unemployment. The sequence of boom and bust was the fruit of uncertainty, not of greed or structure, a technical problem whose solution required sound reasoning at the Treasury, not fighting the class war. In a well-known passage, Keynes wrote, 'I can be influenced by what seems to me to be justice and good sense; but the class war will find me on the side of the educated bourgeoisie.'[2]

The flavour of Keynes's New Way emerges in an essay he wrote in 1940, when everyone was clamouring for the conscription of supply to mobilize the population for total war. Keynes had presented a scheme for paying for the war which involved withdrawing private purchasing power through a system of deferred pay, but avoided rationing and industrial conscription. In these passages, which he wrote in the *New Republic* on 29 July 1940, one can see his political hopes for post-war society:

I am seizing the opportunity to introduce a principle of policy which may be thought of as marking the line of division between the totalitarian and the free economy. For if the community's aggregate rate of spending can be regulated, the way in which personal incomes are spent can be safely left free and individual.

The reformers must believe that it is worth while to concede a great deal to preserve that decentralization of decisions and of power which is the prime virtue of the old individualism. In a world of destroyers, they must zealously protect the variously woven fabric of society, even when this means that some abuses must be spared . . .

The old guard of the Right, on their side, must surely recognize, if any reason or prudence is theirs, that the existing system is palpably disabled, that the idea of its continuing to function unmodified with half the world in dissolution is just sclerotic.[3]

THE DOCTRINE OF PRUDENCE

Prudence was the underlying idea behind Keynes's political philosophy, and he got it from the eighteenth-century political philosopher Edmund Burke, on whom he wrote a hundred-page essay in 1905 – about the same time as he was working out his ethical philosophy and his theory of probability, the three forming the foundational nexus for all his subsequent thinking. While ethical ends were known intuitively, behaviour – action to achieve those ends – had to be governed by expected probable consequences of achieving one's goals. Here Keynes's theory of probability kicked in, with its view that all consequences of our actions, except those in the very near future, occur in a 'twilight' zone, and are necessarily opaque. This dictates a statesmanship of extreme caution:

Burke ever held, and held rightly, that it can seldom be right . . . to sacrifice a present benefit for a doubtful advantage in the future . . . It is not wise to look too far ahead; our powers of prediction are slight, our command over results infinitesimal. It is therefore the happiness of our contemporaries that is our main concern; we should be very chary of sacrificing large numbers of people for the sake of a contingent end, however advantageous that may appear . . . We can never know enough to make the chance worth taking. There is this further consideration that is often in need of emphasis: it is not sufficient that the state of affairs we seek to promote should be better than the state of affairs which preceded it; it must be sufficiently better to make up for the evils of the transition.[4]

Burke has been called the first philosopher of conservatism, and Keynes was a lifelong liberal. But there were at least two Burkes. Before the French Revolution he attacked George III's attempt to establish permanent royal government on the basis of patronage and corruption. But the violence and regicide of the French Revolution repelled him, and it was in the aftermath of this political watershed that he developed his characteristic conservative doctrines. The important point here is not what Burke said, but what Keynes took from him. He drew on both the liberal and conservative elements in his thought, and was not uncritical.

Politics was, for Keynes, a branch of practical ethics: it was the science of how governments should behave. The purpose of government was not to bring about states of affairs 'good intrinsically and in isolation', but to facilitate the pursuit of such goods by members of the community. The presumption was that the more prosperous and contented a community is, and the fairer its social arrangements, the better will be the states of mind of the inhabitants. Politics should be so arranged as not to distract people unduly, and certainly not continuously, from the cultivation of good states of mind.

Ignoring the claims of Hume, the undergraduate Keynes commended Burke as the first utilitarian political philosopher – the first to espouse consistently the 'greatest-happiness' principle. But he emphasized that Burke regarded this as a political, and not an ethical, principle, and he agreed with Burke on this point.

The object of politics is social contentment. Keynes emphasizes such goods as 'physical calm', 'material comfort' and 'intellectual freedom'. Throughout his life he was personally affected by what he called 'bad states of nerves' produced by disturbing public events. His political goods were thus designed to minimize the occurrence of such disturbances. He writes that 'the government which sets the happiness of the governed before it will serve a good purpose, whatever the ethical theory from which it draws its inspiration.'

In Burke's thought, expediency takes precedence over 'abstract right'. Keynes quoted with admiration Burke's stand against the coercion of the American colonies: 'The question with me', Burke had said, 'is not whether you have a right to render your people miserable, but whether it is not your interest to make them happy. It is not what a lawyer tells me I *may* do, but what humanity, reason, and justice tells me I ought to do.' This position, in Keynes's view, put Burke into the ranks of the 'very great'. Prudence in face of the unknown is the key to Keynes's philosophy of statesmanship. It insulated him from the extremism of the revolutionaries who were prepared to wade through blood to attain utopias. Less obviously, it protected him against the extremism of the reactionaries who were prepared to *risk* revolution rather than make timely concessions. It set him on his collision course with the Ricardian school, with their indifference to the 'short-run' consequences of their laissez-faire policies. Societies, Keynes would have said, can tolerate only a moderate amount of social damage before they turn sour. His own lifetime amply proved the truth of this proposition. He was the philosopher of an embattled, not triumphant, liberalism.

The undergraduate Keynes criticized Burke not for his 'method', which he regarded as correct, but for his assumption that the best results are to be had, on the whole, from sticking to tradition, even if this is based on prejudice. This was the classical liberal criticism of conservatism. To maintain social peace, Burke was willing to leave prejudice undisturbed, thereby sacrificing truth and rationality to expediency. The nearest he came to forsaking his own maxim was when he protested passionately against the violence of the French Revolution. For on this occasion, wrote Keynes, 'he maintained that the best possible course for a rational man was to expound the truth and take his chance on the event.' What Keynes was arguing against Burke (and in the spirit of Mill) was that, 'whatever the immediate consequences of a new truth may be, there is a high probability that truth will in the long run lead to better results than falsehood.' The politics of lying, as Keynes would later say of Lloyd George, was self-defeating even in its own terms. Keynes had in his sights the windy trash politicians shout when rousing their peoples for violence and war. 'Rocking the boat' in such circumstances was not a vice but a duty. Truth-telling was thus an important element in Keynes's philosophy of practice. His commitment to it is the most important example of long-run perspectives in his thinking. And Keynes displayed a number of these Burkean moments of truth-telling in his own life, notably in his eloquent and devastating attack on the Treaty of Versailles in his *The Economic Consequences of the Peace* (1919). Keynes was not the most 'collegiate' of men. He believed one had a duty to use one's intelligence to speak out against falsehood and self-deception.

Keynes explained Burke's mistrust of truth in two ways. Burke felt the people would be more contented and the state as well as morals more secure if customs were left undisturbed. But he also 'suspected that the current grounds of right action were, in many cases, baseless'. Keynes assumes here that Burke's hostility to reason was directed against the French revolutionary project of reconstructing society on rational lines. Keynes sympathized with this Burkean attitude. In espousing the claims of reason, he was always conscious of how limited was its scope to penetrate the future.

Keynes went to some lengths to argue that rationality is compatible with democracy because, in practice, the scope of democracy is severely limited, and because over time its exercise might improve the rationality of citizens. However, democracy was never an important strand in his thinking. People, he said, had a right to good government, not to self-government. He looked to an 'educated bourgeoisie' to set political standards for the community, just as he looked to groups like Bloomsbury to set aesthetic standards. His efforts to separate the technical from the political aspects of ruling are consistent with views he expressed in his Burke essay.

If Burke's mistrust of reason pushed Keynes away from political conservatism, another set of arguments in Burke, concerning property rights, pushed him away from socialism. Burke defended property rights on two grounds. First, redistribution of wealth would make no real difference to the poor, since they greatly outnumbered the rich. But, in addition, it would 'considerably reduce in numbers those who could enjoy the undoubted benefits of wealth and who would confer on the state the [cultural] advantages which the presence of wealthy citizens always brings'. Keynes felt that this double argument 'undoubtedly carried very great weight: in certain types of communities it is overwhelming, and it must always be one of the most powerful rejoinders to any scheme which has equalization as its ultimate aim'. However, Burke carried his defence of existing property rights to extremes which conflicted with his own principle of expediency. He was so concerned to defend the 'outworks' of the property system that he did not see that this might endanger the 'central system' itself. Keynes believed that there could be no absolute sacredness of contract. It was the 'absolutists of contract', he would later write 'who are the parents of Revolution' – a good Burkean attitude, but one that Burke himself often ignored.

Later in life Keynes got involved in an argument with his French friend Marcel Labordere, who objected to the phrase 'euthanasia of the *rentier*' in the *General Theory*. The *rentier*, Labordere pointed out, was useful not only for his propensity to save, but because 'stable fortunes, the hereditary permanency of families, and sets of families of various social standings are an invisible social asset on which every kind of culture is more or less dependent.' Keynes replied, 'I fully agree with this and I wish I had emphasized it in your words. The older I get the more convinced I am that what you say here is true and important. But I must not allow you to make me too conservative.'[5] Labordere brought Keynes up against the civilizing face of what he called 'usury'. Keynes just had to live with the tension, rationalizing his animus with the thought that the English dividend-drawing class were insufficiently ready to use their unearned gains to enjoy the good life.

In his political philosophy, Keynes married two key elements of Burkean conservatism – contentment and avoidance of risk as the purpose of government – to two key elements of reforming liberalism – a commitment to truth-telling and a belief in the possibility of rational individual judgement. He rejected those elements in Burke which may be called 'unthinking conservatism' and those elements in socialism which aimed at building new societies on scientific principles.

Keynes offered a sympathetic summing-up of Burke's legacy:

His goods are all in the present – peace and quiet, friendship and affections, family life and those small acts of charity whereby one individual may sometimes help his fellows. He does not think of the race as marching through blood and fire to great and glorious goods in the distant future; there is, for him, no great political millennium to be helped and forwarded by present effort and present sacrifice ... This may not be the right attitude of mind. But whether or not the great political ideals which have inspired men in the past are madness and delusion they have provided a more powerful motive force than anything which Burke has to offer ... For all his passions and speech-making, it is the academic reasoner and philosopher who offers us these carefully guarded and qualified precepts, not the leader of men. Statesmen must learn wisdom in the school of Burke; if they wish to put it to great and difficult purpose, the essentials of leadership they must seek elsewhere.

Keynes was twenty-two when he wrote this essay.

The Burkean precept that Keynes took most to heart was the doctrine of prudence. Two examples of how it influenced him must suffice. The first comes from 1937, when Hitler and Mussolini were starting to rampage over Europe, and war seemed the only way of stopping them. This conjuncture finds Keynes writing:

It is our duty to prolong peace, hour by hour, day by day, for as long as we can. We do not know what the future will bring, except that it will be quite different from anything we could predict. I have said in another context that ... in the long run we are all dead. But I could have said equally well that ... in the short run we are still alive. Life and history are made up of short runs. If we are at peace in the short run, that is something. The best we can do is put off disaster, if only in the hope, which is not necessarily a remote one, that something will turn up ... Britain should build up its naval strength and wait for the dictators to *make mistakes.*[6]

The point here is that we know the state of affairs which exists now, when we are at peace; we don't know what war will bring forth. We should take the gamble of war only if the peaceful state of affairs becomes intolerable, and, even then, only if we have some reason to believe that the peace which follows the war will be sufficiently better than the peace which now exists to compensate for the costs of the war. It is fair to say that statesmen have rarely, if ever, acted on Keynes's precept.

The second example comes from Keynes's response to Hayek's powerful liberal tract *The Road to Serfdom* (1944). Hayek too was a great admirer of Burke. In his book, he argued that 'democratic planning' was the slippery road to totalitarianism. In a letter of warm appreciation for Hayek's essay, with whose moral and philosophical position he found himself 'not only in agreement, but in deeply moved agreement', Keynes nevertheless told Hayek that 'what we need therefore is not a change in our economic programmes, which would lead in practice to disillusion with the results of your philosophy, but perhaps even an . . . enlargement of them.'[7]

Keynes and Hayek shared very similar epistemological positions. Both believed in inescapable uncertainty, and therefore rejected Newtonian thinking. Hayek thought that such knowledge as people had was dispersed through society; much of it was 'tacit'. His conclusion was that the stock of government knowledge was inevitably inferior to that of dispersed knowledge. This was his trump card against central planning, and it was valid. But it was a weak argument to use against Keynes's statesmanship. Keynes certainly did not believe that government knew, or could know, more than 'society'. But he did believe that it was in a position to take precautions against the consequences of uncertainty which private individuals or even informal social arrangements could not do. The 'conventions' which society erects to guard against uncertainty break down in moments of great stress. Hence a full-employment policy was not the thin end of the wedge to serfdom, but a prudent precaution against a situation developing which would destroy the values which he and Hayek jointly shared – exactly the point he had made in his student essay on Burke. We know enough to have a rational belief that 'moderate planning' will be an improvement on laissez-faire; we have no basis for saying that it will inevitably lead to serfdom or slavery further down the line. Therefore it is rational to act so as to improve the situation in the near future, and simply not bother about further consequences about which we have no knowledge at all.

But Keynes was not blind to the possibility of a Hayekian drift to totalitarianism, and sought to guard against it by preserving a certain kind of society. 'Dangerous acts', he wrote to Hayek, 'can be done safely in a community which thinks and feels rightly which would be the way to hell if they were executed by those who think and feel wrongly.'[8]

KEYNES'S MIDDLE WAY OF THE 1920S

In abeyance through the Keynesian era, Keynes's Middle Way ideas of the 1920s were revived in the 1990s as a counter to the free-market ideology of Reagan and Thatcher, when they travelled under such labels as 'the Third Way' and 'stakeholder capitalism'. This Middle Way revival followed the breakdown of Keynes's macroeconomic revolution, which left the cupboard of social democracy bare.

In his 1924 Sidney Ball lecture, 'The End of Laissez-Faire', and subsequent talks and essays, Keynes provided the framework within which his Middle Way arguments developed in the five years leading up to the slump. He traced the origins of laissez-faire ideas to the eighteenth century. 'Suppose that by the working of natural laws individuals pursuing their own interests with enlightenment in conditions of freedom always tend to promote the general interest at the same time! Our philosophical difficulties are resolved . . . The political philosopher could retire in favour of the businessman – for the latter could always attain the philosopher's *summum bonum* by just pursuing his own private profit.' The synthesis between private and public interest was powerfully reinforced by Darwin's theory of natural selection. 'The principle of the survival of the fittest could be regarded as a vast generalization of the Ricardian economics. Socialist interferences became, in the light of this grander synthesis, not merely inexpedient but impious, as calculated to retard the onward movement of the mighty process by which we ourselves had risen like Aphrodite from the primeval slime.' It is not a coincidence that Darwinian ideas were, once again, transferred from the natural to the social world in the Reagan–Thatcher era of 'creative destruction'.

Keynes is scornful about the Darwinian hypothesis in economics. It ignores the existence of uncertainty, the costs of the competitive struggle, and the trend to concentration of production and wealth.

Keynes then develops what is essentially a public-goods argument for state intervention. Each age must 'distinguish afresh the Agenda of government from the non-Agenda'. Services which are technically social must be separated from those which are technically individual, the most important new items on the agenda being control of currency and credit; dissemination of information to remedy the evils arising from 'risk, uncertainty, and ignorance'; collective decision concerning the allocation of capital between home and foreign investment; and a population policy paying attention to quality as well as numbers.[9]

The first three requirements were carried over into Keynes's New Way of the 1930s, but his insistence on population control was dropped. In his 'classical' days, Keynes worried that the fruits of technical progress would be swallowed up by the growth of numbers. Once he identified insufficient aggregate demand as the problem, he started to welcome population growth as a source of extra demand and output. His concern with the quality of the population never left him, however. The higher the quality of the people, the more productive they would be, and the quicker economies would pass from poverty to plenty. In this, as in other areas of Keynes's thinking, it is important to remember from which periods of his life – and the affairs of the world – his thoughts were coming.

Keynes's leading idea in this period was that the individualistic capitalism of old was mutating into the corporative capitalism of big business and banking. Whereas the capitalist system had never been smoothly adjusting, a decentralized economy of individual proprietors could adjust to shocks much quicker than a concentrated one of big institutions. Influenced by the American institutionalist economist J. R. Commons (1862–1945), Keynes had the economic system moving from an epoch of scarcity ('feudalism') to one of growing abundance ('individualism') to one of stabilization. 'Stabilization' in this historical scheme was the alternative to Marx's communism. Individual liberty would diminish 'in the transition from economic anarchy to a regime which deliberately aims at controlling and directing economic forces in the interests of social justice and social stability'.[10]

Keynes argued that the old economics depended on the 'principle of diffusion', or rapid adjustment to shocks. With the slowdown in economic growth, growth of big business and trade-union power, and the onset of unemployment benefits, the economic system had become rigid, but the authorities still acted on the assumption that it was flexible. They presumed, for example, that one could alter the value of money and leave the consequential adjustments to be brought about by the forces of supply and demand.[11] So 'the first and most important step . . . is to establish a new monetary system based on a stable level of internal prices, which will not ask from the principle of diffusion more than it can deliver.'[12]

Keynes suggested that, partly to minimize risk in a changed environment, the economy was 'socializing itself'. He pointed to the growth of 'semi-autonomous bodies within the State' like public utilities, universities, the Bank of England, statutory authorities, perhaps the railway companies. More important was the trend of joint-stock companies, when they had reached a certain size, to start acting like public corporations rather than individualistic capitalists. A point arrives in their growth at which the owners – or shareholders – become entirely disassociated from the management, whose direct interest is not to maximize profits but to avoid criticism from the public and from their customers. He suggests that this tendency to enlargement of the public sphere was a 'natural line of evolution'.[13]

These speculations concerning the evolution of capitalism coincided with the period of Keynes's life when his ruminations on the 'love of money', described in the previous chapter, were at their height. In fact Keynes's commendation of 'semi-socialism' was closely linked to his preference for 'arranging our affairs in such a way as to appeal to the money-motive as little as possible, rather than as much as possible'. In history, as indeed in the choice of occupations, love of money had played a larger or smaller part. 'Most religions and most philosophies deprecate . . . a way of life mainly influenced by considerations of personal money profit. On the other hand, most men to-day reject ascetic notions and do not doubt the real advantages of wealth.' So 'our problem is to work out a social organization which shall be as efficient as possible without offending our notions of a satisfactory way of life. We need a new set of convictions which spring naturally from a candid examination of our own inner feelings in relation to the outside facts.'[14]

Keynes was well aware of the deficiencies of the form of social organization he was commending. It led to conservatism and a waning of enterprise.[15] However, the strength of his aversion to basing society on 'love of money' led him to overlook another crucial weakness of his Middle Way ideas – what economists have since called the principal–agent problem. Keynes thought that, with the separation of management from ownership, public motives would increasingly come to dominate in the conduct of large enterprises. He did not foresee that the private interests of managers would come to take precedence in both private and public spheres – a tendency powerfully boosted by the growth of the financial sector. Keynes (like Anthony Crosland in the 1950s) thought that managerial control of large corporations would expand their 'public motives'. He did not foresee the explosion of the bonus culture, which would give managers incentives to rip off both shareholders and the wider public.

Perhaps the muddles into which these ideas were leading him, or perhaps just the changes in circumstances, led him to drop most of these Middle Way thoughts in the 1930s. The notion of running a capitalist economy on the Victorian ideal of public service faded, to be replaced by a different plan of salvation, in which the state provided enough demand, and the private sector was left free to satisfy it. His moral distaste for love of money as the basis of social organization did not diminish, but he now accepted that it was fittest for the task of getting humanity through the tunnel of scarcity as quickly as possible to the slopes of abundance.

THE AFTERMATH

The non-Communist post-war settlement owed much more to Keynes's New Way than to his Middle Way. Of course, different countries had their own versions of the social contract, with more or fewer nationalizations, smaller or larger public sectors, and different forms of co-partnership and industrial collaboration. But the predominant fact was that for thirty years full employment was maintained, real wages rose continually, economies were relatively stable, and wealth and income inequalities were reduced. The class war went into abeyance, to such an extent that disappointed radicals and conservatives talked about the 'euthanasia of politics' and the 'age of apathy' – developments which Keynes would have welcomed. Keynes's doctrine of prudence was also in the ascendant: neither side of the political divide carried its conflicts to the extent of seriously endangering social equilibrium, and the equilibrium between the non-Communist and Communist worlds was also maintained.

Then, in the 1970s, this whole structure of 'rules and conventions skilfully put across and guilefully preserved' started to crumble. There were a number of reasons for this collapse – flaws in theory, mistakes in policy, changes in the external environment – but it amounted to a swing in the political cycle back to a much less restrained version of market capitalism. With the full-employment commitment abandoned, and the class war heating up again, Middle Way ideas returned as an antidote to distintegration of social cohesion, but got very little further than when Keynes wrestled with them. Now the free-market system, hailed as the solution to the problems of the Keynesian era, is imploding.

8

Keynes for Today

THE NEED TO RETHINK

Any great failure should force us to rethink fundamental ideas. The present economic crisis is a great failure of the market system. As George Soros has rightly pointed out, 'the salient feature of the current financial crisis is that it was not caused by some external shock like OPEC . . . The crisis was generated by the system itself.'[1] It originated in the US, the heart of the world's financial system and the source of much of its financial innovation. That is why the crisis is global, and is indeed a crisis of globalization. But the crisis also reveals an ideological and theoretical vacuum where the challenge from the left used to be. Capitalism no longer has a global antagonist.

One can see that there were three kinds of failure. The first was institutional: banks mutated from utilities into casinos. However, they did so because they, their regulators and the policymakers sitting on top of the regulators all succumbed to something called the efficient financial market theory: the view that financial markets could not consistently misprice assets and therefore needed little regulation. So the second failure was intellectual. The most astonishing admission was that of former Federal Reserve chairman Alan Greenspan in autumn 2008 that the Fed's regime of monetary management had been based on a 'flaw'. The 'whole intellectual edifice', he said, 'collapsed in the summer of last year'. Behind the efficient market idea lay the intellectual failure of mainstream economics. It could not anticipate or explain the meltdown because the majority of economists are committed to the view that markets are self-correcting, sooner or later. The economics profession both sanctioned and rationalized a business model of society which supported a minimally supervised rule of markets. As a consequence, the failure of markets has marginalized economics itself. It is left on the sidelines as politicians try to salvage something from the breakdown of the market order.

But the crisis also represents a moral failure: that of a system built on money values. At the heart of the moral failure is the worship of economic growth for its own sake, rather than as a way to achieve the 'good life'. As a result, economic efficiency – the means to economic growth – has been given absolute priority in our thinking and policy. The main moral compass we now have is a thin and degraded notion of economic welfare, measured in terms of quantity of goods. This moral lacuna explains uncritical acceptance of globalization and financial innovation, and the sanctification of those practices which give the pursuit of wealth priority over other human concerns.

Keynes distinguished between recovery and reform. Recovery is essentially a matter of treating symptoms. Global aggregate demand is collapsing; extra spending is needed to revive it. But, beyond this, what kind of permanent system should be created to minimize the risk of Black Swans emerging? Recovery and reform sometimes point in different directions.

If one wants to keep the capitalist system going – and there is no alternative – confidence, especially the confidence of the business community in the policies of the government, is essential. Reforms should not be pressed prematurely, because they may cut off recovery by denting business confidence; and they should follow a deep, not superficial, attempt at understanding what went wrong. Keynes was very clear about this in the early 1930s. It might even be necessary to balance budgets in a depression, he said, if that was what the business community expected governments to do. And the trouble with being a Keynesian only in the foxhole is that the business community has not been provided with any theory of the economy which would justify the reforms which the politicians are now contemplating. Indeed, as long as the business community's model of the economy is that of efficient markets, with its corollary of correct risk pricing, they are likely to regard these reforms as threatening the future of profits.

Just as there is no single Keynesian way out of depression, so there is no single Keynesian system of political economy. Keynesianism can at best be a common element in very different systems of mixed economic life. In terms of economic policy it has only one proposition: that governments should make sure that aggregate demand is sufficient to maintain a full-employment level of activity. By what mix of politics, policy and institutional innovation this is to be done is a political-economy question. One thing of which we can be tolerably sure is that the next phase of political economy will see less reliance on export-led growth, a more restricted financial system, an expanded public sector, and a more modest role for economics as tutor of governments.

POLITICAL BUSINESS CYCLES

Historians have always been fascinated by cyclical theories of history. Societies are said to swing like pendulums between alternating phases of vigour and decay, progress and reaction, licentiousness and puritanism. Each outward movement produces a crisis of excess which leads to a reaction. The equilibrium position is hard to achieve and always unstable.

In his *Cycles of American History* (1986), Arthur Schlesinger Jr defined a political-economy cycle as 'a continuing shift in national involvement between public purpose and private interest'. The swing he identified was between 'liberal' (what Europeans would call social-democratic) and 'conservative' epochs. The idea of the 'crisis' is central. Liberal periods succumb to the corruption of power, as idealists yield to time-servers, and conservative arguments against rent-seeking politicians win the day. But the conservative era then succumbs to a corruption of money, as financiers and businessmen use the freedom of deregulation to rip off the public. A crisis of under-regulated markets presages the return to a liberal era.

This idea fits the American historical narrative tolerably well. It also makes sense globally. The era of what Americans would call 'conservative' economics opened with the publication of Adam Smith's *The Wealth of Nations* in 1776. Yet, despite the early intellectual ascendancy of free trade, it took a major crisis – the potato famine of the early 1840s – to produce an actual shift in policy: the 1846 repeal of the Corn Laws, which ushered in the free-trade era.

In the 1870s, the pendulum started to swing back to what the historian A. V. Dicey called the 'age of collectivism'. The major crisis that triggered this was the first great global depression, produced by a collapse in food prices. It was a severe enough shock to produce a major shift in political economy. This came in two waves. First, all industrial countries except Britain put up tariffs to protect employment in agriculture and industry. (Britain relied on mass emigration to eliminate rural unemployment.) Second, all industrial countries except the US started schemes of social insurance to protect their citizens against life's hazards. The Great Depression of 1929–32 produced a second wave of collectivism, now associated with the 'Keynesian' use of fiscal and monetary policy to maintain full employment. Most capitalist countries also nationalized key industries. Roosevelt's New Deal regulated banking and the power utilities, and belatedly embarked on the road of social security. International capital movements were severely controlled everywhere.

This movement was not all one way, or else the West would have ended up with Communism, which was the fate of large parts of the globe. Even before the crisis of collectivism in the 1970s, a swing-back had started, as trade, after 1945, was progressively freed and capital movements were liberalized. The rule was free trade abroad and social democracy at home.

The Bretton Woods system, set up with Keynes's help in 1944, was the international expression of liberal/social-democratic political economy. By providing an environment that reduced incentives for economic nationalism, it aimed to free foreign trade after the freeze of the 1930s. At its heart was a system of fixed exchange rates, subject to agreed adjustment, to avoid competitive currency depreciation, and short-term financial help for countries in balance-of-payments difficulties.

The crisis of liberalism, or social democracy, which unfolded with stagflation and ungovernability in the 1970s, broadly fits Schlesinger's notion of the 'corruption of power'. The Keynesian/social-democratic policymakers succumbed to hubris, an intellectual corruption which convinced them that they possessed the knowledge and the tools to manage and control the economy and society from the top. This was the malady against which Hayek had inveighed in his classic *The Road to Serfdom*. The attempt in the 1970s to control inflation by wage and price controls led directly to a 'crisis of governability', as trade unions, particularly in Britain, refused to accept them. Large state subsidies to producer groups, both public and private, fed the typical corruptions of behaviour identified by the new right: rent-seeking, moral hazard, free-riding. Palpable evidence of government failure obliterated earlier memories of market failure. The new generation of economists abandoned Keynes and, with the help of sophisticated mathematics, reinvented the classical economics of the optimally self-correcting market. Battered by the crises of the 1970s, governments caved in to the 'inevitability' of free-market forces. The swing-back became worldwide with the collapse of Communism.

A conspicuous casualty of the swing-back was the Bretton Woods system, which succumbed in the 1970s to the refusal of the US to curb its domestic spending. Currencies were set free to float, and controls on international capital flows were progressively lifted. This heralded a wholesale change of direction towards free markets and the idea of globalization. This was, in concept, not unattractive. The idea was that the traditional nation state – which had been responsible for so much organized violence and wasteful spending – was yielding to a 'market state' whose main job was to integrate its population into the global market, to the great advantage of prosperity, democracy and peace. All this Panglossian rhetoric is now in abeyance.

Today we are living through a crisis of conservatism. The financial crisis has brought to a head a growing dissatisfaction with the corruption of money. Neoconservatism has sought to justify fabulous rewards to a financial plutocracy while median incomes stagnate or even fall; in the name of efficiency, it has promoted the offshoring of millions of jobs, the undermining of national communities, and the rape of nature. Such a system needs to be fabulously successful to command allegiance. Spectacular failure is bound to discredit it.

The situation we are in now thus puts into question the speed and direction of progress. Will there be a pause for thought, or will we continue much as before after a cascade of minor adjustments? The answer lies in the intellectual and moral sphere. Is economics capable of rethinking its core principles? What institutions, policies and rules are needed to make markets 'well behaved'? Do we have the moral resources to challenge the dominance of money without reverting to the selfish nationalisms of the 1930s?

One thing is clear enough. Political economy no more swings back and forward round a Newtonian equilibrium than does economics proper. History is more like a spiral staircase than a swingometer. Some learning does take place, and one of the things we surely have learned – or relearned – since Keynes is that governments can fail as well as markets. We need a new synthesis, in which government is accepted as non-benevolent, but the market is not thereby totally rehabilitated.

So what system would Keynes be trying to set up today? I will try to use my knowledge of what he said and thought to speak as far as I can in his own accent. But he did not cover the whole ground, and, though I believe he was the wisest and most intelligent economist of the last century, much of what I say is an extrapolation of what he might have thought had he lived through the last sixty years.

TAMING FINANCE

Uncertainty tends to turn long-term investment into short-term speculation. Denial of the need to guard against uncertainty allows what Keynes called the 'financial circulation' to expand exponentially at the expense of the 'industrial circulation'. This has been happening everywhere – but notably in the UK, where the financial system has become master, not servant, of production, the royal road to paper wealth. Any reform of our present system will require restricting the role of finance, and adopting a highly sceptical attitude to the claims made on behalf of financial engineering.

Keynes had little specific to say about financial regulation, since the banking system was not at the centre of the storm of the early 1930s; even in the United States it was an induced casualty. So it is not from Keynes that we should seek to learn the specifics of legislation or regulation for financial markets. Nevertheless, use of his theory can show up deficiencies in current thinking on financial reform.

What distinguishes Keynes's theory from today's mainstream thinking on financial markets is the distinction he makes between risk and uncertainty. If financial markets are merely risky, the important reform is to develop better measures of risk and better techniques of risk management, and, if necessary, enforce them on financial institutions. If on the other hand there is bound to be irreducible uncertainty in financial operations, the state has an additional role, which is to protect the economy as a whole against the consequences of uncertainty.

Within the risk-management paradigm there are two main approaches to reform. The first is to allow market forces to create *more* and *better* markets for risk – new derivative products, more extensive financial intermediation – in quest of the holy grail of ever more complete markets for contingencies. According to this view, the financial system is like an early aircraft. Just because it is prone to crash, we shouldn't abandon the attempt to make it reliably airborne. This ignores Keynes's distinction between risk and uncertainty. We simply cannot fit all the contingencies we face into a Gaussian bell curve, so there will always be a role for state policy to reduce uncertainty arising from finance.

The alternative approach is to force better risk-management measures and techniques on financial institutions through regulation. This is the standpoint of Britain's Financial Services Authority's *The Turner Review* (March 2009). This identifies an 'inadequate focus on the analysis of systemic risk and of the sustainability of whole business models: and a failure to design regulatory tools to respond to emerging systemic risks'.[2] The nub of the argument is that risk-management methods did not adequately reflect the new risks created by the spread of derivatives. There are fleeting moments of doubt as to whether even improved risk-management techniques can make financial markets more 'efficient' in the sense of being able to price risks correctly. 'Recent events', the review notes, 'have raised fundamental issues about the extent to which different markets are or can be made to be efficient, rational, and self-correcting. They suggest that there may be inherent limits to how far problems of market irrationality can be overcome by measures designed to make those markets more transparent, liquid and technically efficient';[3] and, in another place, 'If liquid traded markets are inherently subject to herd/momentum effects, with the potential for irrational overshoots round rational economic levels, then optimal regulation cannot be based on the assumption that increased liquidity is always and in all markets beneficial.'[4] Except for stigmatizing as irrational all behaviour that doesn't fit the classical model of rationality, this is the right issue to raise.

Having delivered itself of these warnings, the review nevertheless concludes that the challenge to efficient market theory doesn't require a 'fundamental shift from the FSA's current policy stance'.[5] What it does require is regulation of system risk. The previous assumption was that if individual banks were safe, the financial system would be stable. But, in trying to make themselves safe under stress, banks can act in ways which undermine collective stability.

The review emphasizes the need for increased flow and accuracy of information ('transparency') to be made available to market participants. External 'stress tests' should replace internal assessments of banks' capital adequacy, to reduce banks' vulnerability to solvency crises. 'Dynamic' accounting conventions should replace the static ones agreed at Basel II (2004), so that agents can anticipate future losses before they become evident in trading-book values or loan repayments.[6] As part of its proposal for 'dynamic' accounting, the review suggests that banks create a non-distributable economic-cycle reserve, which would set aside profit in good years to anticipate losses arising in bad years. Bonuses should be based on distributable profit after the deduction of this reserve, thus ensuring that 'such systems reflect a reasonable estimate of future possible credit losses and impairments, rather than a point-in-time calculation of profit which may subsequently prove illusory'.[7] This proposal – similar to 'balancing the budget over the cycle' – of course assumes that cycles follow a Gaussian pattern.

The Turner Review consistently rejects the radical option of reducing the scope of financial intermediation. This is because it continues to believe that the world of derivative instruments has, by diversifying risk, made the economy less shock-prone. It ignores the evidence from the present crisis that the diversification of risk can increase the danger of cumulative and self-reinforcing price movements. In sum, the review proposes a modest increase in regulation, chiefly by imposing higher information and capital-adequacy requirements on banks and other financial institutions, which should be made internationally effective.

The review is worth special attention because it is by far the most able of the conventional responses to the slump, with reforms closely linked to diagnosis. It does not of course exhaust the proposals for taming finance. Other types of reform proposal are aimed at improving 'corporate governance'. A familiar litany includes strengthening shareholder rights, increased disclosure and transparency requirements, better selection of board members, and so on.

It is hard to be against measures to make the financial system less opaque. But, just as it is wrong to believe that asymmetric information was at the root of the financial breakdown, so it is a delusion to believer that more 'transparency' will prevent future breakdowns. For behind this thought lies the belief that all risk is calculable and that its management requires only better tools: more information, better directors, better regulation. Keynes's distinction between risk and uncertainty led him in a different direction. Risk could be left to look after itself; the government's job was to reduce the impact of uncertainty. Risky activities, Keynes implies, should be left to the market, with entrepreneurs being allowed to profit from good bets and to suffer the consequences of bad bets. On the other hand, uncertain activities with large impacts should be controlled by the state in the public interest. How to make this distinction operationally significant should be the major object of the reform of financial services in the aftermath of the crisis.

One obvious application of this distinction is to banking reform. Here, the radical approach to reform is to reinstate the Glass–Steagall philosophy of separating 'utility' from 'investment banking', with retail banks – those which serve the public – allowed to take only moderate risks, leaving high-risk lending to the investment banks. The clear principle is that banks enjoying deposit insurance and access to lender-of-last-resort facilities should not indulge in gambling with depositors' or taxpayers' money; investment banks, which would be free to gamble with their investors' money, should be debarred from accepting retail deposits, and excluded from any public bailouts. The logic is impeccable, but it would mean ensuring that no investment banks become 'too large to fail'. This implies that, apart from Glass–Steagall, there needs to be some restriction on multinational banking. The alternative approach would allow retail and investment banking to be combined, as now, but would impose higher capital and liquidity requirements, which could be varied over the cycle. My own scepticism about the ability of the authorities successfully to carry out such 'macro-prudential' regulation leads me to favour a return to the Glass–Steagall philosophy of 'narrow' banking, which I would argue is desirable anyway on general social grounds. However, retail banking has also succumbed to the financial virus by abandoning prudent limits for lending. Both sellers and buyers of mortgages would be protected by limiting home loans to, say, 75% of the value of the property and three times the income of the borrower. This would reduce reliance on credit agencies. Except for the last, the reforms above would require international agreement to be effective.*

MACROECONOMIC POLICY

Since the economic hurricane struck there has been much talk about the need to develop new principles of macroeconomic policy. The reputation of inflation targeting as the best framework for managing economies has been tarnished, as stable inflation did not prevent asset bubbles. Also gone is the Greenspan doctrine of avoiding pricking bubbles and instead cleaning up the mess after they burst under their own pressure: the mess can be too big. But so far there has been little consideration of an alternative macroeconomic framework, with most attention being rightly focused on the 'stimulus'.

Central-bank inflation targeting does leave some scope for stabilizing output, by allowing the bank some discretion in how long it takes to hit the inflation target. Thus interest-rate policy can to some extent be used to manage output and employment as well as to control inflation. The trouble is that interest-rate policy is the *only* macroeconomic tool currently available to most governments. This reflects the recent conventional intellectual consensus that economies are

*See p. 193 for the latest developments.

cyclically quite stable, and therefore a little gentle 'managing' of expectations is enough to keep them on their optimal growth path. In reality they are cyclically quite unstable, and may become violently so. Recognition that this is so lies behind proposals to add 'macroprudential' banking regulation to the armoury of inflation targeting. But no one has yet suggested reviving Keynesian fiscal policy to stabilize economic activity at a high level.

Fiscal policy, as currently pursued, does have some steadying influence through the operation of the 'automatic stabilizers'. In a downturn, a budget deficit automatically develops as tax revenues fall and spending on unemployment benefits rises. A surplus automatically develops in an upswing for the opposite reason. But the steadying influence of the automatic stabilizers is quite small. The United States also practises a kind of crude Keynesianism based on budget deficits which has done much to give Keynesian policy a bad name. These budget deficits are by-products of periodic defence build-ups, wars and tax cuts, rather than the result of any coherent steadying philosophy. The Bush deficits were large enough to produce a fragile bounceback from the collapse of the dot-com bubble in 2001, but did nothing to set the US economy on a sustainable recovery path. If we agree with Keynes that a money-using economy is prone to internally generated shocks, we should also agree that discretionary fiscal policy needs to be added to governments' depleted macroeconomic toolboxes, minus the 'fine-tuning' obsession which marked their earlier use.

CURING THE SAVING GLUT

In the orthodox economic theory of Keynes's day, the notion of a saving glut made no sense. Saving and investment were continually adjusted to each other by changes in the interest rate (shorthand for the term-structure of interest rates). Any tendency for saving to run ahead of investment would lead to a fall in the interest rate, which would simultaneously reduce the propensity to save and increase the inducement to invest. In Keynes's theory, the interest rate did not play this adjusting role. Determined by people's liquidity preferences, it could remain higher than needed to equalize saving and investment at full employment. The equalization between the two was therefore achieved by a fall in income, which reduced the quantity saved to the level of what people wanted to invest. Keynes believed that, under laissez-faire, full-employment levels of investment were achieved only in moments of excitement strong enough to overcome the uncertainty normally attaching to estimates of future returns. The normal tendency was for the propensity to save to be stronger than the inducement to invest. Moreover, this problem would grow more acute the richer societies became, because people tended to save a higher fraction of higher incomes even as perceived (and actual) opportunities for profitable investment declined. If full employment was to be maintained, therefore, policy was needed to offset the growing deflationary pressure of saving unmatched by new investment.

Keynes's big idea was to use macroeconomic policy to maintain full employment. His specific suggestion was to use monetary policy to secure a permanently low interest rate and fiscal policy to achieve a continuously high level of public or semi-public investment. Over time, as the returns on further additions to capital fell, the high-investment policy should yield to the encouragement of consumption through redistributing income from the higher to the lower-saving section of the population. This should be coupled with a reduction in the hours of work. In short, the object of macropolicy policy should be to keep the economy in 'quasi-boom' till the economic problem was solved and people could live 'wisely, and agreeably, and well'.

This macroeconomic strategy had an international dimension. As Keynes saw it, the gold standard of his day played a large part in transmitting deflationary pressure from one part of the global economy to another. Countries running trade surpluses accumulated gold reserves, which imposed deflation and unemployment on the gold-losing deficit countries. Global aggregate demand would run down as deflation was diffused throughout the system. Keynes attributed the Great Depression of 1929–32 to a global saving glut, whose main source was the United States. The orthodox economists of his time would have regarded this as a fanciful idea. In the 1740s David Hume had pointed out that a country's attempt to accumulate gold was self-defeating, since the inflow of gold would cause its prices to rise, making its exports less competitive, and thus causing gold to flow out again. Keynes's heresy was to point out that this 'automatic' adjustment mechanism was not automatic.

'The process of adjustment', he remarked, 'is *compulsory* for the debtor and *voluntary* for the creditor.' The creditor had the option of reducing tariffs, expanding its domestic economy, investing abroad, or sterilizing – hoarding – its surpluses. The debtor had no option but to deflate and allow unemployment to rise. (A fixed-exchange-rate system ruled out adjustment by exchange-rate appreciation or depreciation.) Keynes believed that the success of the pre-1914 gold standard had depended on a *de facto* system of creditor adjustment, pivoting on London. London had directed the global flow of rich-country savings towards investing in the developing world. In the interwar years, the United States had become the world's leading creditor, but failed to live up to its creditor responsibilities. Reserves had drained out of the rest of the world 'to pay a country which was obstinately borrowing and exporting on a scale immensely greater than it was lending and importing'. The United States was *hoarding* its reserves rather than using them to expand its own economy or invest in other countries. And such foreign investment as it did make no longer 'corresponded to the development of new resources' which would yield an income stream to service the loans. Rather, it was directed to financing debt obligations arising from the war, or to speculation in stocks and commodities – as Keynes himself had engaged in as a private investor in the late 1920s. By the end of the 1920s much of the world owed debt to the United States which it could not repay. When US savings were diverted from foreign loans to the speculative boom on Wall Street, the unsound investment machine went into reverse. Capital flight back into dollars brought the system crashing down.[8] In terms of Keynes's theory, the much greater uncertainty arising from unsettled conditions after the First World War had brought about a big increase in liquidity preference, whose international expression was the hoarding rather than spending of reserves.

Keynes's plan for a Clearing Union, worked out in 1941, was specifically designed to prevent creditors from hoarding reserves by trading in undervalued currencies.* All capital flows would be channelled through his new Clearing Bank, and their destabilizing potential would be excluded. Keynes's Clearing Bank would thus discharge automatically the duty which creditor nations in the past had performed fitfully and voluntarily. A surplus country hoarding its surpluses in reserves rather than lending them abroad would not be able to deprive deficit countries of their use, since the latter would receive corresponding credit balances in the Bank up to the level of their quotas, which were determined by their share of world trade. In this way a global balance between saving and investment would be secured through a balanced-trade position, which would in turn allow a fixed, but adjustable, exchange-rate regime.†

In place of the Keynes plan, the Bretton Woods agreement of 1944 adopted the US Treasury's proposal for an International Monetary

---

*Keynes's plan for an international Clearing Union dates from 8 September 1941. See Skidelsky, *Keynes*, vol. 3, pp. 199–209, and the summary of the Clearing Union proposals on pp. 231–2.

†Formally, the International Clearing Union aimed to secure creditor adjustment without renouncing debtor discipline. All residual international transactions – those giving rise to surpluses and deficits in the balance of payments – were to be settled through 'clearing accounts' held by member central banks in an International Clearing Bank. Member central banks would buy and sell their currencies against debits and credits with the ICB. These balances would be held in 'bank money' ('bancor'). Each member bank would have the right to draw on a quantity of bank money (its quota) equal to half the average value of its country's total trade for the five last pre-war years. This was its overdraft facility. The ICB's total overdraft facilities came, therefore, to half the value of pre-war international trade – $26 billion. (This was later revised upwards to $37.5 billion.) Each national currency would have a fixed but adjustable relation to a unit of the ICB's bank money, itself expressed in terms of a unit of gold. Bank money, though, would be the ultimate reserve asset of the system.

The Keynes plan sought to bring a simultaneous pressure on both creditor and debtor countries to 'clear' their accounts. Creditor countries – those with positive bancor balances – would be allowed or required to revalue their currencies and unblock any foreign-owned investments, and be charged rising rates of interest (up to 10%) on balances running above a quarter of their quota. Any credit balances exceeding quotas at the end of a year would be confiscated and transferred to a Reserve Fund. Debtor countries would be allowed or required to depreciate their currencies, to sell the ICB any free gold, and to prohibit capital exports. They would also be charged interest (at lower rates than creditors) on excessive debits. A persistently profligate member could be expelled from the Union.

Fund. Each member subscribed a small proportion of its gold reserves to the Fund, which would then lend foreign exchange to countries in temporary balance-of-payments difficulties. The important difference from the Keynes proposal was that national reserve accumulation was not excluded. In practice the 'Keynes problem' of creditor hoarding was solved by the United States taking the place of Britain as the chief supplier of foreign-investment funds in an updated version of the pre-1914 system. The United States, that is, applied its savings to foreign investment. Despite the US developing a current-account deficit in the 1960s, countries continued to hold their reserves in dollars. This meant that the US did not have to deflate its economy to correct its deficit, while the surplus countries – especially Germany and France – could keep their exchange rates undervalued in order to preserve their competitive position against the US. But growing doubts about the convertibility of the dollar into gold brought the system down in 1971.

In theory, floating exchange rates, which succeeded the collapse of the fixed-exchange-rate regime in 1971, removed the need for any reserves at all, since adjustment of current-account imbalances was supposed to be automatically effected through the demand for, and supply of, currencies in the foreign-exchange market. But the need for reserves unexpectedly survived, mainly to guard against speculative movements of 'hot money' which could drive exchange rates away from their 'equilibrium' values. Starting in the 1990s, Asian governments unilaterally erected a 'Bretton Woods II', linking their currencies to the dollar, and holding their reserves in dollars. This reproduced both the benefits and the faults of Bretton Woods I: it avoided global deflation, but undermined the credibility of the reserve currency.

There were two motives for the Asian decision. The first was to accumulate a large stock of US dollar reserves for the governments concerned to insure themselves against a repeat of the capital flight from the region that they witnessed or suffered in 1997/8, and to avoid the humiliating conditions which the IMF imposed for the rescue packages it mounted. The second was to keep exports growing very rapidly in order to boost employment and growth. Exchange-rate undervaluation was the policy weapon used to carry out both the accumulation of reserves and the export drive. Asian governments intervened massively to buy dollars and resist market pressure for currency appreciation. Investing their dollars in US Treasury bills was a way of sterilizing their dollar purchases, thereby preventing domestic price increases that would otherwise have eroded their export competitiveness. This has enabled the United States to run a current-account deficit equal to a seventh of global gross savings. It has been able to do this since it can borrow virtually without constraint in its own currency at low interest rates. This is a consequence of the 'exorbitant privilege' bestowed on the US as the issuer of the world's key currency and of the confidence of the market that foreign governments will step in to support the dollar should it prove necessary. Thus the deflationary consequence of reserve accumulation by East Asia has been offset by the reserve position of the US dollar, which enabled Americans to 'live beyond their means'. To update Keynes's 1941 remark: adjustment is now voluntary for both creditor and debtor.

According to historian Niall Ferguson, 'Chimerica' seemed 'like a marriage made in heaven ... East Chimericans did the saving. The West Chimericans did the spending ... The more China was willing to lend to the United States, the more Americans were willing to borrow.'[9] The trouble with Chimerica is that the Americans didn't *invest* East Asian savings: they *consumed* them. East Asian investment in US Treasury bills failed to correspond to the development of new American assets producing a flow of income from which to service the debt. True enough, it enabled Alan Greenspan to run an exceptionally cheap money policy in the first five years of the new millennium. Yet, as he acknowledges, cheap money had only a 'modest effect on recorded developed country investment'. Despite the fall in the long-term rate of interest, investment in the United States and much of the rest of the developed world remained a 'stable share of GDP'.[10] Martin Wolf believes that the 'savings glut ... might be better thought of as an investment dearth'.[11] As a result, it was not eliminated in the run-up to the 2008 collapse. Indeed, with Asia growing faster than the US and Europe, the gap between intended saving and intended investment grew. The US consumption boom was at best a short-term answer to the increasing gap between the two. It offset the deflationary force of the saving glut without eliminating it. It was essentially a race between whether the housing bubble or the dollar collapsed first.

The stimulus packages now being implemented may restore the world economy to its previous rickety condition, but they will do nothing to address the structural imbalance between saving and investment; indeed they will aggravate it, since the stimulus will replace private debt by public debt, without creating new resources to finance it. Any deeper scheme of reform must address the twin problems of reserves and exchange rates, or the world is likely to limp out of this crisis to the next. The 'new Bretton Woods' which some world leaders call for should aim to adopt an updated version of Keynes's rejected Clearing Union plan, as proposed by Paul David-son.[12] That is, it should aim to meet countries' reserve needs for crisis insurance, while preventing the use of national currencies as international reserves. The decision of the G20 Summit at its 2 April 2009 London meeting to increase the IMF's resources to $750 billion may turn out to be a first step towards creating an international reserve asset to replace the dollar, as China and Japan have both urged. However, such a reserve asset could not come about without agreement on rules governing its ceation and distribution. Some restriction on capital movement would probably be needed, as no country will agree to surrender control of its reserves as long as capital flight remains possible. Similarly, there are no signs yet that developing countries will agree to forgo the advantages of undervalued exchange rates, developed countries the monetary independence given by float-ing currencies, or the United States the advantages of being able to live beyond its means, both economically and geopolitically. There are two possible lines of reform. Exchange rates between major currencies could be allowed to float in unmanaged fashion most of the time, but with occasional policy cooperation and coordinated intervention to prevent gross misalignments. Or, more ambitiously, as suggested by John Williamson, the major countries could decide to practise man-aged floating of a structured kind. They could periodically agree on exchange rates that are appropriate for global adjustment, inter-vention being permitted only if undertaken to influence market ex-change rates in the direction of the agreed rates. These reforms would require the agreement of the key countries in the world's monetary system – the US, Europe, Japan and China. Although they do not go far enough, they go far beyond the *ad hoc* patching currently on offer.[13]

NORMATIVE LIMITS TO GLOBALIZATION

Apart from prudential reasons, Keynes would not have been an enthusiastic globalizer. He produced a scatter of reasons against the globalizing trends of his own era, many of which became permanent parts of his mental fabric and are relevant to two canons of orthodox thinking today: capital mobility and free trade.

Keynes had a bias against foreign lending as such. Not only did he think that the ownership of national assets by foreigners would 'set up strains and enmities' in moments of stress, but he believed that domestic investment was *better*, because inherently less risky, than foreign investment. 'To lend vast sums abroad for long periods of time without any possibility of legal redress if things go wrong is a crazy construction; especially in return for a trifling extra interest.'[14] He liked to point out that practically all foreign loans had been repudiated, and wrote in 1924, 'With home investment, even if it be ill-advised or extravagantly carried out, at least the country has the improvement for what it is worth. The worst conceived and most extravagant scheme leaves us with some houses. A bad foreign investment is wholly engulfed.'[15]

Coming from an impeccably liberal Cambridge family, Keynes started his economic career as an orthodox free-trader. Attacking the Conservative demand for protection in 1923, he deployed the whole free-trade case, emphasizing, 'If there is one thing Protection can*not* do, it is to cure unemployment.'[16] The Black Swan of the Great Depression changed his view. In 1930 he advocated protection – as a cure for unemployment! It would give direct relief to the business community by raising prices at unchanged costs of production. It was better for Britain to produce motor cars inefficiently than produce nothing at all.[17] Protection remained Keynes's 'second-best' employment policy, for use in emergencies. Free trade was best, provided unemployment could be avoided by other means. Nevertheless,

Keynes was never to recover his earlier faith in unfettered free trade, some characteristic attitudes of his protectionist period staying with him for the rest of his life. The depression turned him against the fetish of export-led growth. He gave two reasons. First, excessive reliance on export-led growth soured political relations.[18] Second, while Keynes agreed that 'the advantages of the international division of labour are real and substantial,' he thought they had been over-played.[19] 'Experience accumulates', he wrote in 1933, 'to prove that most modern mass-production processes can be performed in most countries and climates with almost equal efficiency . . . Moreover, as wealth increases, both primary and manufactured products play a smaller relative part in the national economy compared with houses, personal services, and local amenities which are not the subject of international exchange.'[20]

Keynes also came to attach increasing value to a 'balanced' economic life. A 'balanced' economy was not just one that secured full employment, but one which enabled a people to display the full range of its national aptitudes in mechanical invention and agriculture, as well as preserving traditional ways of living. If all this cost a bit more, so be it. 'To say that a country cannot afford agriculture is to delude oneself about the meaning of the word "afford". A country which cannot afford art or agriculture, invention or tradition, is a country in which one cannot afford to live.'[21] Just as he loved shops 'which are really shops and not merely a branch of the multiplication table', so he would have welcomed banks which were not merely branches of a giant global casino, paying scant attention to the needs of ordinary depositors. He also wanted to preserve the freedom for 'politico-economic' experiment: 'We each have our own fancy. Not believing we are saved already, we each would like to have a try at working out our own salvation. We do not wish, therefore, to be at the mercy of world forces working out . . . some uniform equilibrium according to the ideal principles of *laissez-faire*.'

He summed up the several strands of his protectionist argument as follows:

But it does not now seem obvious [he wrote in 1933] that . . . a close dependence of our economic life on the fluctuating economic policies of foreign countries [is a] safeguard and assurance of international peace. It is easier . . . to argue quite the contrary. The protection of a country's existing foreign interests, the capture of new markets, the progress of economic imperialism – these are a scarcely avoidable part of a scheme of things which aims at the maximum of international specialization and at the maximum geographical diffusion of capital wherever its seat of ownership. Advisable domestic policies might often be easier to compass if 'flight of capital' could be ruled out. The divorce between ownership and the real responsibility for management is serious within a country . . . But when the same principle is applied internationally, it is, in times of stress, intolerable – I am irresponsible towards what I own and those who operate what I own are irresponsible towards me . . . For these strong reasons, therefore, I am inclined to believe that . . . a greater measure of national self-sufficiency and economic isolation than existed in 1914 may tend to serve the cause of peace, rather than otherwise. At any rate the age of economic internationalism was not particularly successful in avoiding war.[22]

So, in conclusion, 'Ideas, knowledge, art, hospitality, travel – these are things which should in their nature be international. But let goods be homespun whenever it is reasonably and conveniently possible and above all let finance be primarily national.'[23]

The idea that 'globalization' can lead to war, national self-sufficiency to peace, was of course a complete reversal of the traditional teaching. Nevertheless, Keynes endorsed a qualified internationalism:

If nations [he wrote in 1936] can learn to provide themselves with full employment by their domestic policy . . . there would no longer be a pressing motive why one country needs to force its wares on another or repulse the offerings of its neighbour . . . with the express object of upsetting the equilibrium of payments so as to develop a balance of trade in its own favour. International trade would cease to be what it is, namely a desperate expedient to maintain employment at home by forcing sales on foreign markets and restricting purchases which, if successful, will merely shift the problem of unemployment to the neighbour which is worsted in the struggle, but a willing and unimpeded exchange of goods and services in conditions of mutual advantage.[24]

RECONSTRUCTING ECONOMICS

The chief argument of this book has been that underlying the escalating succession of financial crises we have recently experienced is the failure of economics to take uncertainty seriously. It has covered up this neglect by means of sophisticated mathematics.

Keynes did not believe that all economic life was uncertain. Classical theory was appropriate for many markets and problems – for most markets in consumer goods, for pricing policies in particular firms and industries. In these cases it was reasonable to assume that self-interested agents had enough knowledge of market conditions to achieve their goals. The trouble was that classical theory had colonized the whole domain of economic activity, including all those activities whose outcomes were inescapably uncertain. As a result, it greatly overestimated the stability of the market economy, and drew misleading conclusions for policy. Keynes's attack was not on classical theory as such, but on its scope and applicability.

The correct division of economics, Keynes suggested, was between the study of those economic activities in which 'our views of the future are . . . reliable in all respects' and the study of those in which 'our previous expectations are liable to disappointment and expectations concerning the future affect what we do today'.[25] This is Keynes's familiar distinction between risk and uncertainty. This does not correspond to the conventional division between microeconomics and macroeconomics, since economic agents have varying states of knowledge in all their activities. Nevertheless, uncertainty is strongest in those markets which have the greatest influence on the stability and growth of a modern economy, namely, investment and financial markets. The fact that in these markets there is a lot of uncertainty can cause the whole economy to boom or slump.

Macroeconomics is the study of the forces determining aggregate outcomes like the volume of output and employment, the rate of inflation and growth. One can certainly analyse these outcomes as the sum of myriad individual choices, but only if one understands that these choices are governed by *conventional*, rather than rational, expectations. Macroeconomics should therefore be the study of conventional expectations in the fields to which they apply: why and how they arise, what they are, and how they might be improved. Macroeconomic policy boils down to reducing the amount of uncertainty in the economic system as a whole. In short, economics should abandon the quest for uniting the whole of theory under the umbrella of rational expectations, and should recognize that different knowledge assumptions are appropriate for different kinds of activity.

To equip economists to understand the proper scope and method of their discipline, two reforms, I suggest, are necessary to the way it is taught in universities. First, undergraduate degrees in economics should be broadly based. They would take as their motto Keynes's dictum that 'economics is a moral and not a natural science': that the economist should be 'mathematician, historian, statesman and philosopher . . . in some degree', and that 'no part of man's nature or his institutions must be entirely outside his regard.' First degrees in economics should therefore contain not just the standard courses in macro- and microeconomics (which require some mathematics), but economic and political history, the history of economic thought, moral philosophy, sociology and politics. Although some specialization would be allowed in the final year of a standard degree, the mathematical component in the weighting of the degree should be sharply reduced. This would avoid the absurdity of a student being able to achieve a first-class honours degree (or summa cum laude) in economics simply by being good at maths.

My second reform would be to separate the postgraduate study of microeconomics from macroeconomics. Taught postgraduate courses in microeconomics should concern themselves, as at present, with the building and testing of models based on a narrow set of assumptions. Such courses could probably best be taught in business schools, where they could be combined with wider business studies. By contrast, master's degrees in macroeconomics should be joint degrees, with an equally weighted non-economic component. It could be history, philosophy, sociology, politics, international relations, biology or anthropology. There is something to be said for locating such degrees in the departments of the non-economic disciplines which contribute to them. It would be splendid if teachers and students of economics could be forced to talk to teachers and students of philosophy or history; better still if they were partly knowledgeable in matters outside their specialist disciplines. Both sides would benefit. A broadly based postgraduate course in macroeconomics would study not just the implications of particular policies for economic stability, growth and development, but also their social and moral implications.

The obvious aim of such a reconstruction is to protect macroeconomics from the encroachment of the methods and habits of mind of microeconomics. Only through some such broadening and dispersion, I suggest, can we mitigate the departmental concentration of maths-driven economics and provide a proper education for those whose main value to society will lie as much in their philosophical and political literacy as in their mathematical efficiency. Such a reconstruction would loosen the discipline's Newtonian anchor and give it a less regressive research programme.

I don't expect this to happen quickly: economics as it now exists is far too firmly entrenched as a distinctive expression of Enlightenment thought. But it may come about gradually with the shift in power and ideas from the United States and Europe to Asia and Latin America. As this happens, the prestige of the great schools of economics at Chicago, Harvard and MIT might start to wane, allowing a more modest economics to grow up.

KEYNES'S VISION OF A HARMONIOUS WORLD

If Keynes's vision can be summed up in a phrase, it is that of the 'harmonious society'. The idea of social harmony is more attractive than its social-science equivalents 'social cohesion' or 'consensus', as it emphasizes the importance of variety. Keynes's economics of harmony was both national and international in scope. Full employment at home by means of investment and income redistribution would take the pressure off foreign trade, slow down the pace of globalization, and ease the social tensions arising from it. A Clearing Union for international payments would bring to an end global macroeconomic imbalances, automatically creating a more plural world. Nations and regions would rediscover and further develop their own identities. If imbalances caused by geopolitics were eliminated, currencies would become more stable.

Some who see no alternative to Washington Consensus globalization will see such ideas as purely utopian, even fraught with dangerous potential for protectionism and war. Others will see natural tendencies pointing in this direction, which the present slump will accelerate if we can learn its lessons. The entry of China, India and other major powers into key global directorates (G8 up to G20) recognizes the emergence of a more plural world. China, in particular, is no longer a passive actor in international relations. The new emphasis of its rulers on creating a 'harmonious' pattern of economic development points to less emphasis on export-led growth. Above all, the reorientation of American foreign policy under President Obama is set in the direction of multilateralism and regionalism. The United States will remain for the time being the only genuine world power, but its natural evolution is towards it becoming the fifth wheel on every coach, rather than the driver of the whole team. And its economic and political future will depend on its being able to pay its own way by its own productivity.

Important arguments still have to be won. A willingness to end macroeconomic imbalances depends on a willingness to accept geopolitical balances – a point which David Calleo has long argued.[26] If the United States wants to run an empire, it has to be in a position to tax the rest of world. Piling up debt is a shadow tax, but payment is voluntary and depends on the perception that the US is providing public goods for the whole world. In the Cold War era this was taken for granted: America was protecting much of the rest of the world, in particular western Europe and Japan, from Communism. A great deal of cooperation is required to meet the new global challenges of terrorism, environmental damage and climate change. But, with the emergence of a more plural distribution of power and resources, the case for the rest of the world allowing the United States to run permanent current-account deficits for the benefit of all is far from self-evident. If an American empire on borrowed money is rejected, then other political centres – the EU, China, Japan, Latin America, the Middle East – will have to assume responsibility for their own security by way of regional alliances, in which the US can take part, but not the dominant part.

Keynes's ideal of a harmonious national life as an alternative to an extreme division of labour is in tune not only with important currents of opinion in the secular West, but with the main thrust of religious teaching the world over. But, in line with the trend to globalization, Keynes's rebalancing ideas can best be applied in regional settings with a common culture, rather than in national or imperial settings. The most advanced such regional grouping is the European Union. In the circumstances of Keynes's time, Britain – and in economic affairs that meant Keynes – had no alternative but to rope itself to the United States. But Keynes was also a product of the old Europe, of which Britain was an integral part. He was brought up by a German governess, married a Russian ballerina, and was at home in France and Italy. He looked forward to an era of small political and cultural units combined into 'larger, and more or less closely knit economic units'.[27] Sketchy though these ideas are, they point to a very different model of globalization from that projected by today's apostles of that concept.

Strange visions for an economist! But then Keynes was not primarily an economist, only the most brilliant mind of modern times who devoted himself to the study of economics, a contemporary of Einstein, Freud and T. S. Eliot who absorbed the mental and cultural vibrations emitted by their worlds, and used them to revolutionize a science which had not progressed since the eighteenth century. His friend Oswald Falk has left the most penetrating analysis of that mind:

I wonder [he wrote to Keynes on 2 February 1936] . . . whether analysis is your fundamental mental process, whether it doesn't follow, with a somewhat grudging struggle at rational justification, rather than precede, synthetic ideas, which are your real delight, and with which from time to time you startle and shock the majority. And isn't there something in the view that a new idea . . . may be the product of the moral feeling of an age, floating around us, and ready for apprehension by the most *sensitive* minds by other than reasoning processes? And isn't it the artist rather than the scientist who apprehends these ideas? Is your mind really so typically western as superficially it appears to be? I believe not. Brilliant as your analysis may be, I believe it is a veneer rather than the substance of your mental fabric. And that explains perhaps . . . the hostility which you arouse amongst the more truly western minds of your fellow economists, scientists in the narrow sense, bogged down in the muddles of their analysis.[28]

Keynes is not just for the foxhole, but for the emerging world order.

LATEST DEVELOPMENTS

Proposals for financial reform issued by the UK and US Treasuries (8 July and 29 June 2009 respectively) and being discussed by the EU have rejected the 'Glass–Steagall' approach of separating retail and investment banking in favour of 'macro-prudential' bank regulation. Basically, they call for stronger regulation of all banks, stronger rules on corporate governance, and higher capital requirements for internationally important banks. The UK Treasury is considering imposing a levy on banks to insure deposits against future losses. The American proposals call for originators of mortgages to retain a 'material' financial stake in the loans they issue.

These proposals are not without merit. However, they have two weaknesses. First, they would require international agreement to be effective, otherwise banks would have opportunities for 'regulatory arbitrage'. Second, even if this problem could be overcome, banks would find it too easy to 'game' the system, i.e. cheat on capital and liquidity requirements. Investment banks like Goldman Sachs and Barclays Capital are already busy inventing new types of securities which promise to reduce the capital cost of holding risky assets.[29] The deeper criticism, however, is continued reliance by both regulators and bankers on mathematical financial models for measuring and containing risk which promise more than they can deliver. This is a consequence of ignoring Keynes's distinction between risk and uncertainty.

Bibliography

BLOGS

'Angry Bear', various contributors – http://angrybear.blogspot.com/
'Baseline Scenario', Simon Johnson and James Kwak – http://baseline
scenario.com/
'The Conscience of a Liberal', Paul Krugman – http://krugman.blogs.
nytimes.com/
'Econbrowser', James D. Hamilton and Menzie Chinn – http://www.
econbrowser.com/
'Economist's View', Mark Thoma – http://economistsview.typepad.com/
'Grasping Reality with Both Hands', Brad DeLong – http://delong.typepad.
com/sdj/
'Maverecon', Willem Buiter – http://blogs.ft.com/maverecon/

ARTICLES

Abramovitz, Moses, 'Catching up, forging ahead, and falling behind', *Journal of Economic History* 46 (June 1986)
Bordo, M., 'Exchange rate regime choice in historical perspective', *IMF Working Paper* WP/03/160 (1993)
Congdon, Tim, 'Here is the way to end recession with speed', *Financial Times*, 25 February 2009
Coval, Joshua D., Jurek, Jakub, and Stafford, Erik, 'The economics of structured finance', Harvard Business School Finance Working Paper 09–060 (2008)
Danielsson, Jon, 'Blame the models', *Journal of Financial Stability* 4, 4 (December 2008)
Friedman, Milton, and Schwartz, Anna, 'Money and business cycles', *Review of Economics and Statistics*, Supplement, 1963

Galbraith, James, 'Inequality, unemployment and growth: new measures of old controversies', *Journal of Economic Inequality* 7, 2 (June 2009)

Hnatkovska, Viktoria, and Loayza, Norman, 'Volatility and growth', *Policy Research Working Paper Series 3184* (World Bank, 2004)

Leijonhufvud, Axel, 'Mr Keynes and the Moderns', in Pasinetti and Schefold (eds.), *The Impact of Keynes on Economics in the 20th Century*

Matthews, R. C. O., 'Why has Britain had full employment since the war?', *Economic Journal* 78 (September 1968); reproduced in Feinstein (ed.), *The Managed Economy*

Partnoy, Frank, 'Prepare to bury the fatally wounded banks', *Financial Times*, 19 January 2009

Patinkin, D., 'John Maynard Keynes', in *The New Palgrave Dictionary of Economics* (Macmillan, 1987), vol. 3

Singer, K., 'Recollections of Keynes', *Australian Quarterly*, June 1949

Stiglitz, Joseph, 'The financial crisis of 2007/8 and its macroeconomic consequences', presented at the Initiative for Policy Dialogue Task Force meeting on Financial Markets Reform (June 2008)

BOOKS

Akerlof, George, and Shiller, Robert, *Animal Spirits: How Human Psychology Drives the Economy, and Why It Matters for Global Capitalism* (Princeton University Press, 2009)

Aldcroft, Derek, and Morewood, Steven, *The European Economy* (Routledge, 2001)

Aldred, Jonathan, *The Skeptical Economist* (Earthscan, 2009)

Biggs, Barton, *Hedge Hogging* (John Wiley, 2006)

Bronk, Richard, *The Romantic Economist* (Cambridge University Press, 2009)

Butler, Samuel, and Hamlin, Alan (eds.), *Market Capitalism and Moral Values* (Edward Elgar, 1993)

Cable, Vincent, *The Storm: The World Economic Crisis and What It Means* (Atlantic Books, 2009)

Cairncross, F., and Cairncross, A. (eds.), *The Legacy of the Golden Age: The 1960s and Their Economic Consequences* (Routledge, 1992)

Calleo, David P., *Follies of Power: America's Unipolar Fantasy* (Cambridge University Press, 2009)

—— and Rowland, Benjamin M., *America and the World Political Economy: American Dreams and National Realities* (Indiana University Press, 1973)

Chick, Victoria, *On Money, Method and Keynes: Selected Essays*, ed. Philip Arestis and Sheila Dow (Macmillan/St Martin's Press, 1992)

Congdon, Tim, *Keynes, the Keynesians and Monetarists* (Edward Elgar, 2007)

Davenport, Nicholas, *Memoirs of a City Radical* (Weidenfeld & Nicolson, 1974)

Davidson, Paul, *Financial Markets, Money and the Real World* (Edward Elgar, 2002)

—— *John Maynard Keynes* (Palgrave Macmillan, 2007)

Ebenstein, Alan, *Friedrich Hayek: A Biography* (Palgrave, 2001)

Feinstein, Charles (ed.), *The Managed Economy: Essays in British Economic Policy and Performance since 1929* (Oxford University Press, 1983)

Ferguson, Niall, *The Ascent of Money* (Allen Lane, 2008)

Friedman, Milton, and Schwartz, Anna, *The Great Contraction 1929–1933* (Princeton University Press, 1965)

Galbraith, John Kenneth, *The Great Crash 1929* (Penguin, 1973)

Greenspan, Alan, *The Age of Turbulence: Adventures in a New World* (Allen Lane, 2007)

Harrod, R. F., *The Life of John Maynard Keynes* (London, 1951)

Kay, John, *The Truth about Markets: Their Genius, Their Limits, Their Follies* (Allen Lane, 2003)

—— *The Long and the Short of It: Finance and Investment for Normally Intelligent People Who are Not in the Industry* (Erasmus Press, 2009)

Kindleberger, Charles P., *The World in Depression 1929–1939* (Allen Lane, 1973)

Klamer, Arjo, *The New Classical Macroeconomics: Conversations with New Classical Economists and Their Opponents* (Harvester Press, 1984)

Krugman, Paul, *Conscience of a Liberal* (W. W. Norton, 2007)

—— *The Return of Depression Economics and the Crisis of 2008* (Allen Lane, 2008)

Kuhn, Thomas, *The Structure of Scientific Revolutions* (Chicago University Press, 1962)

Layard, Richard, *Happiness: Lessons from a New Science* (Penguin New York, 2005)

Leijonhufvud, Axel, *Keynes and the Classics: Two Lectures on Keynes' Contribution to Economic Theory* (IEA, 1969)

Lekachman, Robert (ed.), *Keynes's General Theory: A Report of Three Decades* (St Martin's Press, 1964)

Liesner, Thelma, *Economic Statistics 1900–1983: United Kingdom, United States of America, France, Germany, Italy, Japan* (Economist Publications, 1985)

Lucas, Robert E., Jr, *Lectures on Economic Growth* (Harvard University Press, 2004)

McCraw, Thomas M., *Prophet of Innovation: Joseph Schumpeter and Creative Destruction* (Harvard University Press, 2007)

Maddison, Angus, *Dynamic Forces in Capitalist Development: A Long-Run Comparative View* (Oxford University Press, 1991)

——*The World Economy* (OECD, 2006)

Minsky, Hyman P., *John Maynard Keynes* (Macmillan, 1975).

Mitchell, William C., *Government as It Is* (IEA, 1988)

Moggridge, D. E., *The Life of John Maynard Keynes: An Economist's Biography* (Routledge, 1992)

Moore, G. E., *Principia Ethica* (Cambridge University Press, 1959 edn)

Morris, Charles R., *The Trillion Dollar Meltdown* (Public Affairs, 2008)

O'Donnell, R., *Keynes: Philosophy, Economics and Politics* (Macmillan, 1989)

Olson, Mancur, *The Logic of Collective Action: Public Goods and the Theory of Groups* (Harvard University Press, 1971 edn)

Parsons, Wayne, *Keynes and the Quest for a Moral Science: A Study of Economics and Alchemy* (Edward Elgar, 1997)

Pasinetti, Luigi, and Schefold, Bertram (eds.), *The Impact of Keynes on Economics in the 20th Century* (Edward Elgar, 1999)

Robbins, Lionel, *Essay on the Nature and the Importance of Economic Science* (Macmillan, 1935 edn)

Rynes, Thomas K. (ed.), *Keynes's Lectures, 1932–35* (Macmillan, 1989)

Schlesinger, Arthur, Jr, *The Cycles of American History* (Houghton Mifflin, 1986)

Schumpeter, Joseph A., *Ten Great Economists: From Marx to Keynes* (Allen & Unwin, 1952)

Shaw, G. K., *Rational Expectations: An Elementary Exposition* (Harvester Press, 1984)

Skidelsky, Robert, *John Maynard Keynes*, 3 vols. (Macmillan, 1983, 1992, 2001)

——*John Maynard Keynes 1883–1946: Economist, Philosopher, Statesman* (abridged version of the above) (Macmillan, 2003)

Snowdon, Brian, and Vane, Howard R., *Modern Macroeconomics: Its Origins, Development and Current State* (Edward Elgar, 2005)

Soros, George, *The Alchemy of Finance* (Simon & Schuster, 1987)

——*The New Paradigm for Financial Markets: The Credit Crisis of 2008 and What It Means* (Public Affairs, 2008)

Stein, Herbert, *The Fiscal Revolution in America* (University of Chicago Press, 1969)

Taleb, Nassim, *The Black Swan: The Impact of the Highly Improbable* (Allen Lane, 2007)

Temin, Peter, *Did Monetary Forces Cause the Great Depression?* (W. W. Norton, 1976)

Togati, Teodoro Dario, *Keynes and the Neoclassical Synthesis: Einsteinian vs. Newtonian Macroeconomics* (Routledge, 1998)

The Turner Review: A Regulatory Response to the Crisis in Global Banking (Financial Services Authority, 2009)

van Dormael, Armand, *Bretton Woods: Birth of a Monetary System* (Holmes & Meier, 1978)

Walsh, Justyn, *Keynes and the Market* (John Wiley, 2008)

Wolf, Martin, *Fixing Global Finance* (Johns Hopkins University Press, 2008)

KEYNES

References to Keynes, unless otherwise indicated, are to *The Collected Writings of John Maynard Keynes*, 30 volumes, including bibliography and index, published by Macmillan/Cambridge University Press for the Royal Economic Society, 1971–89. The citations are in the form 'JMK, *CW*, vol. no, page reference'. The volumes of the *Collected Writings* which have been most relevant to the writing of this book are:

(II) *The Economic Consequences of the Peace* [1919] (1971)

(IV) *A Tract on Monetary Reform* [1923] (1971)

(V) *A Treatise on Money*, vol. 1: *The Pure Theory of Money* [1930] (1971)

(VI) *A Treatise on Money*, vol. 2: *The Applied Theory of Money* [1930] (1971)

(VII) *The General Theory of Employment, Interest and Money* [1936] (1973)

(VIII) *A Treatise on Probability* [1921] (1973)

(IX) *Essays in Persuasion* [1931] (1972 – full text with additions)

(X) *Essays in Biography* [1933] (1972 – full text with additions)

(XII) *Economic Articles and Correspondence: Investment and Editorial* (1983)

(XIII) *The General Theory and After*, part 1: *Preparation* (1973)

(XIV) *The General Theory and After*, part 2: *Defence and Development* (1973)

(XIX) *Activities 1922–9: The Return to Gold and Industrial Policy,* 2 vols. (1981)

(XX) *Activities 1929–31: Rethinking Employment and Unemployment Policies* (1981)

(XXI) *Activities 1931–9: World Crises and Policies in Britain and America* (1982)

(XXV) *Activities 1940–44: Shaping the Post-War World: The Clearing Union* (1980)

(XXVII) *Activities 1940–46: Shaping the Post-War World: Employment and Commodities* (1980)

(XXVIII) *Social, Political and Literary Writings* (1982)

(XXIX) *The General Theory and After: A Supplement* (to vols. XIII and XIV) (1979)

Notes

Full details of works cited only by author and short title can be found in the bibliography.

Introduction

1. Quoted in Justin Fox, 'The comeback of Keynes', *Time*, 27 January 2009.
2. JMK, *CW*, vii, p. 383.

1 What Went Wrong?

1. Taleb, *The Black Swan*, p. xviii.
2. Greenspan, *The Age of Turbulence*, p. 507.
3. Martin Wolf, 'US housing solution is not a good one to follow', *Financial Times*, 9 September 2008.
4. Partnoy, 'Prepare to bury the fatally wounded banks'.
5. Peter Thal Larsen, 'Goldman pays the price of being big', *Financial Times*, 13 August 2007.
6. Danielsson, 'Blame the models', p. 3.
7. Sam Jones et al., 'Moody's error gave top ratings to debt products', *Financial Times*, 21 May 2008.
8. See John Gapper, 'How banks learnt to play the system', *Financial Times*, 7 May 2009.
9. Warren Buffett, *Berkshire Hathaway 2002 Annual Report*, p. 15.
10. Transcript, *C-Span's 'Washington Journal'*, 6 February 2009, see video on YouTube: http://www.youtube.com/watch?v=pD8viQ DhS4, beginning at 2 minutes 20 seconds.
11. Joe Nocera, 'As credit crisis spiralled, alarm led to action', *New York Times*, 1 October 2008.
12. Mervyn King, speech to the CBI, Institute of Directors, Chamber of

Commerce and Yorkshire Forward, at the Royal Armouries, Leeds, 21 October 2008, p.2.

13. Martin Wolf, 'Who will pick up the thread after the great unwinding?', *Financial Times*, 20 November 2007.

14. Justin McCurry, 'Fallout from US financial crisis blights Japanese growth', *The Guardian*, 16 February 2009.

15. IMF, *World Economic Outlook: Crisis and Recovery*, April 2009, p. 6.

16. Partnoy, 'Prepare to bury the fatally wounded banks'.

17. Krishna Guha and Edward Luce, 'Greenspan backs bank nationalisation', *Financial Times*, 18 February 2009.

18. Andrew Ross Sorkin, 'Obama's bailout challenge', *New York Times*, 19 January 2009.

19. JMK, CW, xxi, p. 60.

20. Jeffrey Sachs, 'The Tarp is a fiscal straitjacket', *Financial Times*, 27 January 2009.

21. Kathryn Hopkins, 'Britain cannot afford any further fiscal stimulus, King warns', *The Guardian*, 24 March 2009.

22. Ben S. Bernanke, speech at Richmond 2009 Credit Markets Symposium, Charlotte, NC, 3 April 2009.

23. Congdon, 'Here is the way to end recession with speed'.

24. JMK, CW, vii, p. 173.

25. Vincent Cable has recently published a book, *The Storm: The World Economic Crisis and What It Means*, in which he further develops these themes.

26. Will Hutton, 'Yes it's bad, but at long last the government is getting it right', *The Observer*, 25 January 2009.

27. Jonathan Guthrie, 'Look out for a rash of new business myths', *Financial Times*, 12 February 2009.

28. Lloyd Blankfein, 'Do not destroy the essential catalyst of risk', *Financial Times*, 8 February 2009.

29. JMK, CW, ix, p. 158.

30. Partnoy, 'Prepare to bury the fatally wounded banks'.

31. Donald McKenzie, 'An address in Mayfair', *London Review of Books*, 4 December 2008.

32. Gillian Tett, 'A harmful hedge-fund fixation', *Financial Times*, 8 May 2009.

33. Andrew Smithers, 'Take heed of Cassandra's warning against imminent ruin', letter to *Financial Times*, 24 April 2009.

34. Michael Lewis and David Einhorn, 'The end of the financial world as we know it', *New York Times*, 3 January 2009.

35. Paul Kennedy 'Read the big four to know capital's fate', *Financial Times*, 13 March 2009.

36. JMK, *CW*, vii, p. 383.

2 The Present State of Economics

1. Willem Buiter's blog, 3 March 2009: http://blogs.ft.com/maverecon/2009/03/the-unfortunate-uselessness-of-most-state-of-the-art-academic-monetary-economics/.

2. Robert Waldmann on 'Angry Bear' blog, 27 January 2009: http://angry bear.blogspot.com/2009/01/background-on-fresh-water-and-salt.html.

3. Willem Buiter's blog, 3 March 2009: http://blogs.ft.com/maverecon/2009/03/the - unfortunate - uselessness - of - most - state - of - the - art - academic - monetary-economics/.

4. Shaw, *Rational Expectations*, p. 3.

5. Klamer, *The New Classical Macroeconomics*, pp. 40–41.

6. *The Turner Review*, p. 39.

7. Ibid., p. 87.

8. Greenspan, *The Age of Turbulence*, p. 507.

9. *The Turner Review*, p. 85.

10. Quoted in Walsh, *Keynes and the Market*, pp. 39–40.

11. I emphasize 'best-known': another is Victoria Chick.

12. Taleb, *The Black Swan*, p. xxiv.

13. David A. Shaywitz, 'Shattering the bell curve', *Wall Street Journal*, 24 April 2007.

14. Robert Skidelsky, 'The world on a string', *New York Review of Books*, 8 March 2001. Italics added.

15. Stiglitz, 'The financial crisis of 2007/8 and its macroeconomic consequences', p. 9.

16. Taleb, *The Black Swan*, p. 43.

17. Ibid., p. 44.

18. For example, see Akerlof and Shiller, *Animal Spirits*, and Richard Posner's review of it in the *New Republic*, 15 April 2009.

19. Robert E. Lucas Jr, 'Ben Bernanke is the best stimulus right now', *Wall Street Journal*, 23 December 2008.

20. Paul Krugman, 'Let's get fiscal', *New York Times*, 17 October 2008.

21. Paul Krugman, 'Franklin Delano Obama?', *New York Times*, 10 November 2008.

22. Paul Krugman, 'Depression economics returns', *New York Times*, 14 November 2008.

23. Paul Krugman, 'Deficits and the future', *New York Times*, 1 December 2008.

24. Paul Krugman, 'What to do', *New York Review of Books*, 18 December 2008.

25. William Warren, 'The top ten bottom feeders', at http://alg31blog.timber lakepublishing.com/default.asp?Display=910.

26. Declan McCullagh, 'For many economists stimulus falls flat', *CBS*, 28 January 2009.

27. Fama/French Forum, 13 January 2009: http://www.dimensional.com/famafrench/2009/01/bailouts-and-stimulus-plans.html.

28. John Cochrane, 'Fiscal stimulus, fiscal inflation, or fiscal fallacies?', 27 February 2009: http://faculty.chicagobooth.edu/john.cochrane/research/Papers/fiscal2.htm.

29. Email exchange between Robert Barro and Clive Crook posted on Clive Crook's blog, 10 February 2009: http://clivecrook.theatlantic.com/archives/2009/02/dismal_science_revisited.php.

30. Paul Krugman's blog, 30 January 2009: http://krugman.blogs.nytimes.com/2009/01/30/saving-investment-keynes- evolution/.

31. Paul Krugman's blog, 1 March 2009: http://krugman.blogs.nytimes.com/2009/03/01/equilibrium-decadence-wonkish/?apage=3.

3 The Lives of Keynes

1. JMK, 'Economic possibilities for our grandchildren', *CW*, ix, p. xxx.

2. JMK, *CW*, x, pp. 173–4. Italics added.

3. JMK, 'Newton, the Man', *CW*, x, pp. 363–4.

4. For Freud, see *CW*, xviii, pp. 392–3; for Malthus, *CW*, x, p. 108; for Newton, *CW*, x, p. 365.

5. JMK to Roy Harrod, 4 July 1938, *CW*, xiv, p. 296.

6. Singer, 'Recollections of Keynes', pp. 50–51, 55–6.

7. Davenport, *Memoirs of a City Radical*, p. 50.

8. JMK, 'War and the financial system, August 1914', *Economic Journal*, September 1914; reprinted in *CW*, xi, p. 241.

9. Ibid. – full text in *CW*, xi, pp. 238–71. Keynes's further commentary on the 1914 crisis can be read in *CW*, xi, pp. 278–330.

10. Skidelsky, *Keynes*, vol. 1, p. 208.

11. Davenport, *Memoirs of a City Radical*, p. 50.

12. JMK, *A Tract on Monetary Reform*, CW, iv, p. 34.

13. Notes by Reginald V. Leonard, fellow of Wadham College, Oxford, of a conversation with JMK on the financial policy of colleges, 26 November 1926, item 10, H. Marshall Papers, Miscellaneous I, University Library, Cambridge University.

14. JMK, CW, vii, p. 100.

15. JMK, 'The world's economic crisis and the means of escape', CW, xxi, p. 51.

16. JMK, CW, xx, pp. 345–6.

17. Quoted in Skidelsky, *Keynes*, vol. 2, p. 341.

18. Ibid., p. 341.

19. JMK, *A Treatise on Money*, CW, vi, 176–7.

20. See Deepak Lal, 'A Hayekian recession with Fisherian consequences', *Business Standard*, March 2009.

21. JMK, CW, vii, p. 324.

22. JMK, CW, xxi, p. 390.

23. See Friedman and Schwartz, *The Great Contraction 1929–1933*.

24. See Temin, *Did Monetary Forces Cause the Great Depression?*, for a discussion of the 'money hypothesis' versus the 'spending hypothesis'.

25. Walsh, *Keynes and the Market*, p. 43.

26. Kindleberger, *The World in Depression 1929–1939*, p. 292.

27. JMK, CW, xxi, p. 326.

28. Skidelsky, *Keynes*, vol. 2, p. 401.

29. JMK, CW, vi, p. 323.

30. JMK, CW, vii, p. 155.

31. Skidelsky, *Keynes*, vol. 2, p. 394.

32. JMK, CW, vii, p. 160.

33. JMK, CW, x, p. 447.

34. Quoted in Skidelsky, *Keynes*, vol. 2, p. 526.

35. JMK, CW, vii, p. 157.

36. JMK, CW, xxviii, pp. 399–400.

37. Walsh, *Keynes and the Market*, p. 168.

38. Skidelsky, *Keynes*, vol. 2, p. 526.

4 Keynes's Economics

1. JMK, *CW*, xiv, p. 113.
2. JMK, *CW*, vii, p. 350.
3. JMK, *CW*, xiv, p. 122.
4. Robbins, *The Nature and the Importance of Economic Science*, p. 16.
5. JMK, *CW*, xxi, p. 61.
6. JMK, *CW*, vii, p. 294.
7. Lucas, *Lectures on Economic Growth*, p. 21.
8. JMK, 'Poverty in plenty: is the economic system self-adjusting?', *The Listener*, 21 November 1934, *CW*, xiii, pp. 486–7.
9. Quoted in JMK, 'Thomas Robert Malthus', *CW*, x, pp. 97–8.
10. JMK, *A Tract on Monetary Reform*, *CW*, iv, p. 65.
11. JMK, *CW*, xiv, p. 300.
12. Rynes (ed.), *Keynes's Lectures*, p. 102. See also pp. 101–3 for the whole argument.
13. JMK, *CW*, vii, p. xxii.
14. JMK, *CW*, v, p. 176. See also O'Donnell, *Keynes: Philosophy, Economics and Politics*, p. 58.
15. JMK, *CW*, viii, p. 32.
16. JMK, *CW*, xiv, p. 113–14. Cf. JMK, *CW*, vii, pp. 149–50.
17. JMK, *CW*, vii, pp. 148–9.
18. Quotations from JMK, *CW*, xiv, pp. 285–9, 293–5.
19. JMK, *CW*, vii, p. 211.
20. Ibid., p. 137.
21. Ibid., p. 204.
22. Ibid., p. 149.
23. JMK, *CW*, xiv, p. 113.
24. Ibid., p. 114.
25. For these quotations, see JMK, *CW*, vii, p. 154; xiv, p. 115.
26. See Walsh, *Keynes and the Market*, p. 31.
27. JMK, *CW*, vii, p. 159.
28. Ibid., p. 161.
29. JMK, *CW*, xiv, pp. 115–16.
30. Ibid., p. 116.
31. JMK, *CW*, xxix, pp. 293–4.
32. JMK, *CW*, vii, pp. 5–15.
33. Ibid., p. 30.

34. This account is indebted to Leijonhufvud, 'Mr Keynes and the Moderns'.

35. See JMK to D. H. Robertson, 10 July 1938, in *CW*, xxix, p. 179: 'I hear with surprise that our forebears believed that *cet. par.* an increase in the desire to save would lead to a recession in employment and income and would only result in a fall in the rate of interest in so far as this was the case.'

36. D. Patinkin, 'John Maynard Keynes', p. 25.

37. JMK, *CW*, ix, p. 342.

38. JMK, *CW*, xxvii, p. 322.

5 The Keynesian Revolution: Success or Failure?

1. In Lekachman (ed.), *Keynes's General Theory*, p. 322.

2. This is the view of Leijonhufvud, *Keynes and the Classics*.

3. Friedman and Schwartz, 'Money and business cycles'.

4. Quoted in Klamer, *The New Classical Macroeconomics*, p. 136.

5. For a summary of public choice theory see Mitchell, *Government as It Is*. A related analysis of public-goods provision is Olson, *The Logic of Collective Action*.

6. This is the argument of Herbert Stein, see *The Fiscal Revolution in America*.

7. See Krugman, *Conscience of a Liberal*.

8. Cairncross and Cairncross (eds.), *The Legacy of the Golden Age*.

9. Numbers from Maddison, *Dynamic Forces in Capitalist Development*, table 3.1.

10. World Bank, *World Development Indicators*, December 2008.

11. Hnatkovska and Loayza, 'Volatility and growth', p. 19. Italics added.

12. Bordo, 'Exchange rate regime choice in historical perspective'.

13. Hnatkovska and Loayza, 'Volatility and growth', p. 17.

14. IMF, *Exchange Rate Volatility and Trade Flows: Some New Evidence* (May 2004).

15. Galbraith, 'Inequality, unemployment and growth'.

16. Ibid.

17. Matthews, 'Why has Britain had full employment since the war?', in Feinstein (ed.), *The Managed Economy*, p. 119.

18. Abramovitz, 'Catching up, forging ahead, and falling behind'.

19. Van Dormael, *Bretton Woods*, p. 307.

6 Keynes and the Ethics of Capitalism

1. Mary Riddell et al., 'Alistair Darling: We made mistakes on the economy', *Daily Telegraph*, 3 March 2009.

2. Moore, *Principia Ethica*, pp. 188–9.

3. JMK, CW, x, p. 441.

4. Quoted in Skidelsky, *Keynes*, vol. 2, p. 65.

5. Ibid., pp. 65–6.

6. Unpublished paper, 23 December 1925, quoted in Skidelsky, *Keynes*, vol. 2, pp. 240–42.

7. Walsh, *Keynes and the Market*, p. 74.

8. In CW, vi, p.258n, Keynes cited Freud's *Collected Papers*, vol. ii, clinical paper no. iv.

9. See the exchange in Skidelsky, *Keynes*, vol. 2, p. 239.

10. JMK, CW, ix, pp. 321–32.

11. Ibid., pp. 322–6, 328.

12. Richard Layard summarizes the evidence in *Happiness: Lessons from a New Science*.

13. JMK, CW, xxi, pp. 242–3.

14. See Skidelsky, *Keynes*, vol. 2, p. 223.

15. JMK, CW, vii, p. 374.

16. Ibid., p. 377.

17. Taleb, *The Black Swan*, p. 27.

18. JMK, CW, vii, pp. 375–6.

19. Quoted in Skidelsky, *Keynes: Economist, Philosopher, Statesman*, p. 780.

20. JMK, CW, iv, p. xiv.

21. Davidson, *Keynes*, p. 88.

22. JMK, CW, x, p. 446.

23. Joseph A. Schumpeter, 'John Maynard Keynes', in *Ten Great Economists*, p. 52.

24. William Rees-Mogg, *The Times*, 10 November 1983.

25. JMK, CW, x, pp. 446–7.

26. Ibid., pp. 445–6. 'We used to regard the Christians as the enemy,' he recalled in 1938. 'In truth it was the Benthamite calculus ... which was destroying the quality of the popular Ideal' – JMK, CW, x, p. 446.

27. Quoted in Skidelsky, *Keynes: Economist, Philosopher, Statesman*, p. 515.

7 Keynes's Politics

1. JMK, *CW*, vii, pp. 378–9.
2. JMK, *CW*, ix, p. 324.
3. Quoted in Skidelsky, *Keynes*, vol. 3, p. 68.
4. The discussion of Keynes's essay on Burke draws on Skidelsky, *Keynes*, vol. 2, pp. 61–4.
5. Quoted in Skidelsky, *Keynes*, vol. 2, p. 584.
6. JMK, letter to *New Statesman*, 13 July 1937, quoted in Skidelsky, *Keynes*, vol. 3, p. 33; Keynes's italics.
7. See Skidelsky, *Keynes*, vol. 3, pp. 284–6.
8. JMK, *CW*, xxvii, pp. 385–8; JMK to F.A. Hayek, 28 June 1944, quoted in Skidelsky, *Keynes*, vol. 3, p. 285.
9. JMK, *CW*, ix, pp. 274–5.
10. Ibid., pp. 303–5.
11. Ibid., pp. 305–6.
12. JMK, *CW*, xix, p. 441.
13. JMK, *CW*, ix, pp. 288, 291–2, 289–90.
14. Ibid., pp. 320–22.
15. Ibid., p. 315.

8 Keynes for Today

1. George Soros, 'The crisis & what to do about it', *New York Review of Books*, 4 December 2008.
2. *The Turner Review*, p. 53.
3. Ibid., p. 105.
4. Ibid., p. 112.
5. Ibid.
6. Ibid., p. 63.
7. Ibid., p. 67.
8. JMK, 'Post-war currency policy', *CW*, xxv, pp. 27–31.
9. Ferguson, *The Ascent of Money*, p. 335.
10. Greenspan, *The Age of Turbulence*, pp. 348, 385, 387.
11. Wolf, *Fixing Global Finance*, p. 65.
12. Davidson, *Keynes*, ch. 10.
13. The discussion of the reform of the monetary system draws on the

article by Vijay Joshi and Robert Skidelsky, 'A dangerous free-for-all', *The Guardian*, 11 November 2008.

14. JMK, CW, xix, p. 278.

15. Ibid., pp. 278, 283.

16. JMK, CW, xix, pp. 151–2.

17. JMK's presentation to the Macmillan Committee on Finance and Industry, JMK, CW, xx, pp. 113–21. The Macmillan Committee was set up in 1929 to inquire into the working of the banking system under the gold standard.

18. JMK, CW, vii, pp. 348–9.

19. Ibid., p. 338.

20. JMK, CW, xxi, p. 238.

21. Ibid., pp. 204–10.

22. Ibid., p. 238.

23. Ibid., pp. 240–41.

24. JMK, CW, vii, pp. 382–3.

25. Ibid., pp. 293–4.

26. See Calleo, *Follies of Power*. This has been a continuing theme in David Calleo's writing: see, for example, Calleo and Rowland, *America and the World Political Economy*.

27. JMK, CW, xxv, p. 55.

28. Skidelsky, *Keynes*, vol. 2, p. xxii.

28. See Patrick Jenkins, 'Banks reinvent securitization to cut capital costs', *Financial Times*, 6 July 2009.

Index